Green Business
Opportunities
The Profit Potential

DOMINIK KOECHLIN & KASPAR MÜLLER

FINANCIAL TIMES

PITMAN PUBLISHING

The German physicist and philosopher Carl Friedrich von Weizsäcker, when asked whether he was optimistic or pessimistic (on the subject of an environmentally sustainable world). 'I like to respond to that question with the story of the three frogs that fell into the milk: an optimist, a pessimist and a realist. The optimist and the pessimist both drowned, the first because he didn't do anything, thinking everything would turn out for the best anyway, the latter because he thought the situation was hopeless. The realist said: "All a frog can do is thrash about". So he did. And suddenly there was butter under his feet and he climbed out.'

Die Zeit, June 26, 1992

Pitman Publishing
128 Long Acre, London WC2E 9AN

A Division of Longman Group UK Limited

First published in 1992
Reprinted 1993

British Library Cataloguing in Publication Data
A CIP data record is available from the British Library

ISBN 0 273 03955 5

Phototypeset in Linotron Times Roman
by Northern Phototypesetting Co. Ltd., Bolton
Printed and bound in Great Britain
by Biddles Ltd., Guildford

CONTENTS

LIST OF CONTRIBUTORS

The editors

The editors of this book are the founding partners of Ellipson Ltd, a Swiss-based consultancy (Basel) specializing in environmentally conscious management and strategy

Dominik Koechlin previously worked in the corporate finance department of a bank. He has a doctorate in Law from the University of Bern where his thesis was on the precautionary principle in Swiss environmental law, and an MBA from INSEAD. He was co-initiator of the environmental management elective in the MBA programme at INSEAD. He is also a frequent speaker at environmental management workshops.

Kaspar Müller previously worked as a financial analyst and corporate finance consultant. He is chairman of the Swiss shareholder information committee and member of several national and international accounting standards committees. His first environmental work dates back to the mid-1980s, when he developed a concept for environmentally sound investment. He is a regular speaker and contributor to business journals on financial and environmental issues. Kaspar Müller holds a Masters degree in economics from the University of Basel.

The contributors

Takashi Adachi has a BA in Agricultural chemistry and an MBA from INSEAD. After ten years of marketing pesticides for Nippon Soda Co. Ltd, he now works for L'Air liquide in corporate marketing for the food and agricultural market.

Werner Arber studied Natural Sciences at ETH Zurich and has worked as professor at the 'Bio Zentrum' of the University of Basel. In 1978 he won the Nobel Prize in medicine for the discovery of restriction enzymes and their application to problems of molecular genetics. He is a member of several international scientific academies and Dr. hc. of the University of South California, Los Angeles, and of the University Louis Pasteur in Strassburg.

Richard Ford works as a freelance marketing consultant, based in Central London. He is also a director of Hype Associates Ltd, a company which publishes greeting cards. He has a BA in English from Cambridge University and an MBA from INSEAD where he won the 5000 ECU Minit Prize for the best essay by a European business student. He is also a Member of the Chartered Institute of Marketing and a frequent contributor to marketing and business journals.

H. Landis Gabel is associate professor of Industrial Economics at INSEAD. He has a PhD and and MA in Economics from the University of Pennsylvania and an MSc in Economics from the London School of Economics. He is interested in making businesses see what they can anticipate in the way of environmental policies in the future and what the implications of these policies will be.

Carlos Joly is the founder and president of Skandia Funds, which is a subsidiary of Scandinavia's largest insurance company. His environment fund has been the best performing equity fund in Norway since its launch. Joly was educated at Harvard University, has a Masters degree in philosophy, and worked as a Vice President of Citybank in New York, London and Buenos Aires. He lectures on business ethics at the Norwegian Graduate School of Business.

Douglas Mulhall is Managing Director of the Environmental Protection Encouragement Agency (EPEA), an international scientific institute with offices in Hamburg, Moscow, Kiev, New York, Japan, London and Rio de Janeiro. EPEA specializes in the life cycle analysis of products and processes. The institute serves more than 150 corporate executives, United Nations agencies, community groups, international NGOs, and governments.

Tilman Peter Oehl is a partner of the Munich law firm Dr Grill, Oehl and Partners. His business experience includes 15 years of business practice in law, real estate, franchising and computers, and 10 years with McDonald's Germany where he was Head of the their Environmental Programme. He is a regular contributor to various seminars and conventions on franchising, business cooperation and environmental management and law.

James Otter works for ICI Agrochemicals and is currently the General Manager for the Nordic countries based in Copenhagen. Other assignments for ICI include work in the management team for West Europe and responsibilities for North Africa. As field director with Save the Children Fund in Africa he gained first hand experience of development issues. He was educated at Cambridge University and INSEAD.

Stefan Schaltegger studied economics at the University of Basel where he specialized in economic policy (environmental economics). Since 1989 he has worked under Professor W. Hill as a research assistant at the Institute for business management of the Economics Centre of the University of Basel.

Christian Speich studied zoology and is a publicist and scientific journalist. In

1987 he won the Zurich journalist prize for an article on the language problems in quantum physics in the magazine *Weltwoche Leader*. Since 1988 he is columnist for the scientific section of *Weltwoche*.

Andreas Sturm studied economics at the University of St Gallen where he specialized in business management. Between 1989 and 1992 he worked as a research assistant at the Institute for business management of the University of Basel. In 1992 he joined Ellipson Ltd as a specialist in the field of environmentally conscious management and life cycle analysis.

Piroschka Dossi studied Art History and Law in Göttingen and Munich, and Business Administration at INSEAD. She runs the profit centre of an internationally renowned refractory company. She is a freelance author who writes and publishes in Germany.

For further information, please contact the editors at:
ELLIPSON Ltd, Environmental Management Consultants
Leonhardsgraben 52, CH-4051 Basel, Switzerland

ACKNOWLEDGEMENTS

We would like to thank Helen Pilgrim of Pitman Publishing for her entrepreneurial, easy going way of organizing the publication of this book. We would also like to express our gratitude to Marie-Ann Rijs who, in the same uncomplicated spirit, prepared the book for production.

The spontaneous commitment of the authors at a stage when the book was still only an idea, was a very positive experience. It shows that the greening of business is an issue many people are deeply concerned about and raises hopes for the future.

PREFACE

The growing urgency of issues such as the depletion of the ozone layer, the dangers of global warming and deforestation, have increased the public's, and therewith the consumers', environmental awareness. This means that the success of a company is becoming more and more dependent on its environmental performance. *Green Business Opportunities*, as the title already indicates, is about the challenges and opportunities for companies realizing the need for environmentally conscious business decisions.

Unfortunately, the majority of environmental management initiatives still seem to be confined to a technical, engineering level. They concern themselves mainly with finding a technical fix for an environmental problem. The very diverse, international team of authors tries to get us to realize that successful environmental management pervades all business decisions, and does not limit itself to the technical, single issue approach.

The pace of progress towards a more sustainable world depends on national and increasingly on international policies. Governments and politicians would do well to take this into account. The primer on environmental economics discusses the possible framework for an environmentally sound economy. It shows that there is a distinct trend to move away from public policy of command and control systems towards market-orientated tax and quota policies. This trend implies that the business manager is given more responsibility to manage environmental resources.

The fact that companies should take a proactive approach to environmental issues rather than waiting for regulations, or accidents, to force them into action runs as a main theme through all chapters. It is therefore interesting to note that, as pointed out in the chapter on the changeability of corporate cultures, the environmental management practices of some leading companies are falling more and more in line with practices previously only attributed to environmental pressure groups. The way in which McDonald's Germany was involved in the formulation of the new German packaging legislation can serve as an example to other industries. But what role is there to play for environmental pressure groups in the move towards a more sustainable economy? The chapter on environmental management and pressure groups gives a new insight as to what the business world could learn from pressure groups.

The chapter on environmentally conscious management illustrates that when ecomanagement is a matter of concern to the entire company and the challenges of increased environmental responsibility are met head on, it can lead to almost limitless new opportunities and to a real competitive edge. It makes clear that environmentally conscious management, apart from dealing with the efficiency of a company, also has a strong strategic aspect to it. A good example of this is waste management. From an operational point of view, waste management means using resources as efficiently as possible and making every manager think about the use of resources such as energy and raw material in his daily business. From a strategic point of view, waste management is much broader than just reducing waste from production. It can mean that a company can introduce a recycling scheme in a particular industry to force unaware competitors to bear the high cost of coming up with their own solutions.

This book is based on the assumption that in order to be able to play an important role in calling a halt to environmental destruction – and our environment is in a far worse state than we all seem to think – environmental management needs to accept the complexity and the strategic nature of environmental issues and therefore give them the attention and the organisational backing they deserve. The chemical industry is a good example of an industry where environmental issues play an increasingly important role. Its dynamics are illustrated by the example of ICI's European agrochemical business.

The tool kit of managers needs to be enlarged with tools going beyond the technical fix stage. One of such tools is eco-controlling; a management orientated approach to the analysis of the environmental impacts of a product or process and its financial contribution. This does not mean that traditional management techniques such as investment appraisal methods can be ignored, and this forms the subject of the chapter on environmental management and investment decisions. The chapter on green funds looks at the ultimate referee of economic success: the stock market, and the performance of green funds therein.

Managers involved in environmental management should look into some of the underlying attitudes of today's management practices. The chapter 'One Half of the Sky' argues that the use of more soft factors such as intuition or the so-called female attributes overcomes the linear, technical reasoning of many managers and could therefore prove to be indispensable to the implementation of environmental strategies.

Not only the managers, but their entire organizations need to go through the learning process. Why do so many large organizations find it so difficult to adopt an environmentally conscious management attitude? The chapter on green organizations gives some of the answers and develops a typology of 'green' organizations. Management's understanding of the environment has to translate into the way the company sells its products and services. Despite its misuse in earlier years, green marketing – marketing responsive to environmental issues – remains therefore important.

Because Japanese companies play a major role in most industries, the chapter on Japanese management and the environment looks at the way in which Japanese companies approach environmental issues and how their understanding of environmental management is changing.

Environmental issues often prove to be far more complex and have far more implications than first thought. The chapter on biodiversity deserves its place in a management book dealing with environmental issues because it provides new insights on how far reaching the consequences of the continuing destruction of many species is. It shows how carefully environmental strategies have to be designed and how flexible they have to be as new issues emerge.

The origin of this book is a great example of the importance of environmentally conscious management. Whilst in the MBA programme at INSEAD, some of the authors took the initiative together with a very cooperative professor, to introduce an environmental management elective. From a choice of about 40, this elective is now one of the most popular. It proves that future managers care about the environment and that companies had better get their act together if they want to attract these people!

In the last few years we have attended many seminars and conferences on environmental management and talked to many executives of leading companies. When asked what had led them to environmentally conscious management, they most often answered that it was the comments and questions of their children. To preserve the environment for our children is what the debate on sustainable development is all about and this book describes what role management practices play in a sustainable economy.

The book is therefore dedicated to our children.

Dominik Koechlin and Kaspar Müller, *Basel, June 1992*

1 A PRIMER ON THE ECONOMICS OF THE ENVIRONMENT

H. Landis Gabel

INTRODUCTION

Psychologists who study human learning believe that without a mental model to categorize and organize the stimulae that constantly bombard our brains, none of us would ever learn anything. Without a model of some kind, those stimulae would just be, as Shakespeare said, 'sound and fury, signifying nothing'.

The objective of this chapter is to build a model to make meaningful what might otherwise be just a cacophony of words constantly bombarding those of us who try to understand the nascent environmental movement from the public press. Like all models, this one will be simplistic. It will not be analogous to a house; rather it will be like its framework. But with a good physical framework, a house can be built, and with a good mental framework, the reader can in time build a solid understanding of why the environment has become the problem it is, what should be done about it, and what the impact of reasonably likely future changes might be for him or her.

THE ENVIRONMENT AS AN ECONOMIC RESOURCE

In many respects, the environment constitutes a set of economic resources similar to other economic resources at mankind's disposal. The soil, the forests, petroleum reserves, the air, and the ozone layer, are directly valuable to us by providing flows of consumption services such as recreation, aesthetics, and good health. They are also indirectly valuable as inputs to the production of other goods and services we value – food, wood products, and heating, for example. The fact that environmental resources were bequeathed to us by nature and that some or even most are difficult or impossible to regenerate once used does not alter that fact. It only implies that we must be especially careful in our management of environmental resources now and through time.

Although environmental resources are like all other economic resources in some respects, in others they are clearly different. We have misengaged environmental resources to an extent far beyond any mismanagement of resources such as labour or capital. And to understand why we have done such a poor job managing the environment, one must first understand the peculiar characteristics of environmental resources.

A pollution allegory: the farmer and the rancher

As a starting point, imagine a simple situation in which a rancher herds cattle next to a farmer's cropland. The rancher can decide on a herd of different sizes with each head of cattle earning him a profit of £30. But in addition to earning profits for the rancher, the cattle inevitably stray onto the farmer's land and damage his crops. The damage done to the farmer depends on the number of cattle in the rancher's herd. All of this is shown in Table 1.1.

Herd Size	Rancher's Profit	Farmer's damages	Social Welfare
500	£15000	£ 1000	£14000
1000	£30000	£ 2000	£28000
1500	£45000	£ 4000	£41000
2000	£60000	£ 20000	£40000

Table 1.1 Herd size, profit and damages

As a first scenario, imagine that the rancher is entitled to as many cattle as he would like with no need for concern about crop damage. It would appear obvious that the rancher would choose 2000 head of cattle to maximize his profits. But would this be the best outcome from the viewpoint of society in general?

We normally assume that profit maximization in a market economy serves the public interest by the working of the invisible hand that Adam Smith spoke of more than 200 years ago.

'Every individual endeavours to employ his capital so that its produce may be of greatest value. He generally neither intends to promote the public interest, nor knows how much he is promoting it. He intends only his own security, only his own gain. And he is in this led by an invisible hand to promote an end which was no part of his intention. By promoting his own interest he frequently promotes that of society more effectually than when he really intends to promote it.'

But here the market misfunctions. Since there is an input cost (the damaged crops) that is not paid by the rancher but by the farmer instead, the rancher's costs are incorrectly low. With understated costs, he is motivated to raise a herd that is too large and that does too much crop damage. What is the ideal herd size from the viewpoint of the public interest? It is 1500 where the total net value of output – including the reduced value of crops – is at its greatest. This figure is shown in the last column of the table labelled 'Social welfare'.

So it would seem that the existence of this 'external cost', which is often referred to as an 'externality', a 'spillover' or a 'third-party cost' that is not born by the decision maker has upset the workings of the invisible hand.

Now imagine by contrast a second scenario in which the rancher were obliged by law to compensate the farmer for the damage the cattle do to the farmer's crops. It would appear obvious that the rancher would reduce his herd size to 1500. Crop damage is now an explicit cost of cattle raising, and the rancher's profits are given by the fourth column of the table rather than by the second. The herd sizes that maximize the rancher's profits and social welfare are now identical, and the invisible hand is functioning.

In conclusion, it would appear that in order to solve this 'pollution' problem, one must grant the farmer property rights and enforce their protection. Doing so would internalize the otherwise external cost and correct the market distortion. But such a conclusion would be wrong!

Return to the first scenario in which the farmer has no right to compensation for damaged crops. Would it not be in his interest to bribe the rancher to reduce his herd size? This bribe would represent an opportunity cost which the rancher would have to pay for 2000 head of cattle as opposed to 1500. The farmer would be willing to offer the rancher up to £16000 to cut his herd from 2000 to 1500 (the value of the reduced damage). The rancher would accept anything more than £15000 (his lost profit). Clearly, a bargain can be struck. So even with no property rights (or *de facto* rights possessed by the rancher to damage the farmer's crops), the result will be optimal from the viewpoint of society.

From this simple allegory some valuable conclusions relevant to vastly more realistic and thus complex situations can be drawn.

1. The cause of pollution problems in the first instance is that decision makers are not forced to pay the real cost of the environmental

resources they consume (i.e., the cost of the environmental damage they do). This is a common problem with environmental resources because they often belong to society in general and to no one in particular. The air, water, animal species and the ozone layer, for example, are not owned in the traditional sense; they are thus not traded in a market and are not priced. And even if privately owned, as timber, mineral and fossil fuel reserves usually are, much of the cost of their use may be born by future generations, not the current one making decisions on rates of exploitation.

2. Because the environmental resources are erroneously underpriced, they are overused. Environmental resources are used as inputs in production when other resources should be used instead (as is the case with ozone depleting CFCs), and consumer goods intensive in environmental resources are too cheap in the market place. Thus, consumers buy and consume too many of these goods.

3. The problem is not the existence of pollution, per se. As long as pollution is a necessary consequence of the production of goods and services we want, some pollution is inevitable. Few of us would be prepared to completely sacrifice our heating in the winter, all means of transport but our feet, and artificial lighting be it from electricity or even the CO^2-emitting candle. The challenge is not to eliminate pollution but to ensure that we suffer only as much as is worthwhile.

    This point is illustrated in Figure 1.1. As the level of ambient pollution rises, the marginal damage cost (MC(D)) of another unit of pollution increases. This common observation from the medical sciences is indicated by the rising MC(D) curve as pollution increases from left to right in the figure. And reading from right to left, as the level of ambient pollution is reduced, the marginal cost of pollution control (MC(C)) increases. This principle of diminishing marginal productivity of pollution control methods is shown by the rising MC(C) curve going from right to left in the figure. The optimal amount of pollution is the amount that minimizes the sum of both the cost of pollution damage and the cost of its prevention. This is at the effluent level E* where the curves intersect. Slightly more ambient pollution than E* costs more to achieve than the damage it does. (In the farmer and the rancher story, E* is the 1500 head of cattle.)

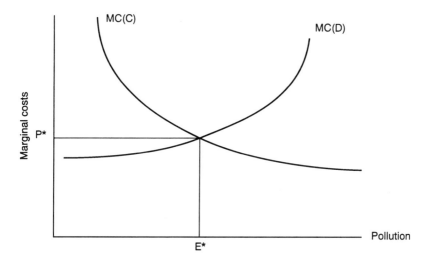

Figure 1.1 The optimal amount of pollution. The marginal cost of pollution damage is defined as the cost of the damage done by one more unit of pollution. The marginal cost of pollution control is the costs of reducing pollution by one unit. Naturally, both these costs depend on the existing state of the environment.

The two curves in the figure can be interpreted as supply and demand curves for environmental cleanup if one were to read the diagram from right to left. (This 'backwards' reading of the diagram is necessary because a cleanup is 'good' while pollution is 'bad'.) The MC(D) curve is the demand curve for cleanup and the MC(C) is a supply curve for cleanup. In equilibrium, the price for a unit of environmental cleanup is P*. The significance of this price will be noted later.

4. The argument that the problem is one of distorted prices and incentives facing decision makers implies that it is best not to view the problem as ethical or moral. We would not say that the rancher was unethical or immoral for herding cattle. It is a useful activity that necessarily causes some crop damage. In fact, even if the rancher felt guilty about the crop damage, it is not clear what he should do about it. He might consider paying the farmer damages even if not required to do so by law. Yet if other ranchers did not do likewise, our 'socially concerned' rancher would be driven out of business by the others with lower costs.

In short, finding and achieving the right balance between the production of goods and of by-product pollutants is better viewed as a question of economics than of ethics.

5. The definition of property rights in this simplest case was irrelevant to ensuring the appropriate output of goods and by-product pollutants. The socially optimal result (1500 head of cattle) was achieved irrespective of whether the polluter paid compensation to the victim or the victim paid a bribe to the polluter. What differed in the two scenarios was the fairness of the allocation of the burden of solving the problem. In the former case, it was born by the polluter; in the latter by the victim.

    This discovery will prove important when we discuss public policy. Whether we fashion a system based on a 'polluter pays principle' or a 'victim pays principle' will not affect the efficiency of resource use. It will only affect the wealth of victims and polluters.

6. Little of the foregoing analysis would be changed if technology were available to solve the pollution problem. Assume, for example, that a fence could be maintained for an annual cost of £10000. Under the first scenario, the farmer would maintain it; under the second scenario, the rancher would. And society would want the fence. For an annual cost of £10000, damage of £20000 would be avoided.

    Next assume that the fence costs £25000 annually. Neither party would have a financial motive to keep the fence, nor would it be socially desirable to spend £25000 annually to avoid an annual cost of £20000.

    We often find that technology can reduce pollution more easily than can reduced production. Yet technology is rarely either perfect or cheap, and we will normally still face a trade off between costs of damage and of control.

7. Although the allegory was one of production and not consumption, the principles it revealed suggest that one might be sceptical about 'green' consumerism. If a 'green' product – i.e., one that does not damage the environment – offers the consumer better personal value for money, it obviously will be demanded. Products that offer consumers better value for their money will be demanded irrespective of their greenness. The interesting case is the green product that is either more expensive for the consumer for the same quality, or equal in price but functionally inferior. Will it then be demanded?

    It may be, but one should appreciate that a consumer who makes such a purchase has decided to spend his or her money mostly for the benefit of others. This is altruistic behaviour. Of course, most people are altruistic some of the time and some people may even be altruistic most of the time. Yet it would be unrealistic to expect that most people are altruistic most of the time, and it would be unwise to predicate public policy on such an assumption. Thus, we appeal to consumers' pockets to sell unleaded gasoline and not to their greenness.[1]

This model is, as noted before, a very simple one which neglects many possible complexities. What are some of them? One is the possibility that environmental damage is irreversible. If so, it would not be possible to move back and forth along the horizontal axis of Figure 1.1. This is especially problematic if we are uncertain about the long-term consequences of environmental damage done now. Complexities such as these have been treated in the environmental economics literature, but they are beyond the scope of this 'primer'.

The case of many parties
One simplification in the allegory is particularly important, especially for the conclusion that pollution problems can be negotiated away. That is the assumption of one farmer and one rancher. With only two parties, a negotiated resolution of the conflict is a reasonable outcome to expect. And if this were always the case, there would be no need for public policy intervention. All conflicts could be left to the affected parties to resolve by themselves. But suppose there were many farmers being harmed by many ranchers. In such circumstances, it would be unreasonable to assume that the parties could coordinate negotiations.

Suppose, for example, that victims' rights were not protected, and they sought to bribe polluters to reduce pollution. Each individual victim would have a motive to let the others raise the bribe money and then enjoy the resulting lower pollution. This would be possible if there were no way of excluding the would-be 'free rider' from the benefits purchased by others. Since the possibility of a free ride would occur to most if not all of the victims, little bribe money would be raised and pollution would remain excessive.

Because in the common situation of many parties, direct negotiations

---

[1] Unleaded gasoline is more expensive to produce for equivalent octane than is leaded gasoline. Thus, it would normally sell at a higher price. But when offered at a higher price, there was little demand. Consequently, in Europe, differential government tax rates were set on the two gasoline types to bring the pump price of unleaded below leaded.

would likely fail, one may need some collective agreement in the political arena to compel affected individuals' participation. Such a system of 'mutual coercion, mutually agreed upon' takes us into the domain of public policy for environmental protection.

THE FOUNDATION OF PUBLIC POLICY

Having made the point that public policy for environmental protection is likely to be necessary in all but the case of few parties, it remains to discuss how that policy might be designed and enforced. And the first step is to define criteria by which we can judge various options that are being or might be used. The criteria listed below have been articulated in policy-making discussions in the European Community.

1. **Is the policy efficient?** This question has three elements.
   - *Will it result in the appropriate amount of pollution?* In Figure 1.1, this is E*.
   - *Will the appropriate amount of pollution be achieved at least cost?* An efficient policy will start to reduce pollution where it is cheapest and then move progressively to more and more expensive means of control. In other words, we want to move along the MC(C) curve from the right to left to the point E* in Figure 1.1 rather than to be above it.

     As an example of what this implies, Germany should focus all its resources on its eastern part where the environment is so despoiled that much can be done reasonably cheaply. In Western Germany, the cheap steps were taken long ago and should be neglected until the marginal cost of eliminating a unit of pollution is equated in both areas.
   - *Will the pollution that we are willing to tolerate do the least possible damage?* Just as Boy Scouts learn to put the latrine downwind of camp, we should ensure that effluents are emitted where they do least damage. In other words, we should end up at E* and on the MC(D) curve rather than above it.

     Whereas this might sound reasonable, it can be controversial. For example, it implies that nuclear waste should be dumped in remote locations like the Sahara rather than in populous locations in Western Europe. This is opposed by many environmentalists who argue that such cheap disposal is inequitable (even though presumably the export of wastes involves compensation) and that it obviates the necessity to find less polluting energy sources in Western Europe.

One should acknowledge that no policy can hope to satisfy this criterion perfectly. Yet even so, the principle of efficiency should not be ignored.

2. **Is this policy fair?** Every policy will necessarily have income distributional consequences, and these can be completely independent of the policy's efficiency. We already saw that efficient policies can require either that polluters pay or that victims pay. In addition, policies may have an impact on the competitiveness of particular firms and countries, and they may cause income transfers between rich and poor countries. In the end, fairness is a value judgement rather than a scientific matter, yet it must be considered as a relevant criterion for comparing alternatives.

3. **Is the policy easily implementable?** As we will see, different policies have different information requirements and institutional costs for their administration. We should not be surprised to find that there is a trade off between the benefits of more sophisticated policies and the possibly greater costs of running them.

4. **Is the policy flexible enough to accommodate changing circumstances?** Environmental policies should provide an incentive to seek new technologies to reduce pollution and to employ them once found.

5. **Are all the affected parties – and only the affected parties – involved in designing the policy?** This criterion, called the 'principle of subsidiarity', implies that the political forum for policy making should be coterminous with the boundary of the pollution externality. If pollution is local, as in the case of a land fill, the political venue should be, too. If pollution is global, as in the case of greenhouse warming or ozone depletion, then so should policy be made globally.

Environmental policy options

With our simple model of pollution and the criteria of policy evaluation above, we can now examine some generic policy options. Before starting, however, one should note that while each of these policy options has been used at one time and place or another, never is it as perfect as described. And frequently, the policies are mixed. We are again simplifying in order to highlight the essence of the possible alternatives.

Negotiations

This policy was already discussed. It passes all the criteria as long as there are few parties on each side. If there are many parties, it will not be appropriate. Where might we find a setting in which there are few parties? There are basically two. One is in local affairs. Siting an incinerator in a local community might be handled by competitive bidding whereby the incinerator owner could offer to pay a community to accept the nuisance. And the *New York Times* has reported that major oil and chemical firms are buying out home owners around their plants at prices well above market in order to reduce the risk that residents are harmed by accidents.

The other situation is in international affairs where there may be few parties and where there is no supra-national government to enforce alternative policies. Here we can find examples of victims bribing actual or future polluters to reduce their pollution. For instance, the developed countries essentially bribed several developing countries including India and China to join the Montreal Protocol to phase out CFC production. Similarly, the US has paid for Mexican equipment to reduce emissions that caused acid rain which entered the US.

These examples have proven feasible either because there were few countries affected by regional pollution (acid rain depositions) or because there were few producers of a global pollutant (CFCs). But global emissions of greenhouse gases will be vastly more difficult to cope with via negotiations because there are many more polluting and victimized countries.

Tort law

Tort law, or civil law, is the body of law that allows an injured party to sue the injuring party for damages. (Presumably, it was the law that allowed the farmer to sue the rancher). As we saw, it is efficient, fair, and it involves the relevant parties and no others.

The failing of tort law is that because it is administered through the courts, it is both slow and costly. So it is not surprising that tort law is generally reserved for infrequent and significant accidents rather than for continuous emissions doing minor damage. That is, it is more suited to a case like the Exxon Valdez oil spill, which cost Exxon over $2 billion in damages, than to the case of automobile exhaust emissions.

But might not insurance coverage reduce the threat of a law suit and thus undermine the incentive for a firm to reduce the risk of an accident? Why should a company spend money to reduce that risk if a judgement would be paid by an insurance company and thus by its many policy holders? This problem is known as 'moral hazard' in insurance markets and is essentially the same problem of an external cost that caused excessive environmental damage in the first place.

There are various ways to mitigate the disincentive effect of insurance. One is to base insurance premia on the actual risk. For example, oil tankers with double bottoms pay a lower premium than single-bottom tankers. And tanker fleet with higher accident rates will face higher premia. Thus the expected accident cost is brought home to the decision maker who then has the appropriate incentive to invest in risk reducing activities.

But there may still be a problem. Ultimately, companies and their managers are insured by their limited liabilities. For a corporation, that limit its net worth. For a manager, it is his or her job. For enormous companies like Exxon, this insurance 'deductible' is very high, and thus the problem is not significant. But after the Exxon Valdez accident, Shell terminated all shipping in US waters. That job is now done by much smaller shippers with which Shell contracts. And in general, there is little to prevent a large company from subcontracting a risky operation to a smaller firm whose sole competitive strength is its low capitalization and thus its cheap limited liability insurance.

Resolution of this problem – at the level of both the corporation and its managers – can be found in the criminal law.

Criminal law

In the United States and in many of the European countries, violations of major environmental laws carry personal criminal sanctions. As Samuel Johnson said, 'the prospect of being hung has a way of focusing the mind', and the prospect of a jail term or heavy and uninsurable personal fines that cannot be reimbursed by an employer is sure to provide a strong incentive for managers to take due diligence in reducing the risk of an accident.

Public investment

Public sector bodies can and often do invest in pollution abatement activities. This investment can be direct, as in the case of municipal waste treatment facilities, or indirect in terms of subsidies to private companies earmarked for pollution abatement.

This policy approach satisfies many of the criteria we have noted. And if there are economies of scale such that, for example, one waste treatment plant serving many firms is more efficient than several, each operated by a single polluter, then public provision of the service is sensible.

There is one problem with this approach, however, and that is its fairness. First, it may mean a double burden for the victims. Community residents may suffer the pollution and also pay for the clean up through their taxes. Secondly, if some countries require victims to pay, there may be a competitive inequity when companies in the two countries compete in international markets. It is for this reason that OECD countries have collectively agreed upon the 'polluter pays principle'.

'Command and control' standards

The traditional and still most common environmental policy approach has been for the regulatory body to define ambient or emission standards that must be attained and often to dictate the specific technologies that must be used to achieve those standards. Good examples are automobile emissions and power plant sulphur emission standards .

Command and control policies might be considered fair if their cost were born by the polluting companies and if all competing companies faced the same requirements. And enforcement is relatively simple since it often can be carried out simply by observing installed technology. Yet on other criteria, command and control policies are flawed. In particular, they are often inefficient. An example illustrates why.

In the US steel industry in the 1970s, standards existed on permissible emissions of particles from furnace chimneys. And the regulations required particle precipitators to be installed to control those emissions. This technology eliminated a pound of particles at a cost of about $20. At the same time, particles entered the atmosphere from wind blowing across ore piles around the mills. If water sprinklers were placed on top of these ore piles, particle emissions could have been reduced for only $0.013/lb. Was this done? No!

Having spent millions of dollars on particle precipitators, the companies had no incentive to undertake even relatively inexpensive pollution reduction actions that were not stipulated by the regulatory authorities.

Stories like this are commonplace in industrial circles. Government authorities are rarely as aware of inexpensive opportunities to control effluents as are the managers on the spot. And command and control policies do not harness the creativity of managers. For example, in the automobile industry, the US emission standards, which were written specifically to force the development of catalytic converters, have recently been criticized for discouraging investment in alternative technologies that may be superior but yet could never satisfy some of the particular requirements of the standards.

Effluent taxes

To avoid the inevitable inefficiencies of centralized command and control policies, two different decentralized market-oriented policies have recently been introduced in many European and US industries. Effluent taxes is one of them.

The idea behind effluent taxes can best be shown by Figure 1.2. Imagine that there are two different sources of the same pollutant. These could be two different sources within a single company, two different companies in the same industry, or two different industries that emit the same pollutant. Each source can be controlled but at a progressively rising marginal cost. This is the curve marked MC(C) and is the same as in Figure 1.1. The key point of the figure is that the curves are different between the two sources. Source 1 finds cleanup relatively expensive and Source 2 finds it cheaper.

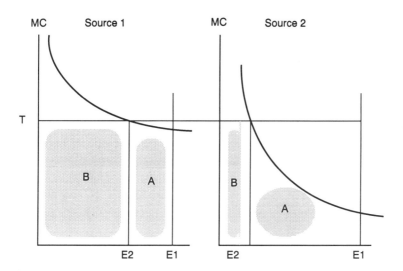

Figure 1.2 Effluent taxes

If one were to establish a tax T per unit of the pollutant in a situation where each source was initially emitting E_1 units of pollution, what would happen? Each source would have a profit motive to reduce its emissions rate step by step as long as the unit tax exceeded the unit cost of that reduction. The reduction would stop when it became cheaper to pay the tax than to continue with further cleanup. This is the point marked E_2 in the figure. The area marked A is the total cost of effluent reduction while the area marked B is the tax paid for the remaining effluent. (The area under the marginal cost curve measures the total cost. It is the sum of the costs of each unit of pollution reduction.)

In terms of efficiency, the tax policy ensures that the pollution abatement is done at least cost across different sources of pollution. And if the unit tax is set equal to the price P* in Figure 1.1, the result is the optimal balance of goods and pollutants. In short, the result is in theory fully efficient.

Is it not possible that some firms would go out of business? Yes. With the cleanup cost and the tax burden, the firm's production cost will rise, and it will naturally try to pass that cost on to its customers. But will they pay it? If they want the product badly enough, they will. If they are unwilling to pay it, they are signalling that the product is not worth its full cost of production – environmental costs included. It only looked attractive to consumers when its price was partly subsidized by victims of pollution. Clearly, society is better off when such products are removed from the market.

But the tax policy, while attracting a lot of attention recently, has its drawbacks. An important one is enforcement. To be correctly taxed, a source of emissions must be monitored. Given the importance of monitoring, there is a natural link between this policy and the various initiatives to establish formalized environmental auditing schemes. If auditing practices were formalized and routinized, the data needed for the tax policy would be generated and reported by the firms themselves with only the need for sample auditing falling on the enforcement agency. The parallel with financial auditing and taxation is obvious.

Taxes on emissions are now policy in many European countries including Denmark, Germany, Italy, France and the Netherlands. They are applicable to many pollutants including pesticides, fuels, packaging, water emissions and aircraft noise. Within the next few years, a CO^2 tax is likely to appear in the European Community.

Tradeable pollution quotas

The second market-oriented policy is tradeable pollution quotas. The idea behind tradeable quota rights is in many respects similar to the idea of effluent taxes. But instead of setting a price and letting the market determine the quantity of effluent, one sets a quantity and lets the market set the price of the quota right. This is shown in Figure 1.3.

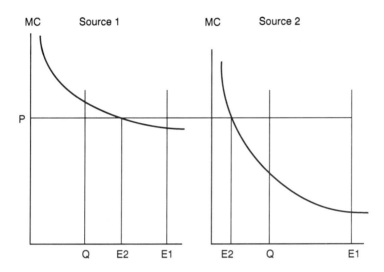

Figure 1.3 Pollution quotas

Suppose that two firms were initially emitting E1 units of pollution, each as shown in the figure, but were given a right to emit only Q effluent. If the firms were allowed to trade the rights with each other, what would happen? Source 1, which finds it very expensive to live within its quota allocation, has a motive to buy extra quota rights at any price up to its avoided abatement cost. Source 2, for which cleanup is relatively cheap, has a motive to reduce effluent beyond its quota and to sell its unused quota rights for any price above its experienced abatement cost. Clearly, there will be trading between the two sources whereby quota rights go from Source 2 to Source 1 in return for money. The trading will stop at unit price P for the rights when each source is emitting E2 effluent.

The results in terms of efficiency will be identical between the effluent tax policy and the quota policy as the similarity of Figures 1.2 and 1.3 suggests. The quota price will equal the tax rate, and the effluent will be identical. In both cases, the cleanup will be done at least cost. The amplification of this approach taken in the case of particles at an American steel mill such as was mentioned previously, resulted in a $13 million annual saving compared to the command and control policy alternative.

In terms of fairness, however, the tax and the quota systems are quite different. With the tax system, environmental resources in effect belong to the public, and private companies that want them must buy them from the public. This provides the motive for the cleanup – i.e., the motive to reduce the need for the resources to the extent that the unit tax makes it worthwhile. But even after cleanup, the firms continue to pay a tax to the public for the continuing emissions.

With the quota system, by contrast, environmental resources in effect belong to private sector companies rather than to the public. The public gave away those resources when the public policy agency gave away the quotas. In Figure 1.3 the analogy to the tax that appears in Figure 1.2 is the value of the quotas. In principle, this value should appear on the companies' balance sheets. Since the quota rights trade and thus command a price, the system does provide a motive for some cleanup to reduce the need to use rather than to sell the quotas. In that sense, it is a polluter pays system. But the polluter pays only for the cleanup. It does not pay the public for the environmental resources that continue to be used.[1]

The tradeable pollution quota system has been used in the US in many areas including CFCs, the phasing out of lead in gasoline, and in hydrocarbon emissions into the air.

Summary of public policy

A number of summary conclusions can be drawn from this discussion of public policy.

● There is a clear albeit slow evolution of public policy away from command and control systems and towards market-oriented tax and quota policies. This change is consistent with the shift in the broader international arena toward reliance on markets as opposed to command and control allocation of resources.

[1] There is another troubling issue with the quota system in terms of fairness. The typical way by which quotas are allocated is as a proportion of existing output. This means that the wealth that is given away goes to those firms that are the biggest polluters. Firms that reduced their pollution prior to the implementation of the policy lost the opportunity to get quotas.

- The implication of this evolution is that business managers will be given more responsibility to manage environmental resources, just as they now have general responsibility to manage the other resources that their firms use. This responsibility will not be absolute – it is not absolute for any resources – but it will expand nonetheless.
- The mechanism by which the devolution of authority to the private manager can still ensure environmental protection is price. Environmental resources will become much more expensive in the future. This expected rapid and enormous rise in prices for environmental resources will provoke many changes – all driven by competition in the marketplace. Less polluting and thus cheaper inputs will be substituted for more polluting and thus more expensive inputs. Higher input costs will be passed on to consumers who will shift to cheaper goods and services which generate less waste or use fewer environmental inputs.
- As these prices rise, firms will find many opportunities to create competitive advantages or many threats to their competitive survival. Cost accounting systems that today do not allocate environmental costs to specific products will have to be changed. Incentive and compensation systems that reward managers who find ways to increase short term profits at the expense of higher risks of environmental accidents or higher long term costs to be born by his or her successor will have to be changed. Product market managers must find lower cost products. Design engineers must consider not just the costs of making products, but the costs of disposing of them as well. And there will be tremendous opportunities to develop patentable new technologies. The pollution abatement and control industry had sales estimated to exceed $115 billion in 1990. By the end of the next decade, that will seem pitifully small.

References

Bodily S. and Gabel L., 'A New Job for Businessmen: Managing the Company's Environmental Resources', *Sloan Management Review*, Summer 1982
Hardin G., 'The Tragedy of the Commons', *Science*, December 13, 1968.
Smith A., *An Inquiry into the Nature and Causes of Wealth of Nations*, 1776

'Man has long forgotten, that the earth was given to him for usufruct alone, not for consumption, still less for profligate waste.'

John Perkins Marsh, Man and Nature, 1863

2 WHY THE EARTH'S GENETIC DIVERSITY CANNOT BE A MATTER OF INDIFFERENCE

by Christian Speich and Werner Arber

TRAPPED IN THE SCURRILOUS GAME OF CHANCE

Tomorrow is the draw and we stand a good chance of winning. A whole table full of draw tickets is standing in front of us, almost bending under the strain of the potentially win-laden paper. However, there is a tremendous draught in the room. With every gust of wind the lottery tickets whirl a bundle at a time out of the window where they disperse in the storm, never to be retrieved. A few people, filled with consternation, complain the window should be closed. But this is only possible using special winders and these are only to be found in the pockets of those for whom the great lottery has long since lost its importance, because they are totally taken up with getting hold of the small change out of gaming machine.

This kafkaesque picture we present: the human species, or actually rather – its usurping representatives – the industrial nations of the First World. The lottery depicts what the publicity surrounding the World Conference on Environment and Development in June 1992 in Rio de Janeiro under the slogan of biodiversity has at least placed within the passive vocabulary of representatives of industry, though may all attribute very different ideas to this abstract concept.

THE PROFITABILITY OF OUR BIOSPHERE

There can be little doubt that uppermost will be those properties in living creatures, unknown or overlooked up till now, that can be exploited in agriculture or pharmaceutics. The acquisition of a heightened duty of care in the treatment of the whole biosphere from the possible existence of such a bonanza in the wealth of living forms on earth seems to be quite unusual. And even in the fields mentioned, the concern with how to protect potentially profitable forms of life takes priority over the general protection of life against the damaging effects of civilization.

Or to remain with our analogy: instead of first of all preventing a further reduction of the stock of lottery tickets, avid discussion and argument ensues about claims on possible profit. This is a case of not simply trying to sell the proverbial bear skin, rather it is the bear himself that is on the line. In the end it will not be possible to shoot any more bears because the bears will meanwhile have been moved from the red list of endangered species to the black list of those that are extinct.

However, anyone seeing such scurrilous behaviour as simply fooling about, an endearing manifestation of human shortcomings, is forgetting that we are not talking here about the tombola at a charity bazaar. The great lottery of which we are speaking, biological evolution, presents not just a matter that is deadly earnest, but it is also bound up with conditions that are totally unusual for raffles and whose severe harshness we are only too ready to forget.

THE RELEVANCE OF EVOLUTION

Even amongst those having some general understanding of natural science, unless they have expressly concerned themselves with the subject, the view predominates that the evolution of life on earth is a piece of ancient history documented in stone in museums. At least since the advent of modern man, homo sapiens, who has now attained briefcase and tie, such events seem to no longer have any relevance.

However, not only does evolution still continue to operate and will do so for as long as living substance is to be found on the planet, but we as humans are also closely bound up with the co-evolution of all forms of living things. Even if it were possible for us to feed ourselves from non-organic material, as do plants, our prosperity or ruin would depend on the co-operation of all forms of life and their interaction with the properties of inanimate nature.

It is then a lottery with inescapable participation. But this is not the only serious deviation from a normal lottery. Whoever participates in it – must participate – must not only reckon with many blanks and rare wins – the draw can also assign losses, and actually in every scale as far as the absolute, the deletion from the list of participants.

It must be mentioned that the participants in this game are individuals whose lots, in the form of their manifest and hidden biological characteristics, their inherited life information, are put into a permanent lottery, but that the actual winner or loser is always a collective, within which the genetic information of those entitled or obliged to participate survives by way of the sexual and a-sexual reproductive mechanisms and so can only then come to fruition.

To complicate the issue even more, it is not only the individual lots, or more precisely, those in the reproduction collective, which are placed in the drum, but the outcome of the lottery depends also on idiosyncratic combinations of meaning with completely alien packets of draw tickets. As even here the trivial basic rule is confirmed whereby the chances in the lottery increase with the number of lots entered by one participant. Every participant therefore, must, if the participation takes place willingly and after consideration and because of the dependence referred to, have a great interest in seeing that everyone else is able to submit as many draw tickets as possible. The dependencies between biological information alien to the species belong to the field of work of ecological research. This comparatively young science has very quickly been able to show that there is much more here than simply the rules of the game and a network of relationships involved in a 'eat or be eaten'. Living things are not just determined by the chemo-physical characteristics of their environment, but they also influence and modify them all the time.

The global dimensions of evolution

Such restructuring can take on global dimensions. That our planet is today completely different than at the beginning of biological evolution of over more than two thousand million years ago cannot just be attributed to its cosmic ageing, its cooling for example. Also quite decisive is the operation of the growing and ever-changing society as a whole of all living things: and the restructuring did not always take place quietly and slowly. The biological 'discovery' of molecular energy changers in the nature of e.g. chlorophyll has brought with it virtually revolutionary changes. From this has come the composition of the earth's atmosphere containing oxygen, absolutely essential to life. And these drastic changes brought terrible difficulties for oxygen-hating life forms. The oxygen revolution has had the effect of being a catastrophe for them.

That the activity and inaction of human civilized society brings with it similar radical global changes is already a truism and not the least also the reason for the publication of this book. Pointing out the similar events in the past history of the earth and thereby denying the acute danger for the survival of mankind would mean to neglect the time frames in which such changes occurred and occur today.

The pressure on the earth's atmosphere due to additional carbon dioxide to an extent which threatens to throw the earth's climatic system into confusion has been achieved in just two centuries with the main contribution in the last forty years. The enrichment with oxygen in the atmosphere through the photosynthetic activity of the plants has, in comparison, only reached today's somewhat stable degree after millions of years.

The increasing speed of evolution

The release of completely new types of chemical material – classes with which no earthly being has ever previously had contact, takes place at a rate of millions of tons within a few years. If in the progress of evolution at any one time a combination hitherto unknown appeared for the first time, it would initially have been synthesized in single cells in amounts of thousandths or millionths of a gramme. Until its spread in the biosphere would have been considered globally as relevant, the number of cells being able to perform the new synthesis would have to have grown over thousands of years.

These differences in speed are of crucial significance. Translated into the analogy of the lottery, they must be understood as differentially restrictive conditions of gain – but equally, as already mentioned, also of loss. The slow change in tiny steps corresponds then to a drawing of lots with one or few winning figures; to quick changes due to the achievements of civilisation on the other hand the effect in the draw is a long combination of figures. In the first case gain or loss distribute themselves to a modest extent to many participants. In the latter, however, it is a question of a jackpot.

And as on the one hand the negative wins predominate in the history of biological evolution, just as on the other hand the magical information connections of the groups of lots amongst each other do not permit the identification of winners or losers as individuals, but the luck of the draw is carried over to the whole of the participants, such a jackpot is virtually always fatal for all those taking part, which can have a drastic effect on the variety of the biosphere.

THE HUMAN ANGLE

Seen from this point of view it would appear to us who are favoured with having the role of beings gifted with reason who organize their fate with far-sightedness and where-ever possible to their own advantage, that for us as managers it must be very useful in all areas of life to ascertain more about the mechanisms of this strange world-lottery and above all about the nature of the lots.

We humans all belong to one and the same species. We are one amongst, as biologists estimate, 10 million species of life forms, who, according to the present level of evolutionary history inhabit the planet. This number is currently in decline, whereby the extinction of single or multiple-cell plants and animal species in by far and away most cases is caused by the fact that their living conditions have been changed to such an extent through the activities of a minority of the almost six thousand million human beings making up what is known as the First World, that they can no longer be meaningfully be responded to through the inherited biological programme of regulation.

FIGHTING AGAINST THE GREAT VANISHING ACT

The disappearance of species marches so frightfully quickly forward, that the systematists amongst biologists and zoologists have probably been unable to identify and describe many of them. For up to the present only a small part of the surviving wealth of life forms on earth has been entered in scientific literature, roughly 1.4 million species. Every species then, has at its disposal specific equipment to enable it to work together with its environment, so that its survival through the succession of generations is thus made possible. This specific set of 'physiological responses' to the specific conditions presented by their living space is contained in every cell of an individual of that respective species in a information packet, that is further inherited by derivatives of the cells. This set of inherited material is called genome.

Diversity

The genetic information contained in species-typical genomes controls the shaping of its form and its life functions. However, we all know from our own perspective that no individual is normally completely the same as another and that there are within one species groups with certain feature combinations, variations or races, that can more or less be distinguished from one another. The biological diversity on earth is then far greater than the number of scientifically defined species.

The genetic diversity actually realized is the basic precondition for the ability of the phenomenon of life to outlive the permanent and often very abrupt change of living conditions on the planet. The ability of species to adapt to new conditions had made it possible time and again for ecosystems of species, working purposefully together, to adapt to water, to land and to the atmosphere, even if in the course of millions of years continents have moved, lifted and sunk, ice ages have changed the face of the planet and complete oceans have opened up and others closed.

However, what appears in the fossilized documentation of evolutionary history as a purposeful direction of the principle of life through the movements of the geological revolutions, rests, as geneticists have recognized, on the success of a random mechanism, whose basic prerequisite is the variability of inheritance material. As each time a sufficient supply of inheritance information was available for deviation in the shaping of form and functions – lottery numbers perhaps – the conflicting conditions were able to have a selective and not simply a terminal effect. It was therefore possible to have winners when making the lottery draw.

The considerable diversity of life forms rests on genetic instability. In order to be able to understand it one needs to know that genetic information – common to all, even if basically different, forms of life – is contained in a sequence along so-called nucleotide pairs that can be compared with letters in a written message. Such a 'genetic letter' would then include, in a bacterium for example, around five million letters – a really thick book then.

Our human body cells require uncommonly more of such 'genetic literature'. Their information content corresponds to a library of over 1000 volumes each the size of the bacterium book. In every cell division this library is passed on the daughter cells, which, according to their function in the body, only consult a few volumes, or even single chapters.

Mutations

Genes, which are much spoken of outside the scientific world, represent such a chapter of genetic information. Their length is very varied and extends from about a hundred to several thousand letters. The genetic diversity then comes about because these texts are not fixed for all time in letters of stone but are subject time and again to little changes. One then speaks of mutation. Basically, mutations of different kinds can be due to changes in the text, i.e., by exchanging letters, deleting letters, adding letters as well as to the breaking up of a series of letters into fragments and the rearrangement into a new combination.

The causes of these text changes are quite different in each case. First is a certain inaccuracy in copying the text. Every time a cell divides copies must be made for the daughter cells, and in this process mistakes creep in the form of the substitution of letters, omissions or erroneous insertions. The more often the text has to be copied the stronger will be the effect of the unfaithfulness of the reproduction. We humans tend to see these changes as errors. In reality, however, they are closely connected with the atomic structure of the gen matter. This matter can assume short-lived changes in appearance, which chemists refer to as tantomere forms.

Genetic information is also mutated through the effect of physical-chemical influences of the environment. In this, high energy radiation – not just from nuclear technologically usage, but also from the spectrum of cosmic radiation and from the B-spectrum of ultra-violet sunlight – can play a part as well as certain chemical substances, as for instance the substance that has become thereby suspect: benzol.

A further source of genetic instability are the transfer processes which are controlled by the genetic apparatus itself and are consequently designed for and important to the meaningful use of the 'genetic library'. The switching of volumes and the swapping of pages which can also lead to new combinations of meaning, genetic mutations, can come about quite by chance.

Mutations across species

And finally, in recent days a quite special type of genetic mutation has occupied research: the direct reception of genetic information. In gene technology the ability of viruses and so-called plasmides, special function forms of bacterial heredity substance, to transfer extracts of genetic information to other organisms is used as a method of working. Certainly such transference from a cell to another cell of a different species, as can be shown in microbiology, also takes place naturally and spontaneously.

And there is evidence to show that this mechanism operates not only in single, but also in the case of multiple cells – also in us.

Micro-organisms play the role of an uncalled for postman in this process, depositing letters in households for which they were actually not intended. The recognition of this is vitally important and requires urgent closer research. It means nothing less than that historical evolutionary related connections of all the quite clearly diverse life forms exist not only indirectly in the form of common previous forms, but can also appear quite directly and spontaneously in new forms. The previous graphic method of portraying the nature of these connections through the passage of time as a vertical family tree requires an additional symbol in the form of horizontal connections, along which far distantly related species of the same time level can be brought together in their genetic relationship.

The complete wealth of life forms on the planet earth, the unnumbered societies of the whole eco-system of the biosphere are thus not just indirectly dependent on one another through the enormously complex ecological network of relationships. The ability to answer the demands imposed upon them by their environment is shared by them also directly.

If however, the acquisition of a new genetic unit of information shows itself to be suitable for such a response, it must first prove itself in the single cell. And whether a mutation can be part of the species-typical information inventory depends on whether it is passed on to descendants. In the case of living things with multiple cells it must be placed in a germ cell that then actually in the process of reproduction becomes a characteristic.

The testing of mutations only occasionally brings about a positive result. All too often it shows the deviation from the previous genetical norm to be lethal; or the carriers of the new information demonstrate at least an insignificant selective disadvantage over the carriers of the conventional combination. In the first case the new software creation disappears as quickly as it comes into being. In the second, at least after a little time.

Often however, the mutation remains initially unsuccessful. It is usual then to speak of a silent mutation. If the living conditions change during a generation, then of course, the combination of silent mutations that have accumulated during the course of thousands of years through a succession of generations can become important. They can contain a response to the new conditions that was hitherto meaningless so that the carriers of the combination possess within their whole population a better chance of surviving. Little by little a previously insignificant portion of genetic information can thus become characteristic of the species so that the non-carriers die out.

To summarize, without the appearance of mutations, life could hardly have continued until the present day. On the other hand, a population must not show too great a rate of mutations in order to continue to exist. And it is tiny little steps of information changes over long periods of time that complete a biologically meaningful pattern. The existence of such for the evolutionary adaptation to new conditions important patterns is only made possible through populations of large enough size to guarantee genetic diversity.

It would be disastrous to assume that sufficient previously inconspicuous recipe books and instructions for use are found in the complete library of the genetic inventory of the biosphere to make the complete life system possible should our civilizing activities continue to change the earth's living space. The frightful speed with which animal and plant species are disappearing from the planet, never to be seen again, speaks against it.

It is just as naive and senseless to rely on the future ability of gene technology which quite clearly, behind the terrific speed of our environmental changes, would have to provide the evolutionary adaptation of the living world with some seven-league boots. Genetic recombination cannot be so easily arranged in test tube: the road from an experiment in a laboratory to a directed mutation in a sufficiently large population is a very long and often inaccessible path. And even anyone involved in the realm of securing food supplies and the correction of environmental damage who is staking everything on this must be particularly interested to see that there is actually a sufficient reservoir of genetic information available for exploitation, because there are no hard and fast rules that genetic information which has disappeared can later be conjured out of a hat again.

BIOLOGIC DIVERSITY AND THE ECONOMY

As human beings are not the only species able to keep their house in order, economic activity must take account of biological diversity. And as this diversity cannot be guaranteed either by a Noah's ark nor in the form of a small nature reserve, neither through seed nor gene banks, conservation must, without fail, go much further than has been the case in nature conservancy up to now when guided by ethical and moral standpoints.

It means preserving sufficient suitable living space for possibly millions of species of life forms from tiny bacteria up to whales and elephants, from mushrooms to giant trees, from gnats through different household vermin to large beasts of prey, not just keeping single specimens alive, but also all these species and possibly many variations and varieties. We as numerically exploding human beings, will have to move closer together.

If we do not do this and insist on our inconsiderate and thoughtless 'business as usual' then the already precarious situation will not hold out for long, when we, as the participants of a compulsory ordained evolutionary lottery, will have changed the conditions of the draw in an irresponsible way so that not only an incredible long combination of numbers will be able to bring about the only possible score – reward: to continue to live. So, we shall at the same time have burned all lottery tickets for the draw except for a few, and even these through the secret lines of communication of ecology will no longer have any connection to the jackpot.

'To recognize environmental management as amongst the highest corporate priorities and as key determinant to sustainable development.'

The first principle of 16, for integrating environmental issues into all aspects of business, prepared by the International Chamber of Commerce, presented at the WICEM II Conference in Rotterdam, April 1991

3 ENVIRONMENTALLY CONSCIOUS MANAGEMENT

by Kaspar Müller and Dominik Koechlin

THE GOOD AND THE BAD NEWS

Let's hear the bad news first: the environment is in a much more critical state than we care to admit. This fact affects every manager of every firm, whether he likes it or not, and ignoring it is bound to lead to a very gloomy future, both for their firm and for their personal career. Admittedly, a great deal has been accomplished so far at management level, but most of the measures instituted are of the defensive, end-of-the-pipe type.

The good news, however, is that, in future, a good manager will be able to use this knowledge to pull ahead of inferior colleagues. Management is going to be more difficult, more exciting and cover a great deal more ground. All areas of a company interact. Environmentally sound management therefore means understanding the complex interrelations and systems relevant to an enterprise. Even when products are only at the planning stage, ways and means of disposing of them at the end of their useful lives must be sought. Environmental consciousness, or rather the lack of it, will be the downfall of the manager who is no more than a highly specialized financial expert or production manager, while opening up almost limitless opportunities for those blessed with it.

It is with these opportunities that we are concerned in this chapter. They still receive far too little attention, even today, mainly due to the defensive attitude of many chief executive officers who feel in their bones that a great deal is going to change but do not know precisely what. There doesn't seem to be a cut-and-dried method of exploiting these opportunities and converting them into market successes and many managers therefore consider a wait-and-see policy to be wisest. They mistakenly believe that their company is not directly affected by environmental problems. They wait and see what happens and hope that their firm will not hit the headlines in the meantime. Such tactics are almost invariably the wrong ones. They mean that managers relinquish control over the situation and once the firm is in deep waters the only course of action is a defensive one. Others will dictate the way in which the firm has to cope. Companies such as Exxon, Union Carbide, Sandoz and many others have first hand experience of this.

Managers who acknowledge their firm's environmental problems and meet them head on have, on the other hand, a good chance of pulling through because they know precisely what their firm's position is and where its strengths and weaknesses lie. They can be active partners in any discussion on the environment and can weigh in with figures, facts and arguments that even critical groups can accept as a working basis in the deliberative process.

A company will benefit from environmentally sound management, or ecomanagement for short, in three simple ways. The first of these is an increase in efficiency because, contrary to a common misconception, environmental management keeps costs down rather than jacking them up. It furthermore can and does lead to the discovery and development of new management techniques which can offer the company a whole range of new opportunities. And finally, the whole pattern of a company's behaviour will bear the imprint of new influences and forms of organization that markedly influence its strategy. In the following paragraphs we will take a closer look at these three topics.

EFFICIENCY

Whenever a company uses natural resources intensively and produces large amounts of waste it runs the risk of being inefficient, which will have a negative impact on its costs. Costs show up in the profit and loss account and also affect the balance sheet, so it is well worth having a closer look at the individual items that make up these two pillars of accountancy.

Income statements will increasingly show signs of higher waste management cost as the costs of dumping and incinerating waste rise dramatically. In addition, insurance premiums, transport costs, taxes, storage costs, authorization costs and interest rates have also risen in response to an increased risk. The balance sheet will be affected by the increased depreciation required on various capital assets because their useful life is being shortened due to new environmental requirements.

The share of environmental costs as a percentage of total costs will continue to rise, but unlike, for example wage costs, which, when expressed as a percentage of total cost, are often used as a target figure for managers, environmental costs are often hidden and therefore not easy to get to grips with.

Outside the chemical industry, virtually no company publishes its pollution prevention or waste reduction costs in its annual report. Accountancy being a mirror of management, and with most accounting systems still ignoring environmentally related costs or treating them under different headings, environmental issues might not be as high up on managers' agendas as many people would like them to be. The fact that through good environmental management the efficiency of an operation can be increased and its costs therefore brought down will only enter into every management's thinking once accounting (and incentive) schemes have been adopted

Much more challenging than just increasing efficiency are the strategic issues raised by environmental management.

The CFC example

The agreement to abandon the manufacture and use of CFCs by 1993 or 1995 is a classic example of inefficiency caused through a collective refusal to heed warnings.

For years scientists had been sounding urgent warnings about the risk of the ozone layer being depleted. Even as far back as the 1970s there was a strong suspicion of a link between the use of CFCs and the destruction of the ozone layer, and from the 1980s onwards these misgivings have hardened beyond dispute. Notwithstanding all the evidence, CFC manufacture continued with the blessing of the law, and it was not until 1985, the year of the Vienna Convention, that a first international agreement laid the groundwork for control measures. Then, in 1987, followed the Montreal Agreement, signed by 24 nations. It limited growth, but allowed production to continue at the same volume from 1986 to 1993, with compulsory reduction not starting until 1993. Already in 1990 the terms of this agreement were toughened during a conference in London, and the year 2000 was set as the year for discontinuation of CFC manufacture to be completed. And then early in 1992 came the urgent warning from NASA, which led Germany, for instance, to take the lead and propose a ban on CFC manufacture by 1993, while the USA still envisage to abandon manufacture by 1995.

Through not heeding the early warnings CFC manufacturing companies are now being forced on the defensive to preserve their image. They must furthermore absorb the costs of decommissioning, converting, or even scrapping their plants in order to avoid harm to the environment.

This entails high write-offs as well as a sizeable leap in development costs because the race for the best substitute products is on, and the winner of this race stands to gain an enormous segment of the market.

High research and development costs for CFC substitutes also affect all the other development schemes of a company because the high priority given to the search for a substitute depletes funds for other projects. And the CFC users also face their share of repercussions: they experience a noticeable change in price structure; they must recycle CFCs or bear the costs of switching to substitutes, and all within a short period of time.

It could have been quite different if the manufacturers and the main users had listened more carefully to the first weak and then strong signals pinpointing very clearly the increasing problems with CFCs.

Ecoefficiency

Efforts to achieve efficiency are part and parcel of standard management science. Even without ecological pressure a good management will seek to improve its efficiency on purely financial grounds. However, the parameters of efficiency are subject to change, i.e. environmental resources that were previously free will be taxed and thus have a price tagged to them. This means that the managerial concept of efficiency becomes increasingly an ecological one. True efficiency will in the long run never be incompatible with ecology and therefore never involves managers in difficult conflicting aims.

The change of the economy will not be primarily because ecoproducts sell better but because only an efficient organization will be able to prevail as competition gets tougher. Only in a second phase will opportunities for offensive action come back into the focus of managerial thinking. How quickly this transformation will proceed depends on the political will to change basic conditions with, say, a carbon tax, and on economic pressures such as high waste disposal costs. This will open up new markets for environmentally friendly products.

The improvement of efficiency is a perennial task for every management and many managers even see it as their prime function. The ecological challenge has merely added a new dimension. This also holds true of companies that still consider themselves to be unaffected by ecology. Such firms simply do not exist. Even banks and insurance companies are undergoing the effects in an ever increasing degree. Apart from ecology at the workplace, banks are finding that the behaviour of investors and the new dimension of risks involved in the granting and supervision of loans are occupying the focus of attention. In this context inherited pollution may lead to major and costly surprises. The sums placed to reserve by insurance companies with worldwide operations have increased by billions as a result of losses due to ecological causes. Both the Allianz and the Swiss Reinsurance Company have informed their shareholders of this in their annual reports.

This case for efficiency is not a completely new one. Similar arguments were heard before when total quality control was under debate. Total quality control means that, on passing through the production process, the products are tested for quality at as many points as possible. In this way defects can be recognized and corrected at once. The main emphasis was on the reduction of production costs and guarantee costs. At the same time, however, it led to available resources being treated with greater care; there were fewer rejects which in turn led to lower material costs. The concept of quality is going to become increasingly important in ecomanagement. On the one hand because there is a direct link between quality and efficiency, and on the other, because in many industries, e.g. foods, white goods, etc. quality is closely tied up with environmental friendliness. In the early eighties AEG gave the concept of quality a new lease of life in its badly dented white goods division and closely associated it with environmental friendliness. With the 'green washing machine' AEG scored a success on a scale that was never anticipated. AEG even succeeded in repositioning itself in the top price segment.

Higher than necessary costs and an uncontrolled change of the cost structure signal inefficiency and are a result of not considering environmental issues in management decisions. Environmental resources which are, for the time being, still free make this possible; but in the long term the introduction of so called economic instruments such as environmental taxes, will put an end to this.

The prisoner's dilemma

The question of efficiency does not arise in the same form for each firm. A crucial factor is the strategy which the company is pursuing in a market sector. Let us suppose that a company is aware that a noxious substance escapes during the production process. This circumstance is still tolerated by the law but it may be anticipated that in three years' time new standards will be imposed and that the emission of this material will be prohibited. Management is now faced with the choice of waiting for another three years or, alternatively, starting to modify the production process, which will cost, say, two million pounds but will halt the discharge of the harmful substance immediately. For simplicity's sake let us leave aside the questions of image and ethics and concentrate solely on the influence of the strategy selected. If a company is successful because it has the lowest production costs and can therefore offer the customers a lower price than its competitors, in other words if the firm is pursuing a 'cost leader' strategy, then additional costs for the elimination of the harmful substances will jack up production costs. The firm's profit margin will drop. For if it passed on the costs to the customers, it could no longer offer the lowest prices and would lose market share.

How, then, should a company with a cost leader strategy react in such a situation? The alternatives are:

1. To accept the additional costs without delay or
2. to wait until the legislator imposes the decision.

What happens if a company decides in favour of the ecologically sound solution and its competitors do not? As long as a firm does not know how its competitors will react, it is in a dilemma described as the 'prisoners dilemma': a prisoner has committed a crime with an accomplice. They are caught and each is confined in a separate cell, not knowing whether and what the other will confess. The prisoner knows that the two of them can count on a lenient sentence if they both deny the deed. So he will not confess to it. If the prisoner denies the deed but his accomplice admits it, then he is in a very unpleasant position. If, on the other hand, he confesses to the deed and his accomplice denies it, the situation is reversed. If both confess to full responsibility, then both will receive a very stiff sentence.

Environmental problems are placing more and more firms in the classic situation of the prisoner's dilemma. Should a company take the lead in environmental performance or should it wait for legislation? What will its competitors do – if the company decides to take the lead, will they follow and join in on restoring the environmental image of the industry?

This dilemma raises the question whether, against this background, more emphasis should be given to industry-wide solutions; or whether, in the light of the ecological dimension, the cost leader strategy is too risky, and the time has come for a realignment. If a firm wants to exploit such a situation to its own competitive advantage, then the cost leader strategy is hardly appropriate any longer. Or should production be altered so that the harmful substance is no longer produced and the additional costs are lower than the savings that can be achieved later?

A firm concentrating, for example, on a market niche which allows higher prices for certain attributes of a product will be less sensitive to the problems inherent to the cost-leader strategy. Customers in this market niche place more emphasis on quality and design features, rather than price and higher production costs can be more readily passed on to them. However, a niche strategy alone is no protection against unpleasant surprises of ecological origin. It simply mitigates the effects of changes in costs.

Efficiency: the other side of the coin

Efficiency is an important building block in ecologically sound behaviour and it is often the trigger that gets managers moving in the direction of environmental management. Cost savings in waste management, lower purchasing costs due to more economical handling of materials, savings in packaging, lower insurance costs – these are the results of ecologically sound business behaviour that concentrates on the cost side. To do more with the same or the same with less is one way of summing up efficiency.

But efficiency in this sense must never be considered in isolation. To build on efficiency alone means neglecting other important aspects that can abruptly negate the improved efficiency achieved. There are several reasons for this. It is perfectly possible to pursue with high efficiency an activity which is ecological nonsense. If, for example, the basic conditions give misleading signals and an important environmental commodity is too cheap, it becomes economically efficient to make excessive use of it. This defeats the entire object. Such a mode of action, irrespective of whether a cost leader or a niche strategy is being pursued, leads into a blind alley and can cause a company or even a whole industry of firms to come in for criticism from a large number of groups: neighbours, shareholders, lenders, personnel, authorities, environmental pressure groups, etc. A firm must be acceptable to such groups if it is to continue its existence. Acceptance is a crucial production factor; only the company who can recruit good staff, who can obtain planning permissions, and who can introduce new technologies has a long-term basis for efficient business operations.

LOOKING FORWARD: THE OPPORTUNITIES

Products that are best-sellers but seriously damage the environment during their life cycle have no future. The same holds true for ecologically acceptable products which do not sell well. It follows that the art of ecomanagement consists in optimizing the relationship between business success and improved environmental acceptability. In other words the environmental acceptability of a product must be enhanced in relation to its economic performance. Such green cash cows, i.e. ecologically acceptable products with a high cash flow, make possible a high level of internally generated financing. Although the efficient capital market will always lend money to successful enterprises, self-financing is and remains important. This is because a high proportion of borrowed capital increases the influence wielded by lenders. Repeated capital increases lead to dependence on the stock market and intensify the pressure exerted by investors. The structure and business climate of the economy are tending towards an industrial landscape in which the environment is a factor that matters. But it is precisely during such times of change that independence is particularly important.

A successful management strategy will always aim to move away from products which have both a low earning capacity and low environmental acceptance. The way ahead should lead to green cash cows. This means that independence and efficiency are fostered because environmentally friendly products are incompatible with inefficiency.

Portfolio methods

It is important for the management of a company to have at its disposal instruments of corporate analysis which enable it to evaluate a situation. More than one half of the Fortune 500 companies in the USA have worked with portfolio methods in strategic planning during the last decades. Portfolios are used to assess, for instance, the relationship between relative market share and growth, or between attractiveness of a market and a company's strength. As a result management can identify the segments it will push or those it should give up.

It could be argued that environmental criteria have received enough attention because they are an integral part of the other inputs in the strategic planning process. But the whole crux of the matter is that just being taken into consideration as one of many aspects is not enough. You cannot afford to just pay lip service to the environmental dimensions of your planning process, because exactly these environmental criteria spark off those dreaded down turns in the economic trend that are occurring at ever shorter intervals. In order to break away from the downward spiral environmental questions must be presented in a systematic and undiluted way within a framework of strategic planning. It is important for managers to be able to detect and interpret the various signals which could predict breaks in the economic trend or crucial changes in a phase early enough to allow a considered and purposive reaction. These signals are very important and could never be detected against a general background. They are an indication of a segment or product group's sensitivity to the environment. They show where and how decisive action in response to environmental problems can make an impact. In an early stage these signals will only be weak, for instance, critical newspaper articles and discussions in the technical press. They become stronger when product ingredients come under scrutiny, product characteristics are queried, recycling systems are started up, disposal costs rise, new routes of distribution are established, the first substitute products appear, legislation is initiated, competitors go in for green marketing, advertising is intensified, advertisers think up new arguments and eventually when industrial associations become active. They then indicate that the environment is becoming an issue.

Ecological portfolio methods
Portfolio methods also have their strong points. They can be rounded off with a control portfolio concerned solely with ecological questions. Basically, this involves a kind of strategic environmental audit. For such an environmental stocktaking strategic planning does not have to be reinvented, but it does need to be supplemented so as to reveal the opportunities and also the risks created by environmental issues and trends.

One of the most exciting questions likely to confront ecomanagers is the problem of knowing what to do when an audit shows that the development of precisely that product segment in which the firm has a major interest performs unsatisfactorily from an environmental point of view. A frequent, but inadequate, answer is the recommendation to diversify into new, environmentally less sensitive, products. But diversifications often involve high costs and the company is suddenly faced with making decisions on products and markets of which it is ignorant. Furthermore, the shareholders will not readily accept a decrease in the earning powers of a company for a diversification they can effect more cheaply by buying shares of different companies. If a company is under environmental pressure to diversify into completely new areas, the capital will be invested unproductively from the shareholders' viewpoint. Their investment loses value. Or might not an environmentally conscious investor ask whether this diminution in value is not the price to be paid for a better positioning of the company in which he or she owns shares? Management, it is usually alleged, diversifies only to increase its own security and power and is indifferent to the value of the company to the shareholders. Will this give rise to a new chain of arguments which will exonerate the management from the charge of consulting its own interests if at the same time clear ecological goals are pursued?

Diversification is not the only possible move towards a solution. The value chain, which was developed by Porter and includes the ecological dimension, allows for other possibilities. It enables us to pinpoint exactly the place in a firm's chain of activities where ecological objections arise and the precise importance of this activity for the buyer's value to be ascertained. This chain includes obtaining raw materials, product development, materials procurement, production, marketing and logistics up to and including waste disposal. The main focus of value creation may suddenly be transposed to another link of the chain because of environmental problems. In the automotive industry, for example, environmentally correct waste management is steadily becoming an important sales argument. A rigorous analysis of the value chain will show that the question of packaging is rapidly gaining in importance for many consumer goods and also influences the customer's purchasing decision but that packaging contains no great value creation. It follows then, that the whole created value can be sold only when the packaging problem for the customer has also been solved.

Ecomanagement means product stewardship in the sense of an all-embracing responsibility for a product's environmental acceptability product, even long after it has left the factory. Consequently the analysis must take cognizance of whether the environmental problems are located in the value chain of the company itself, of a supplier or of a customer. A foodstuff manufacturer, for instance, can attract severe criticism because the packaging he uses is not ecologically unobjectionable. But he obtains this packaging from a supplier. The sins of others, so to speak, are visited upon him. And above all, it is not his incontestably good and healthy food that figures glowingly in reports but rather the unsolved packaging problem. One crucial question here is whether a firm can exert any influence on the solution of such problems. Can the supplier be induced to provide better packaging? Nestlé and Unilever would no doubt have no problems. But what is an entrepreneur to do if he is only an insignificant customer of the packaging manufacturer? His product has fallen into disrepute because of its packaging, but with this product he might achieve a high portion of his sales.

Other management instruments

Apart from the portfolio method and the concept of the value chain, there are other management instruments which help the manager to handle environmental questions more satisfactorily. If one applies Porter's system of strategic planning logically to environmental issues, it will show that they offer enormous possibilities and lines of advance that have previously remained quite unexploited. It will demonstrate that the environment is a factor which exerts an influence on both the attractiveness of an industry and also, within that sector, on the relative status of an individual company which depends on the strategy it has selected.

According to Porter the attractiveness and profitability of an industry depends on the question of how power is shared between supplier, company and customer. Where the power lies the major part of the profit will accrue. Other influential factors are the possibility of new competitors penetrating the market and the danger of substitution. It is obvious that the position of the suppliers and of the customers can be crucially affected by the environmental dimension. The appraisal of a product over its whole lifetime, the assessment of its value creation chain and also of its potential for pollution will alter the rules of the game in many industries. The question of product substitution may, however, be even more momentous: ecological arguments will accelerate possible substitution – a constant threat – and therefore at the same time influence the entry barriers for new competitors into the industry. This threat is increasing in various sectors because new competitors can figure with higher credibility and competence in environmental questions. They have an easier time compared with existing manufacturers who have the laborious task of remedying their image as polluters. The newcomers can use offensive arguments in their communications whereas the others cannot abandon their defensive posture. New firms will never miss the opportunity of pointing out that their products and production processes are more acceptable from the ecological point of view than yours. If you don't make your products obsolete, your competitor will. Changes such as these also influence the power structure and this exerts a potent influence – underestimated by many managers – on the profitability of the industry and also on their own firm.

An aggressive management will exploit the enormous opportunity and try itself to influence these factors. A pacemaker with environmentally sound products can, in particular, mitigate the risk of substitution and erect new barriers to market entry by pleading for higher environmental standards for the industry. Those who take no active measures, on the other hand, are likely to find themselves suddenly out in the cold because the rules of the game have changed. And these changes are today more frequent and come at ever shorter intervals.

We have already dealt with the effects of the strategy adopted when discussing the subject of efficiency. It is important to stress that there are no easy answers. The environmental dimension must be tackled individually for each product segment and each company. The important issue is that each firm should clearly commit itself to a strategy and then pursue this to its logical conclusion, otherwise there is a danger of being stuck in the middle between variant strategies which are mutually exclusive. And precisely this danger will be aggravated by the environmental dimension as long as the economic system as a whole has not switched over to an environmentally acceptable pattern of behaviour. Pacemakers will often – it is inherent in their role – pursue a niche strategy. If the pacemaker role has the result that other enterprises follow suit, a niche can easily turn into a mass business. As soon as niche products – as the result, say, of environmental legislation – become commodities (as happened, for instance, in the case of certain PVC-free packaging) other firms will dominate the competition. In mass production costs are usually the factor that decides between success and failure. However, there can be only one cost leader, and therefore, sooner or later, the question will crop up whether one should return to the niche strategy. This means that a firm must constantly review and possibly change its strategy. It can be assumed that, in the process of an economy changing over to a more environmentally acceptable one, the path leading from a niche strategy via a cost leadership strategy back to a niche strategy will often be encountered.

Once again it is clear that the tasks of management will become more difficult, demanding and complex but also more exciting. A company must have an idea of its way ahead and the limits within which it can operate. But within those limits it must be in constant motion; it must, as Porter puts it, be a moving target.

Every company has to bear an economic, social and ecological responsibility. Although these three responsibilities affect each other reciprocally, it is just about impossible to bring all their components under a common denominator. It is only by studying all three individually and in depth that a properly considered decision can be made on priorities and weightings in the overall strategy. The underlying values of a decision and the trade offs made, for example between the preservation of jobs and the environmental performance, can then be openly communicated.

If a company is to safeguard the environment, much more is involved than when it decides on mere compliance with the law – to which it is obliged at any rate. What is necessary is to optimize managerial and ecological results in a way that makes sense in the long term. If either becomes disequilibrated, it endangers the other. Nor can the relevant factors all be quantified at once. Many of them, e.g. image, acceptance and shorter authorization procedures, pay off only in the long run.

Beware of pitfalls

If a company decides that, in the light of ecological factors, a product should be withdrawn from the market and replaced by a new one, the question of the right timing arises. This is a question which is not posed in the same terms for every firm but depends on its position in the industry. A proactive company with a sufficiently large share of the market can influence the structure of the industry. It is more difficult for a medium-sized firm which is only one player among many. How can it switch over to a more acceptable kind of growth? Is it enough to have a good communication strategy and thus be assured of the customers' cooperation? Are environmental innovations sufficient? Various pioneers with their environmentally acceptable products have staked too much on innovation as the sole factor of success. They came onto the market too early and fell into the so-called innovation trap. For although solutions to many environmental problems are being urgently sought, these markets are also ruled by the classical laws of marketing. One of these laws is the market introduction time, which tends to be long precisely in the case of new, environment-safeguarding technologies. Many firms which are environmental pioneers do not have the time to survive from innovation to market introduction and the first cash inflows. All that often remains to them is the cold comfort of seeing another firm market the technology five years later when the market has become mature because of, say, new environmental standards. This has been the experience of the manufacturers of solar energy generators who reacted in the 1970s to the first oil price shock. The various pioneers of the electric vehicle sector may suffer a similar fate.

Organization and change

Managers who have revised and altered their strategy with a view to the environment are in for a bitter disappointment when trying to put these changes through. Their implementation will succeed only if the basic structural and organizational conditions have been so modified that a change is practicable at all. It is a right and proper step to vest a staff manager with responsibility for the environment, but it falls far short of what is necessary. What is needed is a technical regulator with unlimited authority to inquire and inspect. This can serve as a central starting-up office and stimulate new thinking, but the ultimate responsibility must remain with the line managers. Total quality control has fared similarly; it was found that a quality inspector was counterproductive. Total quality control has gained acceptance only in those companies that have succeeded in making the quality of their products a matter of concern to all their personnel.

Certainly, every firm needs its champion for the environment who creates environmental awareness. When this is a member of the top management everyone will realize that environmental aspects are to be taken seriously. VW, for instance, appointed to its executive committee Professor Steger, an internationally recognized authority on questions of management and environment. The effects of this appointment on the strategy of the company remain to be seen.

And then the form of organization also plays a prominent part. Not all organizational forms lend themselves equally well to ecomanagement. The important thing is that a form should be found which is capable of responding in an early stage to signs and signals and learning from them. Markedly hierarchical forms are unsuitable in this respect. The more pronounced the hierarchy, the more limited the learning ability of the system. The learning ability of firms operating in protected industries is also very low. This has been a painful experience for many companies. For example, the insurance industry in Switzerland or large parts of the car industry in Europe and in the USA are finding it very difficult to adjust to the modern age. The protection afforded by cartels has sapped their ability to learn and adapt.

There is no form of organization preeminently suited to the environment, but it has been found that it helps for authority to be delegated as far downwards as possible and for the structure to be well decentralized. Decentralized production gives the individual a wider perspective, brings manufacturer and customer closer together, and can also improve the results of an environmental audit because of shorter transport hauls. A company has to be close to its markets and stakeholders, for physical presence is important for mutual understanding. Proximity also sensitizes the firm to early signals emanating from such groups. Distant headquarters will never be in a position to identify changes at an early stage, let alone to grasp their proper significance.

Delegation may also have a positive impact, when a motivation gap between the attitude of an employee at home and at his workplace might arise. The managements of Hoechst, ICI and Dupont must ask themselves what the reactions of their own workforce are when they see programmes about the ozone problem on their home TV, discuss them with their children, and go back to work the next day. What goes on in their minds when they go through the factory gate? Do they have to switch off their feelings at this point? Situations like these must never be underestimated by management. They lead employees to quit inwardly. Such a mood will also be reflected outside and will, in one way or another, recoil on the company. If responsibility for environmentally conscious management is delegated to all levels, it becomes the concern of every employee. True, this does not dispose of all the problems, but the employees see that the company they work for is taking the question of environment seriously.

Environmental audits, a multifunctional management tool

Environmental audits are the managerial instrument that is growing fastest in use; they have become indispensable. There are many different types and methodologies of environmental audits and probably it would be more reasonable to talk about life-cycle analysis, when assessing a product's environmental impact. Whatever the methodology, even highly pragmatic procedures reveal immense opportunities for saving and identifying the fields where action is most important. It is similar to the world of sport: top athletes work with video evaluations, top managers with environmental audits. When his run is analysed, the best downhill racer sees where he lost time, where his rivals were better, where his movements were right and where they were wrong. The manager can only assess what is possible for him in ecomanagement when he knows how much energy his firm consumes, what harmful substances his products generate when incinerated, what products he can market with the support of environmental arguments, etc.

Ecology in general, and environmental audits in particular, are constantly criticized for their lack of precision. It is alleged that they lack accuracy, that their pronouncements are not clear, and that the data is vague. Not a newspaper article on ecology is printed without a political demand from one association or another for more investigations! These uncertainties are for many a pretext for pooh-poohing the possibility of management in accordance with ecological criteria. This view must be vehemently contested. For, clearly, the standards applied in environmental questions are stricter by far than in other management problems. If the same exactitude were to be demanded for, say, an investment decision, investment would virtually come to a standstill. Every investment plan is based on forecasts of future trends. And, ecological forecasts, like every forecast, are also bedeviled by major uncertainties. Moreover, predictions in financial forecasts are usually far less assured than ecological facts. We know a great deal more about the increasing pollution of drinking water and its state in five years' time than about the turnover and earnings of a textile machine factory in five years. Major investment decisions are very often actuated by the merely emotional motives of the managers responsible and are not based on purely rational considerations. Yet it is precisely this rationality and precision which is now being demanded from ecology. Just think of all uncertainties contained in financial statements as for instance the valuation of goodwill.

During the last twenty years misguided approaches in communication have destroyed a great deal of trust between the public and industry. For far too long only favourable features were highlighted and adverse ones were passed over in silence or their existence was even denied. Today ecology in particular seems to be paying for these past sins.

It is in this communication process that environmental audits can be especially useful. They are an ideal instrument for actively structuring a development, particularly if an enterprise has the courage to feed the public with information. Of course, in the initial phase, this brings enormous pressure to bear on the company. But as public pressure for environmentally sound management is going to come sooner or later, it is better to seize the initiative. Citizens' action groups and environmental pressure groups are becoming increasingly professional. Their members are often highly educated and experts in a number of fields. They keep an alert eye on developments in business and industry. Impelled by concern for the future, parents are going to ratchet up their demands on behalf and in the interests of their children. So it behoves management to enter into active communication with these various groups and to weigh in with facts and figures in the dialogue on, say, new technologies. The company will then be seen by other groups to be part of an overall social system and not to be one part which considers itself to be its centre. As part of a system one must be prepared to lower one's sights and accept less than maximum demands, for the other stakeholders also have their demands and it is they that supply the company with the resources it needs. If society no longer accepts a firm, or if the bank will no longer make credit available, if the motivation of the workforce flags, the consequences for the firm are disastrous. That is why in a process of negotiation cards must be laid on the table and the differences between the various interests and claims discussed. It is not a question of converting other people to one's own views but rather of understanding what they want. Such discussions will afford the alert listener a number of insights and hints as to future policy. In time the dialogue will be found to build up confidence. And this confidence is in turn the inseparable condition of the production factor 'acceptance'.

New instruments for environmentally sound management will of themselves solve no problems. An environmental audit does not relieve the firm of its worries. The danger is that the introduction of an environmental audit will be mistaken for the implementation of an environmentally conscious strategy. Yet nobody would think that a management strategy can be formulated just by drawing up a balance sheet and profit-and-loss account.

PROVOKING NEW LAWS, AN UNUSUAL OPPORTUNITY

The subject of new thinking is closely linked to strategic planning, otherwise it would not be worth while discussing it here. With this new attitude it should be easier to pinpoint trends at an early stage and institute suitable action. In this way legislation can be headed off – e.g. by voluntarily ensuring a high standard – or deliberately provoked so that one can bring active influence to bear on the attractiveness of the industry. Every company must face the risk that one day new competitors will come into the field. The larger the number of firms competing for the customers' favour, the greater the danger of competition degenerating into a ruinous price war. The wise entrepreneur forestalls this risk by an active engagement in shaping the basic conditions of the sector. New laws setting high standards are a suitable instrument in this, not only because one's own company comes under pressure to perform better but also because every other firm must first satisfy the more stringent regulations before it can become a serious competitor. Limits are thus set to the number of possible competitors. Competitors are, so to speak, saddled with development costs which one has already borne oneself. The Elco Looser group, a Swiss heating engineering firm operating on an international scale, has, for instance, exceeded the stringent Swiss regulations on air pollution and had a say in the negotiation of the still stricter Zurich standards. The firm has thus stolen a march on competitors, and all imitators will have to surmount higher barriers if they want to be equally successful. And Elco has done its image no end of good into the bargain.

There are also other ways of turning legislation to your advantage. In the United States the Environmental Protection Agency has organized workshops on the problems raised by leaking pumps, valves or flanges. This problem is particularly important for the chemical industry, for there are serious leaks from the thousands of hose connections at many chemical plants. Staff of Fisher Controls International, a former subsidiary of the Monsanto Group, have carefully analysed the results obtained at these workshops. They came to the conclusion that it was only a matter of time before new regulations would be issued. So they started work on a new valve long before there was any serious discussion about an amendment to the Clean Air Act. They developed valves which reduce the emission of volatile gases by 95 per cent compared with traditional types. When finally a new standard was decided on, the staff of Fisher Controls were ready with a design that met market requirements to a T. When the new standard was introduced, Fisher had the only control valves specifically designed to meet the EPA's standards for fugitive emissions. Competitors had nothing comparable to offer, and the success was enormous.

With the help of industrial associations, both firms might have pushed for conditions under which no or only very minor requirements would be incorporated in the law. They would then have been able to go on selling their old products for as long as possible. This defensive ploy would have obscured and negated the opportunities inherent in such a situation. By taking their line, the two firms have followed one of Nature's laws. They have not wasted their valuable energies on resisting disturbing forces but rather diverted these forces to work in their own favour. Both have exploited this approach with great success.

A stringent environmental policy in a company's home country has still further advantages. Nowhere else do companies respond to signals and pressures so quickly or so sensitively as on their home market. Strict domestic standards keep firms on their toes, fit them for the future, and are a factor in ensuring that they have good opportunities on foreign markets. Companies who are never under stress in the home market are prone to protect themselves from better trained foreign competition by non-economic means and are hardly likely to stay fit enough to be successful abroad.

In this respect not only legislation but also the existence of active pressure groups and lobbies have an important function. In France no one pressed for the catalytic converter and discussions on PVC-free packages for beverage lagged far behind those in other European countries. In both fields the French missed the bus. The absence of an active environmentalist movement has cost the French economy dear.

The strategies of many industrial associations will have to change. Many of them have slipped into the way of saying 'no' because in most cases they have to represent the interests of those who are losers as a result of environmental measures. The very process of ecologizing industry will find many firms on the losing side. These represent a political force and therefore usually use their power purely to preserve structures and to gain time; but they cannot hold up the march of events. As our two examples have shown, it is open to all companies to change over to the winning side by taking active steps. But there can be no steady economic progress unless the winners stand to gain.

The bottleneck

Back in the 19th century Rockefeller grasped the point: if he controlled the bottleneck, he would control the whole industry. In the oil and gas business the bottleneck was transport. Now there is a new bottleneck: waste disposal. The possibilities of disposal are dwindling while the pressure to dispose is increasing, and as a result the prices for waste disposal are rocketing. This means no more or less than that the power of the waste management firms is increasing. This is particularly marked in those countries in which waste disposal is being privatized. Cases are already known where a disposal firm could ask thirty times the cost of disposing of a ton of hazardous waste. A handsome margin! Manufacturers' profits will therefore become steadily smaller. Although they are responsible for the bulk of the value creation of a product, only a disproportionately small part will remain to them when the profit is shared out. The lion's share will be claimed by the disposal firm. Moreover, it could prove hopeless to try for a fairer share by negotiation. In the public eye the waste management firms are always at an advantage; they provide a solution for the problems which the manufacturing companies have created. More, they apparently spirit away a problem which we are all only too happy to forget.

These are difficulties which many manufacturers can still cope with. But things become critical when the waste management industry can dictate to the manufacturers what they may or may not produce. Managers who want to preserve their independence and continue to make their own decisions about what their company produces will therefore do well to bear these developments in mind. They have to consider all aspects of a product's life cycle and heavily underline in their development engineers' specifications the parts referring to waste disposal. They must devise strategies for avoiding and reducing waste. A favourite scheme for this purpose is recycling.

Recycling: obvious solution or empty gesture?

People use ecological slogans far too readily to connote the contents of a strategy without analysing in detail the ways in which this will affect their own company. Recycling is just such a buzzword. The knowledge that, whenever possible in industry, circuits should be closed, often leads to recycling being proposed as the best bet. In many instances recycling is undoubtedly a rational solution; but it is not always the best. A closed circuit economizes resources and reduces the emissions burdening the environment. But recycling is not a strategy per se, quite apart from the fact that downcycling would be a more appropriate term. In recycling no circuit is actually closed; all that happens is that the economically useful life of the raw materials is prolonged. But along with this goes a diminution in their useful properties. In the great majority of cases the recyclate is of inferior quality and is therefore difficult to market.

Careful strategic planning can no doubt always find a place for the variant recycling. But it must be remembered that there are also other solutions. Recycling euphoria must not blind us to all its implications.

First, from the environmental point of view it is reasonable to ask whether it might not be preferable to prolong the service life of the product rather than introduce recycling. Why should a product not be designed in a modular way so that only one unit out of the whole need be replaced in the event of technical change? Using a strategy of this kind, a firm could forge well ahead of its competitors. A niche would open for the sale of spare parts and also of technical retrofits.

The advantage for the customer would be that, in the event of technical innovation, he would simply have to buy the appropriate module. In this way the manufacturer could also tie his customers closely to his products. Such systems can also make life very difficult for competitors.

Second, in the vast majority of cases recycling requires the recycling system to be an industry-wide solution. That is to say, a company cannot introduce this system on its own. Hence the potential for differentiating from competitors is limited. Product designers no longer have an entirely free hand because a product must subsequently be reprocessed in a recycling plant. Originality and creativity are downgraded. But for a company whose competitive ability rests precisely on these two capacities, a recycling system can lead to disastrous results. The strategic effects of cooperative schemes and joint ventures must therefore be gauged very carefully in advance.

Once recycling is established, the pressure to find new solutions is off. Recycling may even be regarded as a retarding factor on the path to closed circuits. For as soon as a system is introduced, the pressure to find new and technologically superior systems to minimise the use of raw materials will rapidly diminish. To take an example: the new packaging legislation in Germany has caused innumerable organizations to concern themselves with packaging. But at the same time the idea of dispensing with packaging altogether is completely neglected. Motivation to innovate is thus paralysed, even in individual companies. This cannot be the objective of any company. Just the opposite: almost every company has continuous innovation firmly anchored as a goal in its business philosophy. Just as strict legislation raises the entry barriers to possible competitors, thus making the sector more attractive overall, recycling systems can constitute exit barriers to the individual company which wants to innovate its own products. For it is not only a new product that is needed but also a new recycling or disposal system, and the costs also have to be borne for closing down or withdrawing from the old system.

If a manager comes to the conclusion that recycling is the right solution for his products, then there are two further questions he has to face. The first concerns the basic materials which are fed into the recycling system. Tropical wood as a basic material is not a good solution and never will be, even if it can be reused a number of times. The second question: Does the company, or the waste management firm working for it, have the recycling process under such complete control that polluting the environment can be ruled out altogether? These points are important because recycling is often used as an eye-catching advertisement of the company's environmental commitment. It thus becomes a pillar of communication in public relations. Public reaction is then all the sharper if it should be transpire that something is wrong with the recycling. A good reputation and laboriously acquired confidence can be quickly forfeited in this way. This has been the bitter experience of the aluminium industry in Switzerland. A great deal of hard work and lobbying went into building up a recycling system for aluminium packagings. The question whether from an environmental point of view aluminium is the right material for packaging or whether a substitute might be available received too little attention. And it was also found that the recycling process still presented problems. After extensive research Greenpeace discovered that the recycling process is technologically inadequate and that the environment is subjected to unacceptable pollution.

Whose is the responsibility? Own or hire?

What shifts of power take place? We broached this question in the section on bottlenecks. Who, it might be asked, sets up the distribution and redistribution pattern within the recycling system? With this goes the question of responsibility and ownership. Can a company that sells a product ensure that a sufficiently high proportion finds its way back to recycling? Or do other forms of contract other than a straight sale come to mind here?

Quite conceivably, leasing will in future acquire a quite different status in environmental management. With the aid of leasing it is possible to contract with the customer so that he can use the product while the ownership remains vested in the manufacturer. If the owner remains the same throughout an entire cycle, first, responsibility is clearly defined and, second, a code of behaviour can be imposed. When a manufacturer sells a product, he also forfeits a large part of his ability to exert his influence and to organize rational disposal. Companies that reflect on the meaning of ownership in the context of ecomanagement may arrive at new and creative solutions. Ownership may acquire a new meaning when the responsibility for a product extends over the whole of its life cycle. Solutions that have been devised in other industries may point to new approaches. Leasing is a firmly established practice in the case of office equipment. It makes it easier for the distributors to ensure that these machines are disposed off in an ecologically correct way because they take them back at the end of their service life.

This brings up the question whether there is any need at all for us to become the owners of products if we simply want to use them. Why should not more products be supplied on the lines of a lease and then returned to the owner when their useful life is finished? The latter would then have an incentive to reutilize in his new products as many parts as possible from the old so as to keep down disposal costs and also reduce the costs of new materials.

Competition among users

New forms of contract and behaviour patterns are typical signs of a structural change. Above all, they afford enormous strategic opportunities. A number of other points can be made here concerning environmental management. As soon as a resource that was once freely available becomes scarce and hence a price is set on it, there will be competition among users and management will have to deal with new competitors and negotiating parties. The classic example here is the competition between deep-sea fishermen and industry, which has abused the sea as a dumping ground. The same thing will happen with drinking water because many emissions finally end up in drinking water. So before very long, although this is not yet an acute problem in the environmental debate, competition will arise between those who are responsible for the emission of the substances polluting the water and those who are responsible for supplying the population with healthy drinking water. In strategic terms this may confront a food manufacturer with the question whether he will offer the product mineral water or whether he will perform the function of quenching thirst. If, in the light of ecological facts, the emphasis is placed on function, strategy may switch from the acquisition of a mineral spring to the purchase of a water-treatment plant.

Confidence, competence and marketing

Marketers and advertisers realized long ago that environmental acceptability boosts the sales chances of a product. Advertising messages abound in which consumers are persuaded that, if they buy the product advertised, they will be making a notable contribution to environmental protection. Some washing machine advertising almost implies that frequent washdays are a must for saving the environment.

Against such a background, it comes as no surprise that the call is heard for an independent and trustworthy assessor of environmental arguments. Not that there is anything new, of course, about the fact that every purchasing decision rests on incomplete information. To meet such misgivings, brand names have been created whose trustworthiness and good image are intended to relieve the potential purchaser of the need to make a detailed analysis of the product. Instead of having to wrestle with, say, the chemical or technical properties of the product, the customer knows that, because of the brand name, the products made by this company answer his requirements.

Accordingly, one way of radiating competence in environmental questions is to create a new brand. But if too many brand names, even established ones, seek to acquire an environmental aura, the result is renewed bewilderment among consumers. The next step often consists in the dissemination of private labels. The various environmental labels in the field of bio-foods are the best example. The plethora of such labels has, for example, induced the WWF in Switzerland to issue a guide in credit card format, the so-called ecocard. It can be consulted during shopping to check the ecological credibility of the different labels.

Various countries have endeavoured to create national eco-labels because such enormous importance is attached to environmentally acceptable consumption. The pacemaker was the 'Blue Angel', which was introduced in Germany in 1977. It has already been conferred on some 3,500 products which are distinguished from other products of the same category by their greater environmental friendliness. Of these 3,500 products, however, more than 900 fall into the category of 'low pollutant' varnishes. The most serious criticism of the 'Blue Angel' is that it is not awarded to bicycles, because there are no bicycles which are more harmful to the environment than others, but is awarded to cars with catalytic converters because there are cars more noxious, namely those without a converter. In spite of the criticism that the criteria for awarding the 'Blue Angel' are based on the environmental acceptability of a product within its category, and hence it is also conferred on products whose use is ecologically questionable, it enjoys undiminished popularity. Various products were able to increase sales by as much as 40 per cent after the award of the 'Blue Angel'. Various other countries, such as Japan, Canada or the Group of Nordic Countries have also developed an eco-label along the lines of the German model.

With the increasing use of eco-labels in advertising and of actual 'green marketing', these will sooner or later become an issue for every producer of consumer goods. In 1985, 0.5 per cent of all consumer products in the USA were launched with green arguments; in 1990 the figure had already risen to 9 per cent. Experience has shown, however, that marketing with the eco-label makes good sense only if the company tries to conform to ecological principles in all its activities. There is, of course, also a strategic dimension to this development. It again imposes drastic limitations on the ability of a company to acquire a distinctive identity. It is doubtful whether a company can afford not to tie an eco-label to its products. But it can do this only if the company's entire strategy is focused on making its name a synonym for quality in all respects, and especially in environmental matters. In both cases the company will have no alternative but to qualify for its eco-label with the aid of an environmental audit, in this specific case a life-cycle analysis, at product level and also to communicate environmental awareness through all echelons of the company.

DO IT NOW

No management should forget that the products developed today will one day be measured by the standards of the laws of the year 2000. The pressure exerted by the problem is high and continually rising. No great forecasting ability is needed to predict that these laws will be very much tougher than today.

In future a product will be able to hold its market position only if it is compatible with the needs of the environment. And this compatibility will go much further than conformity with the regulations of today.

Environmentally sound management means acting now. Our children will judge us by what we did and not by what we intended to do. Abstract schemes are a thing of the past. It is action that is needed!

References

Christopher/Majaro/Mc Donald, *Strategy Search*, Great Britain, 1987
Monsanto, Annual Report, 1990
Porter M E, *Competitive Strategy*, The Free Press, New York, 1980
Porter M E, *Competitive Advantage*, The Free Press, New York, 1985
OECD, *The State of the Environment*, Paris, 1991
OECD, *Environmental Labelling in OECD Countries*, Paris, 1991

'An image as an environmentally responsible company is becoming an essential part of a competitive strategy.'

Business Week, 18 June 1990

4 GREEN MARKETING

by Richard Ford

In this chapter, we look at the key issues of green marketing – the ways in which the concerns of consumers for the environment can affect their purchasing decisions, and the ways in which companies can influence, react to and profit from these decisions.

Green marketing is central to any analysis of why companies change their business strategy and conduct as a result of environmental pressures. To put it bluntly, all companies could reduce the impact on the environment of their products and processes, but they will choose not to, unless it is profitable to do so – and it will be profitable if consumers will pay more for the changes than the changes will cost.

There are, of course, other factors which affect companies' conduct and policies towards the environment. Competitors' green initiatives can provoke a green response which is immediate and drastic. Similarly, government regulations can force a company to embrace new changes in their products and processes which they would not otherwise have contemplated. However, it is as well to remember that the actions of competitors and of the government are in fact reactions to perceived changes in the attitudes and behaviour of consumers, although in the case of the government consumers happen to be called voters.

So consumers' attitudes and behaviour are central to the greening of competing companies in pluralist democracies. For this reason, green marketing, which we describe as 'profitably satisfying customers' requirements about the environmental impact of the products they use', is critical to a company's success, and understanding what those requirements are should be a key activity even for senior managers.

THE BACKGROUND TO GREEN MARKETING

The importance of green marketing in recent years is the result of a

quarter-century of tremendous growth in ordinary people's consciousness of the beauty and precariousness of the environment. Up until the
late 1960s, the vast majority of the population even in the developed
world neither thought nor cared about this subject. There were probably
two reasons for this.

First, the over-riding preoccupation of most people in the first half of
the twentieth century was with survival – whether from war, disease,
abject poverty, or other evils – so that concern for the natural world was
considered to be an unwarranted indulgence. This was particularly true
among the vast mass of working class people, who lived and worked in
cities and had lost any contact or sense of proximity with the countryside –
and whose standard of living improved dramatically between the First
World War and the sixties throughout the developed world.

Second, the frenetic economic growth in Western countries after the
end of the Second World War led people to believe in the power of
science and technology, and of the man-made in general, to transform,
improve and ultimately perfect their lives. After all, the diffusion of
products like cars, telephones, domestic durable goods, medicines and
new forms of household heating (notwithstanding the fact that many of
these were based on nineteenth century technologies) added immeas-
urably to working people's freedoms and pleasures. Technology was
seldom blamed for causing the destruction of natural resources and
habitats. On the contrary, it was popularly assumed that technology
would always be able to solve any problems it created, and that it would
continue its benign, triumphal march.

Interest in the environment started to flower in the 1960s. Books like
Silent Spring and *Limits to Growth* began to make the intellectual case
against the idea as a self-evident force for good. For the first time, the
downside of progress was described with scientific rigour. Moreover, the
founders of events like the first Earth Day (in 1970) and groups like the
Sierra Club and Friends of the Earth, not only had a strong commitment
to reasoned analysis in defence of the environment, but were also keen to
find ways of bringing environmental issues to the attention of the media
and the public.

Nevertheless, in the 1970s, the environmental movement in Western
countries was still largely confined to relatively affluent, articulate
people, and to the newspapers and magazines they chose to read. Indeed,
and paradoxically, a huge setback to greater dispersion of the message of
the pernicious effect of 'progress' on the natural world came with the first
oil shock in 1974.

This did not vindicate environmentalists' warnings about the West's over-reliance on diminishing natural resources, and thereby provide a fillip for the environmental movement. On the contrary, it sent the West's economic system into a tailspin and led to a fall in real standards of living which made people very reluctant to make the sacrifices which environmentalists were advocating. Faced with a general economic downturn – all the more traumatic since it followed nearly thirty years of dizzying growth – people strove to preserve their lifestyles rather than the planet.

With the improvement in economic conditions in the 1980s, however, the environmental movement once again began to gather pace. Today, awareness of the importance of the environment as a whole, and of specific phenomena like acid rain, global warming and the greenhouse effect, is at an all-time high. And as for attitudes to the environment, there has been a complete *volte-face* since the 1960s. The benefits of technological progress have become unclear to most ordinary people, while the downside of progress, in terms of ecological degradation, is seldom called into question.

Moreover, consumers take for granted the necessity of considering environmental factors in making their consumption decisions. And, astonishingly, even major recessions in many Western countries have not eroded the relevance of environmental issues for consumers. For example, in research conducted in Britain, France and Germany in late 1991, 93 per cent of respondents said that the environment was one of the most worrying problems facing society, significantly more than identified crime, unemployment and the economy as worrying problems.[1]

There are a number of reasons for the massive shift which has taken place in consumer attitudes towards the environment. The most important of these seem to us to be as follows.

Increasing affluence

The 1980s were a decade of economic growth and steadily rising incomes, wealth and living standards throughout the developed world. These gains in affluence were particularly strong for working people in their twenties and thirties, who were able to take advantage of the growing need for flexibility in the work place, as computerisation swept

---

[1] Research conducted by McCann-Erickson and Harris, quoted in *Marketing Week* (31 January, 1992). Crime, unemployment and the economy scored 85%, 81% and 79% respectively.

through factories and offices alike. Even in the recessionary 1990s, these people have continued to improve their living standards.

Increasing affluence has enabled these people to buy 'green' products, even when these have been priced at a premium. But more generally, these people have enough money to satisfy all their low level needs and are therefore able to concentrate on fulfilling relatively high level needs, one of which is their 'need' for environmental posterity[2]. It may seem strange that this is described as a high level need, since it is fundamental for the survival of the human race as a whole. However, for individuals, it is less pressing and important than any of their low level needs, since it is external, impersonal and uncontrollable.

Rational understanding of the ecological threat

In the 1960s and 1970s, environmentalists often argued on the basis of theories and suppositions which were remote from the experience of ordinary people. There was little empirical evidence that any damage to the environment was being caused by the march of the modern industrial system, nor that mankind would be adversely affected by any such destruction.

Times have changed. Most people would now regard the empirical evidence of the reality and impact of environmental destruction as overwhelming. In fact, the 'cranks' today are assumed to be those people who deny this evidence. The shift has come about as a result of the greater amount of scientific data which is being assembled and analysed to study environmental phenomena, and the continually improving coverage of these data in serious magazines and other media.

Emotional anxiety over the ecological threat

As well as thinking more about the environment, people now are also *feeling* more about it. The scientific evidence has been disseminated in highly dramatic ways by mass media throughout the developed world. The rise of colour television as *the* mass medium of the 1980s may even

---

[2] This analysis is based on the work of Maslow, who suggested that people are governed by an "Hierarchy of Needs" in their everyday decision-making, whereby low level needs always take precedence over higher level needs. So, for example, physiological needs (like food and drink) must be satisfied before safety needs (like a secure dwelling), which in turn must be satisfied before self-esteem needs (like a car or fashion goods) and so on.

have improved the visibility of green issues. Moreover, the mass media are increasingly driven by images rather than by statistics or reasoned scientific arguments, and they are concerned above all with disasters that threaten ordinary people – since these are the things which most effectively sell their wares.

Consequently, the mass media have been eloquent and in many cases heart-rending advocates for environmentalism. They have presented key green issues like the depletion of species, global warming, the presence and effect of noxious gases, and the destruction of natural habitats, as a series of media epiphanies – shocking and arresting images like the clubbing of seal pups, children starving in Africa as the Sahel gets drier, the ozone hole in the Antarctic, the burning of the Amazon rain forest, ships beached in the middle of the former Aral Sea, and many more. These have had a power and an immediacy which has cut through the complexity of the green debate, and has made ordinary people much more committed to helping the environment than they ever would have been otherwise.

Demographic shifts

People are growing older in the developed world, and their perspectives are increasingly becoming those of their children and grandchildren. The birth-rate is stable or falling in most Western countries, while improved health care means that people are now living longer. As a result, the median age of the population is rising. The 'baby boomers' of the post-war period are now reaching maturity and having babies of their own (often after delays caused by women pursuing their careers) on whom they are lavishing more money, love and care than ever previously in the history of the human race.

As developed societies become increasingly child-centred, people are paying more and more attention to the world which their children will inherit. Furthermore, because the age at which couples have children is getting higher, parents are now likely to be found in a life-stage where their urge and enthusiasm for achieving things themselves is on the wane. This makes their anxiety about their childrens' environmental inheritance, and their desire to do something about this, all the more profound.

Other crises receding in importance

In the second half of the 1980s, the Cold War was diffused through the efforts of President Gorbachev and the main Western leaders. The threat of nuclear war, which had been a subtext of international relations since the late 1940s, seemed to diminish. The process of liberalisation in Eastern Europe, and in the USSR itself, seemed to remove the danger of conventional war in Europe. And the hegemony of the USA, combined with the co-operation of the USSR, seemed to ensure that the United Nations would become a truly unified force for peace and justice.

This allowed people to look beyond immediate military threats to the world and towards more distant environmental ones. At the same time, the discovery of the ecological damage which had been wreaked by socialist regimes in the USSR and Eastern Europe amplified the need for strong environmental policies and solutions, while appearing to demonstrate that these would not work except in the context of pluralist, capitalist democracies. Thus the end of the Cold War gave the worldwide environmental movement a tremendous boost.

How the uncertain and insecure aftermath of the Cold War will affect green attitudes, however, is at present impossible to say. The Gulf War led to destruction on a grand scale, and to the first appearance of environmental terrorism directed against the rest of the world. Wars and threats of war have reared up in Europe, and four new countries of the old Soviet Union now have nuclear weapons. It is possible that immediate anxieties like these will once again make people less involved in longer-term environmental problems, although this has not yet been reflected in consumer research.

The respectability of being green

During the 1980s, being seen to be green became increasingly important among a broad group of middle-class people throughout the developed world. This was partly a reflection of traditional views that the countryside was physically, spiritually and morally superior to the city. It was also a conscious rebellion against the supposed values of 'grasping capitalism', as witnessed in stockmarket battles and frauds, red braces and fast cars. Being demonstrably green thus became a signal of distancing oneself from uncaring and socially irresponsible behaviour.

As a result, many consumers have been motivated in recent years by the thought of buying environmentally friendly products, since these not only seem to hark back to a meaningful rural idyll, but also demonstrate that the purchaser is not selfish, boorish or otherwise reprehensible. But the upshot of this is that their environmental demands are not stringent –

in effect, they are satisfied so long as products are *not ungreen*, and do not therefore expose them to the ignominy of green criticism from their peers.

Green initiatives from governments and companies

Governments have increasingly championed environmentalist causes. Altruism may have played a part in this, but there have also been sound political reasons. Governments have seen real electoral advantages in throwing their weight behind green legislation, because the relatively small group of people for whom the environment is the single most important political issue also tend to have few existing party loyalties, and are therefore crucial marginal voters in national elections. Attracting and maintaining the support of environmentalists can help to secure their ballots, but requires sensible and well argued green policies, not political flim-flam.

By aiming their green legislation at a demanding, environmentally articulate elite, governments often fire over the heads of the mass of the populace. At the same time, as suggested above, the environment has become relevant, albeit by no means the single most important political issue, across a broad swathe of society, so that new environmental policies, unless spectacularly radical, are unlikely to alienate the rest of the electorate. By appealing to a well informed minority, governments 'trade up' the majority to accepting intelligent, far-sighted environmental policies.

A similar process has been at work among competitive companies. From the middle of the 1980s, they saw that a small group of well informed consumers were willing to pay premium prices for greener products. In pursuit of higher margins, companies sought to appeal to this market niche; and in so doing, they awakened and progressively educated a broad mass market to the benefits of environmentally friendly products. This snowballing process has been rapid in most developed countries, because of the pervasiveness of advertising media and the control exercised by a relatively small number of powerful retailers. For example, the main reasons why the UK's transition from consumer ignorance to mainstream green purchasing in the mid-1980s was so fast that it astonished industry observers, were that the UK has a relatively high concentration of both mass media for advertising and multiple retailers, especially in the grocery trade. Once the leading advertisers and retailers went after high-margin, pioneering green consumers, they could not fail to communicate with the general public.

Thus, by pursuing the 'innovators' and 'early adopters' of green attitudes and behaviour, both governments and companies have broadened the appeal of environmentalism, and hastened its mainstream acceptability. (The terms 'innovators' and 'early adopters' are taken from the literature of the 'product life-cycle'. Innovators and early adopters are the first and second groups of consumers envisioned as starting to use a particular product.) The adoption of green attitudes and behaviour among consumers can be seen as analogous to the adoption of products. Political and market competition to be green has increased the number of people interested in and committed to the environment. The snowballing process has become irresistible.

THE PROBLEMS WITH GREEN MARKETING

These, then, are the main factors which have led to the rise of green marketing in the last few years. But the foregoing analysis suggests that there are problems with green marketing which practitioners need to take into account. The most central of these is that environmental friendliness remains a *motivating* concern for only a relatively small group of consumers. For the rest, it is a *hygiene factor* – something which products need at a minimal level to be satisfactory (that is, they have to be *not ungreen*), but which is seldom the reason for purchase and is typically taken for granted.

The snowballing of green consciousness has led to profound differences in understanding and commitment, even among consumers who all purport to be 'green'. While there has been a strong effort to educate people about green arguments, details and complexities (via pressure groups, schools and universities, quality media and some government publications), it is clear that many of the reasons given above for the growth of green marketing have encouraged a narrow and trivial conception of environmental issues. In particular, the mass media, competitive companies and, on occasion, governments have not been driven by educational goals regarding the environment, so it should not be surprising that they have been poor at putting across objective priorities and principles for green consumption.

Moreover, most people would not welcome an overload of information about the environment, which is generally considered to be distant from their own concerns of doing a job, looking after the family and making ends meet. People constantly complain that their lives are growing ever more frantic and packed with messages, as the 'information age' threatens to overwhelm their senses and mental faculties, so most of them are not interested in complex environmental information which does not even appear to help them with the way they live their lives from one day to the next.

There is, to be sure, a growing minority of people for whom environmental issues are so critical that they are prepared to join green pressure groups or become hyper-loyal customers of committed green companies. But even here, there is little interest in obtaining completely objective information to assist in making green consumption decisions. While pressure groups and avowedly green companies wish to educate their supporters, the 'education' they provide is by no means designed to take account of all currents of green thinking. In fact, it is didactic and propagandist, and seeks to eliminate the contradictions and difficult choices faced in making green consumption decisions.

At the same time, as greater numbers of scientists, economists and other intellectuals have started to consider environmental issues, it is clear that these issues have become more complex and contradictory, not less. Scientific 'proofs' have elicited counter-proofs. Sacred green cows have come under the spotlight, and traditional solutions no longer seem self-evidently and unambiguously correct. Questions and answers lack the certainty which busy, strained and fallible human minds require. For example, should nuclear power now be embraced because it does not contribute to global warming in the same way as plants burning fossil fuels? Is recycling always the best alternative, when the transportation of recycled materials can cause more environmental damage than their destruction? How can environmentalists object to the wearing of fur coats if the animal populations used to produce them are sustainable and are farmed ethically – and if they say that there is a qualitative distinction between using animals for meat and using them for clothing, are they not being motivated by envy rather than ecology?

If coming to terms with questions like these is difficult, people find it even harder to cope with the systemic nature of green decisions – the fact that apparently separate aspects of the environmental debate are interconnected and demand holistic solutions. Most purportedly 'green' consumers are neither willing nor able to supply these.

KEY PRINCIPLES OF GREEN MARKETING

Thus, increasingly complicated green messages are continually being thrown at consumers, many of whom do not have the time, the capabilities or the inclination to handle them. Not surprisingly therefore, consumers' understanding of and commitment to green issues is generally flawed and also varies substantially by consumer segment. Nevertheless, among all groups in society, there are certain principles which seem to be universally relevant to green consumption decisions, and which should therefore inform companies' green marketing.

1. People generally pay more for green products

Environmental friendliness is perceived by consumers as an *extra* benefit, one which its supplier has added to an otherwise less green product. So consumers assume that greener products (however they define these in a particular product category) will be more expensive than other products, and then decide whether they are prepared to pay any extra for the extra benefit of being green, and how much of a premium they will pay. This applies to any product field where some products are perceived to be greener than others. Individual consumers appear to be willing to pay roughly the same premium for perceptibly greener products, regardless of the product field.

One reason why consumers will pay a premium to be green was touched on earlier. Green innovators and early adopters tend to be above average in terms of education and income. They are keen to demonstrate that they are committed to the environment, and they have the money to do so. They also assume that green products forego the advantages of factory-based economies of scale, and that a premium price is therefore justified.

It is ironic that green products portray themselves as more 'natural', less technologically transformed, than ungreen ones. Given that technological transformation usually costs money, it is perhaps surprising that consumers expect to pay more rather than less for green products. This discrepancy indeed accounts for the very high margins on some green products.

2. Green products must be good at what they are supposed to do

The crucial caveat to the previous section, however, is that green products must do as well as any others on the primary performance criteria by which consumers judge products in a particular category. In fact, there is often a trade-off between primary performance and environmental friendliness. For example, greener detergents have tended to be less effective at their primary function of getting things clean.

3. Green claims work best in less demanding product categories

Since consumers require at least parity performance from green products, it follows that green claims will be most salient in those product categories where primary performance is easy for products to achieve or difficult for consumers to judge. Writing paper, for example, is a product category where environmental friendliness is very relevant, because the criteria for parity performance (being easy to write on, not smudging, being pleasant to look at, and so on) are not difficult to achieve and are not at odds with being green.

Moreover, because the categories where environmentally sound products and claims come to the fore are ones with comparatively limited product performance requirements, green products and claims are relatively easy to duplicate. From this perspective, individual green products and claims do not provide a sustainable competitive edge.

4. Consumers use green criteria more in intra-category purchasing decisions than in inter-category ones

Consumers are far more inclined to use green criteria in making purchasing decisions within a product category than when choosing between different product categories. In other words, they are very unlikely to cut down on purchases in a particularly ungreen product category in order to increase their purchasing in a particularly green one. They find it difficult to rank product categories in terms of greenness, and this probably reflects the fact that, for the majority of people, environmental friendliness is a secondary criterion – it does not generally drive decision to purchase in a particular product category, although it influences which product gets purchased in that category. There are very few examples either of new product categories which have grown solely because they are green, or of old product categories which have died off solely because they are ungreen.

5. Green claims are less relevant in technological categories

The more technologically advanced a product category, the less likely that consumers in that category will be swayed and attracted by green claims. Consumers tend to base their purchasing decisions in such categories on criteria of primary product benefits, which are themselves constantly improving as companies compete to provide greater utility. Green benefits are relatively insignificant as purchasing criteria until the rate of technological innovation slows down and most products come to achieve a common level of technical proficiency.

Thus, green claims are seldom seen in categories with a very high degree of 'technical transformation', such as computers, consumer durables, pharmaceuticals and telecommunications, where products require ever-improving performance and do not stand still for long enough for parity performance – with environmental friendliness as the motivating, purchase-determining criterion – to be possible. We might characterize technological markets as 'blue', to distinguish them from markets where green claims can be much more powerful in stimulating consumer purchases.

6. Green claims are also less relevant in luxury categories

Being seen to be green is also comparatively unimportant for products in luxury categories, which by definition have psychological and emotional meanings for consumers far beyond their functional role. Consumers here base their purchasing decisions on highly personal, epicurean, even selfish stimuli – in effect, people want to pamper themselves and to demonstrate to their peers that they have the money to do so. They are aware that they are often buying for the sake of buying, that they are purchasing products more as 'ciphers of luxury' than for their intrinsic value, and that they are suspending their normal criteria of utility and morality in order to derive self-respect from spending extravagantly.

Under these circumstances, consumers are unlikely to consider green claims in making luxury purchases. Environmental concerns are practical, realistic, entailing hard choices – generally the very antithesis of consumers' reasons for buying luxury products. As with 'blue' technology markets above, we might characterize luxury markets as 'red', to point up the limited usefulness of green claims in stimulating consumers' luxury purchases.

7. Green claims are making inroads into blue and red markets

Nevertheless, it is clear that green claims are becoming more salient in both 'blue' and 'red' markets. Consumers are starting to question the green credentials of high-tech marketing companies – to bring green secondary criteria into their purchasing decisions, especially where the pace of innovation slackens, along with the ability of companies to differentiate their products on the basis of primary performance criteria. Furthermore, some luxury markets have been transformed by a new environmental consciousness among particular consumer groups, especially young female consumers.

This has often been shown negatively, for example in the recent collapse of the market for fur coats in Northern Europe. But it is already being seen positively, in the growth of 'green luxury' suppliers like The Body Shop, which offers consumers the opportunity to signal their green commitment while at the same time buying products which are pampering, non-practical, self-indulgent, and expensive (though markedly less expensive than the products of established cosmetics houses). Some environmentalists have questioned the need for the type of products sold in The Body Shop. For example, environmentalist David Bellamy has said of The Body Shop, 'Anita Roddick does a great job educating people but we don't need the stuff she sells.' But there is no doubt that people have a deep-seated psychological need for luxury products, which no amount of earnest exhortations against their frivolity can destroy.

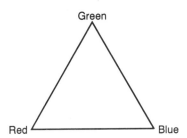

Figure 4.1

8. Emotive green messages are the most immediate for consumers

Some green messages are much easier for consumers to understand than others. In general, images are easier to understand than words, anecdotes are easier to understand than scientific studies, catchphrases are easier to understand than objectively correct but dull statements of fact. In effect, appeals to the emotions have a stronger immediate impact on ordinary people than do carefully reasoned arguments – again a function of the secondary nature of green criteria in most purchasing decisions.

Most consumers are looking for quick and easy ways to show that they are 'doing their bit' for the environment. They do not want to spend too much time thinking about how to make green purchasing decisions, so they are seeking emotive shorthand messages which seem to cut through the environmental debate. Thus, most manufacturers shun excessive detail in making green claims, and prefer platitudes and simplistic diagrams (especially rough-drawn globes).

An excellent example of this was afforded by the launch in the UK of Nouvelle recycled toilet tissue. The launch advertisements showed trees springing up, apparently in the Amazon rain forest, somehow as a result of people using Nouvelle. The opportunism and inaccuracy of the advertising campaign has been much criticised, but its creators did realise that the image of Amazonia mysteriously restored would have much more selling power than learned treatises comparing softwoods with hardwoods, or demonstrating the pros and cons of recycled paper products, or suggesting the socio-economic factors behind the destruction of the world's rain forests and the need for a re-evaluation of global consumption and investment priorities. And they were right: Nouvelle claimed to have achieved a hitherto unheard-of 8 per cent market share as a result of its controversial launch campaign.

9. Established brands find it easy to achieve green parity

It is very difficult for new brands to use the appeal of environmental friendliness to challenge well known brands with high market shares. The reason why some brands become established in the first place is that they offer consumers the right mix of rational and emotional benefits. In other words, consumers not only feel that established brands do their job particularly well, but also feel genuine affection towards them. In group discussions, consumers often use the same language about their preferred brands that they use to describe their friends.

Consumers always want to think the best of their 'brand friends', and need strong evidence if they are even to consider breaking off their brand relationships. So established brands have few problems in countering and combating the green claims of upstart competitive brands with stronger green credentials. They can afford much less rigorous proof that they are environmentally friendly than newcomers. Indeed, their reaction to competitive green attacks is little more than to tell loyal consumers that they can trust their friend Brand X to take care of the environment. Since 'care' and 'trustworthiness' are part of the brand image of most very successful brands, Brand X's consumers are naturally predisposed to believe its green communications.

10. Rational green messages are the most meaningful for consumers

For brands which are comparatively green but are not well established, their best means of improving their market position is to appeal to the reason – to make people think about the brand and put forward its benefits in a strong, coherent way. This is in fact the only way of distancing a particularly green brand from the welter of bland, me-too or fallacious 'green' claims being communicated emotively by its competitors.

In other words, brands with a real green edge must touch people's minds, not their hearts. They must convince consumers of their benefits. In this respect, green marketing brings greater rationality into consumers' purchasing decisions. It also means that green marketers must communicate at the outset with the relatively small group of people who are willing to think carefully about their brand choices in a particular category, although this group may later expand as word-of-mouth spreads from brand users to the uninitiated (it is for this reason that green marketing often appears to be 'educational').

11. The corporate brand is vitally important for green marketers

Just as green marketers trying to break into markets against established brands need to concentrate on rational arguments, so they need to demonstrate a commitment to the environment which runs right through their organisations. Once green marketers start to put across facts about their brands, and to make strong green claims that differentiate their brands from established ones which are also 'household names', they subject themselves to extensive scrutiny. So their whole house needs to be in order before embarking on a campaign of rational green attack.

This means that the lack of blemishes required makes green marketing a difficult and dangerous task. It is also something for which retailers and other intermediaries are naturally more fitted than manufacturers, since the former can pick and choose between suppliers on an ongoing basis as technologies and consumer demands change, whereas the latter become harnessed to their current technology as soon as they purchase it. If a retailer is criticised for selling a particular product with an adverse effect on the environment, it can simply change its supplier; whereas if a manufacturer is thus criticised, it must contemplate massive and expensive changes to its production process. Retailers can therefore afford to be much more environmentally proactive than can manufacturers.

CONCLUSION: WHAT DO GREEN MARKETERS NEED TO DO?

These eleven points, then, are some of the prevailing features of green consumption. Clearly, companies must assess the importance of green criteria in their own markets. How do consumers define performance, and how well do competing products compare with consumers' requirements? Can green claims discriminate between competing products in consumers' eyes? And how can green claims be communicated effectively to consumers?

All companies have a duty to society to compete. This has always been the case. But in recent years their duty to society has expanded. Now they must compete to upgrade their processes and to decrease their impact on the environment. How can a company continue to make a profit while doing this, if its competitors can take advantage of consumer ignorance to blur the distinction between green and ungreen products? There seem to us to be five key steps.

The five steps

- First, green marketers must become more adroit at understanding how their consumers choose between products at present, and how they might react to more environmentally friendly products in the future. This calls for 'visionary' market research, rather than the static and historical sort that normally prevails.
- Second, green marketers must be angels. They must scrutinize every element of their business to ensure that they perform better on environmental criteria than their competitors. They should embrace third-party endorsement from a 'gatekeeper', whether the govern-

ment, a green pressure group, or a private company which has set objectively verifiable green standards. Given the confusion which ordinary consumers feel when confronted with the complexity of environmental issues, such gatekeepers are critically important.

- Third, green marketers must recognize the importance of trying to change laws, regulations and methods of doing business in directions which are ecologically sounder and which expose the obfuscating 'green' claims of their competitors. This calls for lobbying and planned 'contact marketing', not to preserve the status quo (which is its current role for most companies) but to elicit and ensure change throughout the industry.
- Fourth, green marketers must communicate rationally, objectively and intelligently, and thereby 'educate' their consumers, without being patronizing or obviously self-serving. They will also prefer corporate to brand communication, since the former will show consumers that environmental excellence runs right through the company.
- Fifth and finally, green marketers must be open-minded to the ongoing environmental debate, and willing to use their own weight to confront even the deep-seated environmental problems which consumers are often sceptical about being able to solve, such as the abject living standards of people in the third world which can lead to deforestation and other evils which affect the developed world. These grand environmental issues are often fertile ground for initiatives which can move consumers and make plenty of profit, while changing the world for good. Everybody knows that charity begins at home, but it really depends on what people consider to be their home.

'The conflict between environmental protection and economic competitiveness is a false dichotomy. It stems from a narrow view of the sources of prosperity, and a static view of competition.'

Professor Michael E. Porter, Harvard Business School

5 SOME ASPECTS OF ENVIRONMENTAL MANAGEMENT WITHIN A CHEMICAL CORPORATION

by James Otter

ICI is a major chemical corporation. Group turnover, before the company's proposed demerger, is in the order of £15000 million per annum. Businesses range from commodity chemicals, such as chlorine, to advanced materials and pharmaceuticals. Being a manufacturer, and in the chemical sector, some of the company's activities bring it into the 'front line' of environmental issues in business. Like the majority of industrial companies many of its activities which provide benefits for its customers and make money to satisfy its shareholders, affect the environment.

This chapter will focus on the agrochemical division and the way in which ICI personnel have become involved in decisions and changes in attitudes that have contributed to a change, both in the commercial attitude of the business and the general approach towards environmental issues. Views regarding the long term effects on environmental regulations on the agrochemical industry are also expressed.

BACKGROUND OF AGROCHEMICALS

Agrochemicals have made a massive contribution to the world food production and public health. Insecticides such as DDT were used with great success to control malaria and typhus up to the 1960s. Selective hormone weedkillers (such as MCPA) and fungicides (such as mancozeb) contributed greatly to improving crop yields and the so-called green revolution.

Many observers believe that the correct use of agrochemicals is an essential part of an efficient farming system. Herbicides can be used as tools which substitute traditional mechanical cultivation methods. Insecticides can be used to reduce damage to crops and improve quality both in the field and in store. Fungicides can help the farmer reduce the loss of yield from fungal diseases.

In recent years great progress has been made in reducing the amount of agrochemical required to achieve control of the target pest or weed. For example modern synthetic pyrethroid insecticides are applied at doses of 10 – 15 grams of active ingredient per hectare (g ai/ha). Each gram of active ingredient is generally less harmful to the environment than their predecessors, many of which were applied at doses of 250 – 300 g ai/ha.

Modern farmers can also use selective agrochemicals. Some selective herbicides kill only grasses, leaving broad-leaved crops such as sugar beet or oil seed rape unaffected. Certain other chemicals kill only aphids, leaving other insects, including those potentially beneficial to the crop, unaffected.

IMAGE OF AGROCHEMICALS

Despite these economic benefits to agriculture the agrochemical industry enjoys an unenviable position in public perception. A Mori survey published in the *Financial Times* in July 1991 displayed the favourability and familiarity of the public perception of industries. Food, gas, electricity and building societies emerged as the most favoured and familiar industries. In contrast agrochemicals scored the lowest rating of familiarity. The favourablility of the industry was at the same low level as the nuclear industry. The perception of chemicals and fertilisers were only marginally better.

This negative public image is due to many factors. Agrochemicals, by definition, affect the natural environment since they are selected and purchased for their effect on target pests. They can lead to residues and breakdown products in the soil and ground water. The organochlorine family of insecticides (such as DDT), are excreted at a very low rate by most animals and accumulate in fat tissue. As a result they enter the food chain. The use of organochlorines is therefore banned in many countries.

The industry is now very tightly regulated. New agrochemicals, like pharmaceuticals, are subject to long and complex test programmes before they can be sold. These regulatory programmes include complex toxicological tests as well as simulating exposure of operators to the compound and sophisticated studies which trace the fate of the test compound and related breakdown products in the environment. The costs of developing and registering an agrochemical in the major world markets is now estimated at about $50 million, and can take between seven and ten years. If chemicals fail the regulatory standards during the

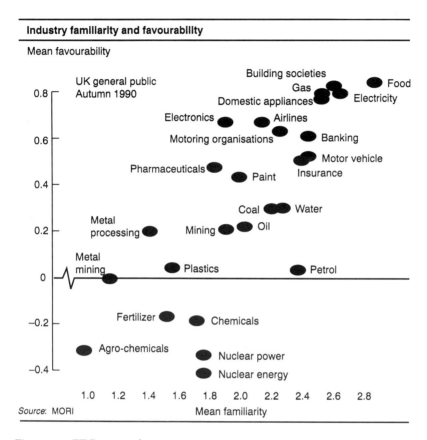

Figure 5.1 FT Perceptual map

long registration process then the commercial investment in research is usually lost. However, the benefits from success are high and the sector, like pharmaceuticals, has traditionally enjoyed excellent levels of profitability.

Patent protection for agrochemicals is about fifteen years. If registration is successful the company has therefore about seven years of sales orders to recover the research and development costs before patent expiry. Not surprisingly the market is dominated by large corporations.

Regulatory standards are high for both agrochemicals and pharmaceuticals. Familiar drugs, such as aspirin, if discovered tomorrow, would be rejected in the regulatory process due to teratogenic effects, which exceed modern regulatory standards. Also some components of a normal diet, such as common salt, would probably be rejected as pesticides on the grounds of chronic toxicity. Safety margins are high. The gap between perceived and scientific risk is large.

Certain products, although approved by government agencies have been subjected to specific targeting by pressure groups. The negative publicity linked to Alar in California led to the destruction of apples of a market value of running to tens of millions of dollars. Uniroyal, the makers of Alar, withdrew the product in the face of negative publicity before Alar's alleged side effects were proven, despite pressure from the industry to maintain sales. This can be cited as a case where emotional arguments, combined with massive media coverage, won over arguments based on scientific evidence, and had severe economic effects on the American apple industry.

Technically-based arguments are often invalid in public debate. Agrochemicals have an image of chemicals that are unnecessary and dangerous contaminants of otherwise healthy food. Assurances based on the evidence required for registration and graphical representation of safety levels rarely sway over emotional concerns about chemical additives.

Economic arguments concerning the effect on local farming interests can have a positive or a negative effect, usually depending on the power of the local farming lobby.

ICI AND AGROCHEMICALS

This perception of agrochemicals as often unnecessary, harmful additives is not restricted to the general public. In 1988 ICI considered that the chemical industries' views on the benefits of pesticides were not being adequately projected to counteract the often emotional arguments put forward by the groups opposed to the use of pesticides.

A survey of ICI Agrochemical employees in the UK revealed that only 30 per cent considered that pesticides were essential for food production. This was not a favourable base on which to build a change in public perception or to continue a drive for increased market share and pro-fitability for the company. This was especially true in an environment of largely negative external, economic forces, which were slowing down the demand.

Therefore, it was opportune for the company to reverse this trend and upgrade the perceived and actual environmental performance of the organisation at all levels. These changes were conducted in a variety of ways.

Corporate initiatives

At a corporate level the ICI Chairman, Sir Denys Henderson, made public statements about ICI's environmental policy and the expenditure on environmental projects. He also announced that ICI would have no double standards and all ICI sites and activities were to be subject to the same stringent regulations irrespective of their location. The company announced that it spent £274 million on environmental improvements in 1990. The 1991 annual report was accompanied by a separate document outlining ICI's environmental activities and performance.

These strategic initiatives coincided with recession, a decline in profits and a possible hostile bid from the Hanson corporation.

For ICI Agrochemicals changes took place in the following areas:

- product
- manufacturing
- publicity

These will be discussed in more detail below.

Product

Since the early 1970s ICI has been subjected to pressure against its product paraquat. This chemical, usually sold under the tradename of 'Gramoxone', is a unique, rapidly acting herbicide and has been in use since the early 1960s. It has a rapid action on plant's photosynthetic tissue and is quickly immobilised in the soil where the molecule binds tightly to clay particles. However, before immobilisation it is toxic if taken internally.

Until the early 1980s paraquat made up the lion's share of ICI Agrochemicals profits. The company has spent much time, money and effort protecting users and sales. Formulations have been changed to include alerting agents such as colour, stench and emetic. Recently, thixotropic formulations have been developed so that they can only be poured if shaken vigorously. This is intended to minimize the accidental exposure to children. Further work has included farmer education and comprehensive pictorial labels for use in less developed countries. Extensive trials have been conducted to test the effect of paraquat on a range of ecosystems. This data is used to support government registrations.

Many of these changes were implemented proactively and before national authorities requested them. Trials and experience from other countries allowed ICI to at least defer the restrictions on the use of the chemical in some countries such as Cameroun, the Netherlands and Colombia. In some markets such as Japan, pressure to reduce the concentration of paraquat in the formulation has led to a decrease in profitability.

Paraquat is on the so called 'dirty dozen' list of chemicals targeted by the Pesticide Action Network (PAN). This international pressure group has started several campaigns specifically to ban certain active ingredients. The campaign has served as a rallying point for many pressure groups calling for a ban of the product.

In the developing world specialist teams train operators on safety and application methods. This technical training is sometimes specified by aid donor agencies as part of a crop protection package. This is a responsible approach to purchasing decisions which used to be based only on the cheapest price of a chemical.

The search for new chemical innovations continues. Traditional screening processes for new agrochemicals mirrored the regulatory requirements and focused on efficacy and toxicity. However, in the late 1970s ICI also incorporated environmental screens early on in the development process. The objective of this change was to avoid costly, unnecessary development of new compounds which, although non-toxic and effective, were harmful to the environment and would be rejected by regulatory authorities. Areas of study include mobility through the soil profile into ground water, persistence of the active ingredient in the soil and the behaviour of metabolic breakdown products, as well as the effect on non-target organisms such as earth worms.

Many of these techniques have to be used in order to generate environmental data to support the re-registration of older active ingredients. In the future it is possible that the fate of volatile breakdown products in the air will also be demanded by the registration authorities.

Not surprisingly the areas of chemistry yielding new molecules which are effective against the target organism, of low toxicity, and rapidly degraded in the environment, are small in number. However, the rewards of success are sufficient for the major agrochemical companies to maintain large research and development budgets, costing up to 10 per cent of turnover.

Manufacturing

ICI corporate environmental policy states explicitly that there will be no double standards for manufacturing. All plants must comply to the same high standards which may exceed local legislation and therefore incur cost not required in states with low environmental standards. However, businesses faced with reduced profits due to the recession in the early 1990's had few spare resources to upgrade plant beyond levels which were strictly necessary. Investment in environmental upgrades were given higher priority than other projects and reported separately in financial accounts.

In the domain of public relations apparent sluggishness in implementing environmental improvements could be a hostage to fortune in the case of a spillage or accident. In order to improve profitability in 1990 ICI made significant provision (£400 million) for the costs of restructuring the business.

Some could argue that the bold allocation of such provisions would send a clear signal of commitment to environmental excellence to shareholders and investors alike. It would have however sharply reduced ICI's profitability and dividend value, during a time of potentially hostile takeover activity by the Hanson Corporation. In the current business environment ICI, like many other corporations, continues to stick to traditional dividend policies.

There is a risk that such radical revisions would be badly received by the equity markets. This risk is likely to continue until methods that can accurately value plants and incorporate an estimate for any environmental liability and clean-up costs are developed and accepted. In some cases ageing plants, instead of being recorded as an asset in a company balance sheet, could be quantified as net liabilities after reevaluation. This practice is the logical extension of formalized, environmental audits. Traditional valuation methods are, however, likely to be widely used for some time. At present there is little perceived advantage of being the first to make the radical step in valuation methods.

However the recently announced proposal to split the ICI group into separate companies provides the opportunity for an intermediate position. The current demerger plans yield two separate companies, one focussing on industrial chemicals, the other focussing on high value chemicals with biological effects. As the companies will be entirely separate they will be able to develop independent asset valuation methods and dividend policies. This could give them possible competitive advantages over rivals still structured as large chemical groups.

In ICI environmental audits are progressively being integrated into normal procedures for manufacturing sites. Safety performance is now linked to remuneration for senior managers. Clean-up costs and liabilities for sites scheduled for divestment are estimated internally.

Publicity

In many situations companies try to create a 'green' image only through publicity. The approach of ICI Agrochemicals has been broader and has linked targeted publicity with a change in attitude to pressure groups and opinion makers.

Following an initiative by the UK operating unit, money was transferred from the routine advertising budget and used on a specific campaign to clarify information about pesticides. This was titled 'Food for Thought'. The centre piece of the campaign was a video made independently by the UK naturalist, David Bellamy. Bellamy is very well known in the UK for his eccentric and enthusiastic approach to natural history. He was given editorial independence for the video in order to preempt any criticism that the company had distorted the information portrayed in the video. The video, tracing the tests and regulations that a new agrochemical must pass, was called 'Safety Side Up' and was targeted at customers, employees and opinion groups. It was enthusiastically received as proved by the several thousand copies requested during the campaign and it was also in demand for use in schools.

Other aspects of the campaign included education in schools and for employees, as well as advertisements in the national press. A new news sheet for employees was produced. One of the objectives of the news sheet was to allow employees to respond to current arguments or television programmes critical of the agrochemical industry. Although the real benefits of such a campaign are impossible to estimate, it was well received at all levels and went some of the way to giving employees counter arguments to criticism from neighbours or other members of their peer group.

Simultaneously, there was a deliberate thawing of relations with environmental pressure groups. For example Friends of the Earth conducted an audit of a paraquat manufacturing plant in the UK.

Higher profile initiatives included the sponsorship of a rain forest conference in Brazil. This deliberated, in conjunction with the British government aid agency and the Brazilian authorities, means of regenerating forest and managing marginal land in Brazil. The 1991 ICI Agrochemical calender entitled 'Disappearing Worlds, The Rainforest' was a marked break with the traditional calendar coverage of more bland subjects linked to agriculture.

The overall effect of the communication campaign was to provide impartial, accurate information to employees and other interest groups. Also, by starting an open door policy with environmental groups, the confrontational nature of previous debates was replaced with one of dialogue. Although sometimes tense, this has often been beneficial to both parties.

In conclusion ICI Agrochemicals has taken a range of actions to improve the organisation's environmental performance and the perceptions of its employees, as well as its public image. This process, like most activities, can constantly be improved.

OPPORTUNITIES FOR AGROCHEMICALS

As national environmental regulations for agrochemicals become more stringent, the use of certain chemicals is being banned or restricted. In 1990 the use of atrazine, a major maize herbicide, was restricted in Germany. The product (the market leader) was shown to generate residues in ground water. This pressure on the market leader caused a reshuffle in the sector. Older, less effective chemicals suddenly jumped in market share and turnover in order to satisfy the demand left by the reduced use of atrazine. These products had previously been superseded by atrazine but returned on the basis of their more benign environmental profile and the best available solution to the weed control problem of the farmer.

Traditionally new agrochemicals fill niches through unique properties linked to technical innovation. The event of chemicals leaving the market due to either bans or companies deciding not to incur the massive costs of tests requested for re-registration can allow old products to return from the marketing death zone. With detailed knowledge of the regulatory criteria and the performance of certain products in the environment, this so-called 'Lazarus effect' can be predicted and should be included in marketing plans. The decisions of registration authorities are already causing market opportunities in a flat, often crowded market.

In similar fashion some companies will take a clear decision to let registrations of certain pesticides lapse. The cash flow predictions from certain minor products cannot justify the costs of meeting demands from certain authorities for additional environmental data before registrations can be renewed. In some cases in the USA the generation of data required for re-registration will cost several million dollars, and carries no guarantee of success.

In some countries, such as Sweden, government policy has a direct effect on the agrochemical market. Taxes are levied on all agrochemicals with the objective of reducing consumption. Also the registration of certain chemicals deemed important for agriculture are retained only until a more benign substitute can be found. Sometimes the processes associated with the registration of the potential substitute are accelerated and the use of the original product is banned as soon as the substitute product passes all the required tests.

These changes will lead to some sophisticated markets, although static in volume, undergoing dynamic change due to the actions and views of the regulatory authorities.

Future for agrochemicals

Upgrading environmental standards for any process is expensive. In times of recession the pressures on agrochemical companies to make immediate profits are high, especially as profits from the industrial divisions falter during the economic downturn.

Actions to meet tougher regulations can also lead to additional costs in other stages of the product life cycle through tougher manufacturing standards, higher transport and warehousing standards and the compulsory recycling of packs. Only a fraction of these additional costs can be passed on to the customer, not least as agricultural subsidies are likely to be reduced in line with possible GATT agreements and CAP reforms. These changes will erode the profitability of the industry.

This decline in profitability could lead to pressure to reduce innovative research. Smaller companies with weak research facilities could decide to cut out research expenditure in order to maximize profitability. They could run for cash, and like the importers of products whose patents have expired, could make excellent short term profits.

Within Europe the planned harmonisation of registration procedures for active ingredients will decrease the barriers to entry for new entrants and facilitate price competition. Profits available for innovative research will decline. For the large, research-led corporations, tougher regulatory standards will favour the introduction of new products that could set new standards of environmental safety. Therefore, in marked contrast to the past, the large corporations wishing to continue to do research should favour tougher, new environmental standards. The regulators, who were considered by some industry observers to constrain the activities of the business in the 1960s – 1980s, now provide the barriers to entry from generic producers as well as the force to maintain the incentive for research for yet further technical innovations.

The scene is therefore set for conflict within the European Community. On the one hand the free traders seek to open the European agrochemical market to world competition and give European farmers access to cheap inputs, enabling European farmers to compete on the increasingly liberalized market for food.

On the other hand, environmentalists and consumer lobbies will argue that free trade should not be allowed to dilute the drive for safer, more benign agrochemicals. They will try to set environmental standards that are met only by modern chemicals or alternative control methods, which may cost the farmer more than the older alternatives. Recent announcements by Ciba Geigy state that their research is targeted towards chemicals that act only on certain pests, thus making the products strong candidates for use in Integrated Pest Management (IPM) programmes.

Biotechnology could also provide innovative solutions, and innovative products already fill some niche markets along with biological control methods. However the issues concerning regulation of biotechnology products are even more complex than traditional chemicals as they concern the manipulation of the genome as well as the environment. Many observers consider it unlikely that biotechnological solutions will be largely used in agriculture before the year 2010.

The large research-led companies therefore have some tough choices. Unilateral investment in environmental standards to meet the requirements of the future would be bold in the present times of economic bleakness, and unlikely to be understood by shareholders. Arguments such as competitive advantage, employee morale and future positioning to justify these investments are difficult to quantify, especially to shareholders expecting healthy dividends.

Short term considerations, such as declining profitability, will force many companies to operate only up to the minimum environmental standards required by law. However, as these laws become more strict and their effects cross international boundaries, then the long term survivors will be those companies who force through bold investment (and divestment) programmes in anticipation of future demands. Only these companies will have core businesses with genuine long-term viability and minimal risks from liabilities hidden in ageing plants and contaminated sites.

The challenge for the manager of today is to judge the speed of change and when to break the drive for short-term profits in order to remain a long-term survivor. The speed of change will be driven by the political will and aspirations of the legislators in the more profitable markets of the developed countries, articulating the effect of pressure from a range of interest groups. (In poorer countries the primary issue is likely to be less sophisticated and based on food availability rather than perceived quality and safety.)

Farmer's representatives are likely to insist that farmers have access to agrochemicals that are as cheap and effective as their competitors in order to compete on the world market.

Consumer lobbies will combat this trend by insisting on increasingly sophisticated reporting of products used to grow the goods available on the supermarket shelves. This trend could create a price incentive for innovative farmers producing 'greener' food that meets the desired standards.

For some countries, notably in Scandinavia, it might be politically acceptable for governments to compensate farmers for using environmentally superior methods, in order to let them compete on the world market with farmers using older, cheaper chemicals. Significantly, part of the objectives of the recent Mac Sharry reforms to the EC's Common Agricultural Policy are to reduce the environmental impact of intensive farming. Shifting the drivers for agricultural subsidies from production quantity to production quality could be a future trend.

The maintenance of existing standards, combined with the arrival of generic producers of products whose patent has expired, could lead to price erosion and reduced profits for the agrochemical companies. This will be pronounced if the generic producers can operate from countries with low standards for the environmental performance of manufacturing plants giving a low cost base through the externalisation of pollution. This liberalisation will reduce the incentive and funds for the continuation of research into improving environmental performance of agrochemicals.

Technical innovation has provided the fuel for growth for the agrochemical industry in the last three decades. Innovation, combined with environmental performance and minimal long-term liabilities, could be a common factor for the research-led companies surviving the period of shake out in the next two decades.

Environmental regulators, following political aspirations determined partly by the demands of increasingly sophisticated consumers, will be asked to provide the legal and technical framework that insists on ever higher environmental standards for agrochemicals. This will provide the incentive for the continuation of costly research into improved solutions for world agriculture.

EXAMPLES OF MANAGEMENT DECISIONS IN AGROCHEMICALS THAT CONCERN ETHICAL AND ENVIRONMENTAL JUDGEMENTS

There is often a gap between corporate pronouncements of intent and actions taken in large organisations. Many decisions that improve the environmental performance of large corporations decrease short term profitability.

Individuals, often at humble levels in the organisation, must make judgements on decisions that define the limit between acceptable business and that should be turned away because the opportunity goes against the long term interest of the company.

Examples of some of these judgements include:

Humanitarian issues

Locusts and organochlorines
Experts from the Food and Agriculture Organisation (FAO) of the United Nations recommend use of organolchlorines in remote desert areas to control locust hoppers in Africa.

The advantages of this recommendation include:

- single spray of low concentration;
- hoppers die within 2 – 3 weeks;
- logistically simple from Land Rover, treatment can be accomplished by locust scout teams;
- minimal risk for 'biomagnification' in food chain.

A leading bilateral donor states explicitly that any government using organochlorines will be exempt from any further assistance in any area from the donor concerned. This is for legal reasons and concerns the financing of agrochemicals that have been banned in the donor country.

The alternative is to use more 'modern' chemicals sprayed from the air. Areas will have to be resprayed every three weeks, increasing costs and the risks of the hoppers developing into swarms of flying adults. These could then fly to the agricultural areas in the South and cause massive damage to crops.

If a chemical company supplied DDT from India and China to meet a local government tender in line with FAO advice the company could face a publicity backlash for supplying a product banned in many developed countries.

Any manager taking the decision to supply is likely to have to justify his decision.

Global issues

Effluent control
Following certain patent agreements often only a handful of companies are permitted to manufacture a certain active ingredient for an agrochemical. The companies then compete vigorously in the market to sell the same product.

In the case of one active ingredient the manufacturing process creates CFCs as by-products. These are usually sold off for use in foam manufacture. However, following the Montreal protocol the CFC market has effectively ceased to exist. Production costs have increased as the manufacturer is now obliged to incinerate the CFCs rather than sell them.

Certain companies, which receive government support, can solve the problem by other means, such as burying the CFCs down deep wells in remote areas. This gives these companies a favourable cost position and they could use their competitive advantage to gain market share through decreased prices.

Companies without access to cheap methods of disposing of the CFCs are being made less competitive. The political steps to show the price of honouring the Montreal protocol and redressing the balance of fair trade would be delicate. Environmental responsibility carries costs.

North – South issues

DDT, who has the right to decide to pollute?
After lengthy debate in Parliament the Indian government decided to approve the sale and use of DDT in India for use in malaria control programmes. However, DDT is banned in developed countries. Trade in DDT to India by a corporation could therefore be categorised as a form of double standards, and therefore against many corporate philosophies.

Alternatively, the decision not to supply could be classed as a racist decision, and contrary to the profit objectives of the company by imposing standards contrary to local law.

This sort of decision helps set the boundaries of corporate ethics. The level at which the decision is made reflects the importance attached by the organisation to the possible effects of an unconsidered decision.

South – North issues

Pollution as a resource and as a competitive advantage
After the breakdown in negotiations with a European supplier for a herbicide for use in Spain you require an alternative supply.

This product is out of patent and can be manufactured in the Far East. Under the new EC directive on pesticide registration you can secure registration within 4 months, in time for the selling season. You require the product to complete a crop treatment package and have already committed costs to advertising, labels and training.

The price from the Far Eastern company is highly competitive, and below the 'full cost' displayed by the European supplier and your own company's estimates; this could be due to low environmental standards and sloppy operating procedures.

Choosing the European supplier will be against the financial interests of the company. Selection of the Far Eastern supplier could cut across your company's environmental objectives.

Intra EC issues

Testing double standards to the limit
Most chemical companies now have issued statements concerning double standards. These normally state that the company will operate only at the highest level of environmental standards, irrespective of local requirements.

However certain agrochemical products are now banned by the German authorities following tough new restrictions concerning levels of leaching through the soil profile and into water courses. These restrictions do not apply in the majority of other EC member states.

Theoretically the companies should therefore restrict supply to other EC member states in order to comply with their pronouncements concerning double standards. In reality most companies place profitability first and continue to supply.

Is this an ethically valid position?

'As the country lost the war, there was the mountain and the river waiting for me at home.'

Tu Fu, Chinese poet of 700

6 JAPANESE MANAGEMENT AND THE ENVIRONMENT

by Takashi Adachi

JAPAN AND THE ENVIRONMENT

Generally, Japan is known for its good environmental management. It owes this reputation, however, to two bitter experiences: pollution and oil shocks. Fortunately, it has been able to rely on two very positive factors to overcome the effects of these. As we will see later in this chapter, government and industry in Japan manage to collaborate and negotiate quite successfully, and furthermore, Japan has a tradition of economizing resources.

Pollution

From the end of 1950 to 1960, a rapid but unequilibrated economic growth caused serious problems of pollution: air pollution from a petro-chemical complex caused severe cases of asthma in Yokkaichi; organic mercury discharged in sea water by a chemical plant polluted fish and caused the notorious Minamata disease in people who ate them.

Even if it took several years to officially recognize the cause and effect and more than ten years to reach a solution, it was clear to everyone that pollution had to be controlled. Today in many areas, Japanese environmental standards are among the toughest in the world, together with those in California or Germany. For example, emissions of NOx and SOx are among the lowest in the industrialized countries. In 1985, the levels of NOx and SOx emitted per unit of electricity generated in thermal power plants were around a third of those in West Germany (but higher than for the by nuclear energy generated electricity in France). When we look at levels of pollution in relation to the GNP or population, Japan is rarely not in the list of best performers.

Oil shocks

Another important issue was the two oil shocks. Japan had been heavily reliant on oil, and the ready availability and cheapness of this resource suddenly changed overnight. Especially during the first oil shock, when Japan did not yet have any economical and political weight, it had to sit tight and await the outcome without being able to do anything – a painful situation for such an oil-dependant country.

It was evident that over-dependence on oil imports is dangerous. Although Japan will always be a transforming and exporting country with a heavy reliance on oil importation, it should use this oil more efficiently than countries less dependant on oil imports to secure its survival in the World economy. The government took wide ranging measures to curb the use of oil which led to a 30 per cent reduction after the second oil crisis. This gave Japanese firms in return a big competitive advantage, and many companies selling energy-saving know-how or equipment, whatever their industry, are those who have been continuing the effort since then.

Officials and industry

In tackling pollution and the consequences of the two oil shocks, the Japanese government adopted a subtle strategy. It was always very demanding, and set relatively high standards but gave companies the time and opportunity to meet them. Evidently, it also benefited from its close relationship with industry which gave it an excellent insight into the capability of companies to improve their efficiency in the use of resources.

Companies were obliged to meet official requirements, but when these seemed not feasible they negotiated with officials and often formed a collaboration with competitors; the objective was the survival of their industry rather than winning the competition. When the Muskie Act, (an early American bill to limit pollution from exhaust gasses, which is often referred to in Japan) did not become law in the USA because its requirements were seen as too demanding, it was the Japanese car industry that took its requirements on board and met them. Minimizing unit consumption became the key for its success.

Tradition of economizing

Some hundred years ago, Japan was one of the main gold suppliers of the world, but today it is evidently not a country rich in resources. To make the best use of scarce resources Japan has a tradition of recycling; except for aluminium cans – a material which was introduced only relatively recently and of which Japan only recycles 40 per cent compared to the US's 60 per cent – most of Japan's recycling rates are among the best in the world.

Even though this tradition is suffering from the effects of increased consumerism, the waste of resources is often criticized. A recent joint attempt of gas suppliers and wash basin manufacturers to promote morning shampooing failed because of criticism regarding its wastefulness, despite the fact that it was in line with the modern western life style which is so much sought after.

The recent moves towards increased environmental consciousness, led in first instance simply to the voluntary collection and recycling of cans, of paper in businesses and even of the plastic trays used to pack meat and vegetables in supermarkets. People immediately saw it as a means to express their concern: recycling equated with environmental protection in most people's minds.

IS JAPAN SO GOOD?

Why is it then that Japan is repeatedly criticized in the world media for its 'environmentally unconscious behaviour'? These criticisms do not simply fall within the frame of the political 'Japan bashing' game.

The mass effect

Even with a relatively efficient use of resources, the size of the Japanese economy is very large, especially in comparison to its population or surface. On 0.3 per cent of the earth's land surface, 2 per cent of the world's population produces 10 per cent of the world's GNP, uses 10 per cent of the world's CFCs and imports 50 per cent of the world trade in tropical wood. The aggregate influence is important. Japan seems to be in a trap here. 'We pollute less than others' may not stand any ground against the hypothesis that the 'right to pollute' is equal to everyone. If every country began polluting, even at the Japanese rate, the earth would not survive. Evidently, Japan will say 'then, please, try to bring all pollution down to our level. . .' . Is the 'right to pollute' given per unit of

GNP or a given surface or a country? A tough question to which Japan seems to think the answer is 'per unit of GNP'.

Market nature

There are two typical aspects in the Japanese market that are often questioned from an environmental point of view.

First to be questioned is its overly competitive nature. In the car or electric appliance industry, for example, new models are being launched twice as often as in Europe, with the sole aim to attract new clients. The famous just-in-time or *kanban* system which minimizes the stock at the assembling factory – a convenience for large manufacturers – is criticized for causing social problems such as traffic jams or overwork at the subcontractors.

The evolution of consumerism in Japan is the second point for criticism. With increasing income and relatively flat wealth distribution, the 'lux' is sought in a massive way. Japanese gourmet food such as tuna fish and crab have been fished out from several seas, and ivory and protected animals continued to be smuggled in until recently. Unfortunately, this pursuit of lux did not go hand in hand with an evolution of consumer's consciousness of environmental problems or social acceptance.

Think locally, act globally

Contrary to the ecological cliché, 'think globally, act locally', Japan seems to ignore its size and influence in world affairs despite its worldwide activities, and thinks locally according to its own reasoning.

Typical cases were observed in the political scenery. Throughout discussions on whether aid should be given to the former USSR, the key issue in Japan was how long it can hang on to its northern islands without becoming too isolated from other world powers who reckon that Japan is only trying to save face by not giving up these islands to Russia. In the discussion on whaling, Japan tried to line up with Eskimos, saying that it is a tradition and local people cannot survive economically without. Even if much more ego is involved in political bargaining, we can see here a certain tendency of 'thinking locally'.

Another example: as an almost subtropical island washed out several times per year by typhoons and massive precipitation, Japan seems to have difficulty in understanding the acid rain problem in Northern Europe.

In short, Japan's achievement in environmental management seems to express itself in the efficiency with which resources are used or in terms of pollution per unit GNP, but it is less evident outside these fields.

CORPORATE JAPAN IN ENVIRONMENTAL MANAGEMENT

Before 1987

Full of confidence in its efficiency, Japanese management has been quite suspicious of the emerging influence of environmental consciousness on business:

'This is a new way of Japan bashing.'
'If the USA could use resources as efficiently as we do, there would be no problem with Iraq.'

Especially on the CFC issue, it was nearly unthinkable to most Japanese CFC users to abandon such a convenient product for cleaning semi-conductors (50 per cent of CFC in Japan is used for this purpose), the real core of Japanese industries.

'Europeans can abandon CFC because they cannot manufacture semi-conductors but neither the USA nor Japan can accept it'.

And if its release in the air is the problem :

'Japan could continue using CFCs because its recycling system is much more thorough than in any other countries. . .'

Triggers

Influence from outside – gaiatsu
Gaiatsu, a word which means external – American – pressure, became one of the common expressions in the past years. Japan has been particu-larly vulnerable to pressure coming from the USA. The American government introduced a new practice of directly requesting Japan to change some traditional, customary or local system. As its influence was so strong and it shortcut the complex decision-making system, this also

had many advantages for Japan in that certain officials used it to by-pass internal political objections. And the strong fear in Japan of being isolated in international affairs also helped *gaiatsu* gain force.

In the case of CFCs, Dupont's decision to withdraw from the hugely profitable CFC business came thus as a shock in Japan. It saw it as a *gaiatsu* and felt it had to follow.

Influence inside Japan

Unlike in many other countries, consumers, shareholders and employees have not been able to exert a great influence on industry. It took a long time for voices of pollution victims to be heard and acted upon. Pressure groups, often supported or formed by students and mothers, lacked money and political influence, but it seems they are finally and slowly gaining force.

The strong influences have come from officials, the media and industrial pressure groups (the ones that have money and favour growth over care for the environment). Administrative orders, which can be issued quite easily by ministries, are almost as binding as laws in Japan. Nevertheless, on environmental issues, a struggle of power exists between several ministries. The Environmental Agency, which advocates the importance of a leading position in environmental protection, is not as powerful as the famous MITI (Ministry of International Trade and Industry) which favours growth. As far as the media are concerned, Japanese companies seem to be positively allergic to scandal, possibly because of a lack in PR. Many companies started positive public relations campaigns with an emphasis on environmental consciousness after 1988, the trigger for which will have been the increasing environmental consciousness of the Japanese consumer.

Influence inside the company

Growth was by far the first priority in the past. Therefore, the strongest internal incentive to pursue environmental management was often an attempt to benefit directly from it. It turned out to be an easy-to-swallow pill, because of its compatibility with the growth supremacy. In other words, 'environmental management' meant becoming more cost effective, saving energy, and selling the techniques developed in the process of doing so, all of which are, after all, cash generating efforts.

Many companies rushed to rebuild and sell their in-house anti-pollution know-how and many of them tried to improve their public green image in the process. Launching tougher environmental standards to gain competitive advantage was often the strategy of a medium-sized company trying to forestall stronger and slower competitors.

Leadership has some influence, but in most cases, it seems to behave as an amplifier of outside pressure rather than a spontaneous independent force.

Reactions

There are at least two factors that discourage immediate actions.

Growth and efficiency supremacy

As mentioned above, Japanese industry is based on a firm belief in growth and efficiency. The aim of Japanese companies was to constantly grow and be more efficient than competitors rather than taking care of, for example, shareholders. This overwhelming obsession with growth meant that, even when receiving small dividends, shareholders felt certain of capital gains as long as growth would be maintained.

Growth-oriented management is generally in direct contrast to environmental management which favours sustainable growth. Growth should not be sacrificed for reducing CO_2 emissions, it could be against the company's or the industry's *raison d'etre* and even against human evolution. And anyway, if there is a problem, a technical solution should be sought instead of suppressing activities.

Collective decision making

Decisions are generally made in a collective manner in Japan, and leadership thus intervenes less than in the Western system. Whereas strong leadership tends to be associated with drastic changes, collective decision making is not . The collective decision-making is slow by its very nature as it is based on the persuasion of all members and it furthermore provides room for political bargaining.

Another disadvantage of this system is that a company cannot make its decision on important issues alone in its branch of industry. It often waits to see what happens within its own industry or negotiates the most acceptable solution with other companies or officials. The more important the problem is, the more protagonists are involved and the longer it takes to find a solution.

There is, of course, an advantage: actions that follow a collective decision normally go smoother than a decision imposed from above. It could be one of the reasons why Japanese decisions are often slow in the coming but are quickly and thoroughly followed by actions. It is commonly known that Japanese companies are slow decision makers, but quick to act on them and continuously try to improve on them.

It is interesting to note, however, that in successful cases of Japanese environmental management, strong leadership often played an important role, and was still followed by a smooth acceptance as if the decision had been made collectively.

Action

As soon as someone, often a high ranked board member, is nominated as responsible, a task force consisting of members from several different activities is formed. They start gathering information from inside and outside the company. There are often continuous contacts with relevant officials and companies in the same group of industry.

They will set a concrete objective which will then be studied by the people concerned who digest it in a feasible manner, a typical collective decision-making system.

A move initiated by the Mitsubishi Corporation and many other trading houses is to try and make the task force a final filter for decisions. Apart from keeping an eye on any possible business opportunity, they can veto a project if they think it is against the global environmental policy.

In general, the ensuing process does not differ much from that in Western companies. The only possible difference lies in the fact that change comes about gradually rather than as the result of bold action, just like TQC or *kaizen*. Gradual improvement does not need complicated collective decisions because it has relatively little implications and is in line with overall decision making.

A TQC programme called 'Do we really have to use CFCs?' and 'Can recycling be better decreased the use of CFC in Epson by 25 per cent. Some Japanese management practices, such as *kaizen*, and worker involvement in continuous quality improvement activities seem to be equally applicable in environmental management.

Canon is known for its continuous environment protective advertisements and for a worldwide effort to collect and recycle used toner cartridges for laser printers, a market in which Canon has a high market share. The company was successful in 'thinking globally', which has not been common in Japan but which is keenly sought today.

Projects

There are several efforts ongoing. What is interesting here is that companies are not bound to their industry and try to find a new use for their resources. Japanese companies' biggest achievement in the field of environmental protection is said to be in air purification. Large manufacturers in heavy industries such as Mitsubishi Heavy Ind., IHI, Hitachi, and others are all involved in this area and see future developments for their business in Eastern Europe.

All major electric power companies such as Tokyo Electric Power or Kansai Electric Power have been studying and formulating a stable and environmentally balanced electricity generation and seem perplexed by this sudden green movement. The difficulty lies in the fact that more than ten per cent of electricity in Japan is generated by nuclear power, thus minimizing its dependence on oil but provoking strong opposition in the wake of Hiroshima. Research is under way to improve storage of electricity by supra-conductivity to electricity generation by wind or wave. Non-electric power generation produces further challenges.

Car manufacturers are careful not to get too caught up in the non-stop stream of regulations, and have asked for a restructuring of the public transport system. Better roads and more regular public transportation will reduce the pollution from cars. All are looking into environmental alternatives such as improvements in catalytic converters in the short term, and at cars running on methanol or hydrogen in the longer term. But again, many companies of other branches of industry, such as Nippon Steel or Hoxan, are also present and competing in such efforts.

Beside Asahi Glass, the largest Japanese chemical manufacturer which works together with Dupont and ICI on CFC substitutes, Organo and Kurita sell water purification systems that can replace CFCs in the cleaning of semi-conductors and many engineering companies sell recycling systems. On the users' side all large electronics manufacturers are also keen to find a solution and are heavily involved in R&D.

In 1990 the paper industry collaborated with photocopier manufacturers on the introduction of recycled paper for copiers and printers. They are now looking for a way to erase printing from copies by means of irradiation so that the paper can be used again. Many attempts by supermarkets and cooperatives to collect the paper packaging of milk to produce paper rolls have taken place.

These projects show the efforts made by Japanese companies to develop their business resources in the environmental field.

Analysis

In addition to the collective decision-making system mentioned above, certain characteristics of Japanese systems which have generally been recognized as good assets do not always seem to be conducive to environmental management.

In the first place, while the famous loyalty of employees and shareholders may support quick and thorough action as an organisation, it may limit the amount of information going in and out. A comfortable but uniform and not freely talking structure may discourage green ideas, especially if these do not fit in with the overall pursuit of growth.

Silent shareholders and docile board members do not play the role of advisor to the company and this carries the risk that the company blindly proceeds on its course. Generally, Japanese companies resemble well-protected fortresses into which only selected bits of information are accepted, although attempts have been made to change this structure because of the recent scandals in financial markets.

The second problem is the large stake in technology which has been a big contributing factor in the competitiveness of Japanese industries. Mr Honda was known for his confidence in technology, and always tried to find a technological solution for a problem. This creates a risk of over-inclination to solve problems by technology rather than nipping the problem in the bud at the early stage. However, any bold environmental investment can be rendered useless by a technical innovation and makes people careful leading the way in this area.

The term 'network economy system' is used increasingly to identify the series of particularities Japanese society and companies display in Western eyes. In short it means that, unlike their Western counterparts, Japanese companies form a 'network' with other companies or officials to pursue business – something which is sometimes even referred to as 'conspiracy' in the Western media. Competing players may have come to the understanding to 'compete in quality'. *Keiretsu*, the famous group structure adopted by Mitsubishi or Toyota, is an extreme network system which is challenged by the US because of its exclusive nature. Even this famous administrative structure could be seen as a sort of 'order' in the 'network'. 'Ostracism is the toughest penalty in Japanese society', says the president of the Chamber of Commerce in Osaka.

This network system which is a collective decision system of the highest level, allows members to adopt a similar attitude to a common problem and then enables them to move very quickly once the decision is taken.

There are, however, two drawbacks to the system. The first one is that it is slow (which is, as we saw earlier, typical of collective decision making), and the second is that the decision-making process and its criteria are not clear to outsiders.

It is interesting to know whether environmental management is located at the free competition side, and thus outside the network – which would mean that members are freer to seek competition on this issue – or not. At present it still seems to be handled within the network, though it appears to be moving outwards. Only the independent companies not in the middle of these systems go for bold action.

Finally, to illustrate the recent change in tone, even the JIT system is publicly criticized for its 'egoistic' nature. Nissan's president admits that the growth supremacy will no longer be acceptable and Japanese companies have to change. Car and electric appliance manufacturers are looking for ways to slow the rate at which new models are launched and to set up a system to collect old equipment for recycling.

This change in attitude became apparent recently in two cases. In contrast to the USA but in line with most of Western Europe, the Japanese government ended up voting in favour of a ban on any development in the South Pole. Furthermore, it will publish a report that admits that the Japanese economy has averse effects on the global environment and should therefore change. And finally, it is planning the launch of an environmental development assistance scheme which would assist Third World countries to acquire advanced anti-pollution technologies.

Keidanren, the Federation of Economic Organizations, which is the most powerful association of industries, has set a charter of environmental management with tough guidelines for its members.

Of course, these positive moves are taking place at the top levels, and in many surveys employees at lower levels confess that the priority is always sales and growth. But, although it may take time for these ideas to filter down through the ranks and to cause a shift in priorities, there certainly is a new degree of determination.

The most difficult, but at the same time most effective development in Japanese environmental management is for it to break out of the network system, especially because of the slow nature of this system. However, once succeeded, it is not difficult to imagine the effect of this massive effort and repeated investments in environmental improvements. The first yard is much longer than the next ten, particularly in Japan.

INSIGHTS

Since World War II, Japan has been putting all its efforts in improving the efficiency of economical activities, and it has been successful. These efforts have been so concentrated that factors with negative impact were sometimes overlooked, especially if the problem was not concrete which occasionally happened to be the case with environmental problems.

If Japan's behaviour in the area of environmental management can be criticized, it would be that such a growth-orientated management system which has been in practice for almost 40 years could not digest the developments in the company's or industry's social role for the environment. This criticism possibly emanated from certain irritated parties in the West who considered Japanese economic growth unpleasant and attempted either to pressurize Japan into cutting back or to extract a proportionate contribution to global affairs.

Not only the issue of environmental protection itself but many of the political issues such as the Gulf War, led Japan and its companies to reconsider their global status. Many important business leaders already admit the need for a change from greedy growth to sustainable growth. This attitude might change suddenly, however, if environmental consciousness in the West were to decrease drastically – 'we have to save the Eastern countries at the cost of the environment' – or if there was a surge of arrogance in Japan – 'we are the best so why should we have to listen to others'. In order to bring Corporate Japan's new approach to environmental management nearer, there are two steps to go through. The first one is to widely promote the view of these business leaders within their own organizations and secondly to put it into practice. Putting it into practice will be the least difficult of the two; promoting the view is totally new as decisions are almost always made without consensus.

Another point of great importance to Japanese industry would be the transparency of the network system, according to Professor Nakatani of Hitotsubashi University. The future environmental decisions should be understandable and synchronized worldwide. Therefore, shaping the network system in that orientation will no doubt be necessary. Particularly in environmental problems insisting on local particularities (Japan is different) is unacceptable.

Consumerism

A free and large society in full growth led to an outbreak of a sudden consumerism which caused other criticisms. It was incompatible with the matured Western, especially European, consumerism which went through this phase a long time ago and now seeks a more balanced system. This disagreement touches on the important discussion between the 'haves' and 'have nots'. Does the rich Western world have the right to limit Third World countries in their use of resources? Though classified as rich today Japan is the last member of the group of rich countries and its behaviour might be referred to later by new comers. Japan's role is important and difficult. Japan's actions now will later be mirrored by newly industrialized countries.

Finally, there is a definite need to develop consumer consciousness. With today's relatively weak consumer consciousness in Japan, industries' efforts can be well promoted horizontally, or across the industry, but less easily vertically. Consumers should play a more important role to promote product stewardship, as manufacturers may be satisfied with the management of only a limited part of the product life cycle. Though segmented efforts exist already, a general consciousness may take time to attain the same levels as in the West.

As the *Kanban* system shows, Japanese industry relies heavily on sharing in business. Subcontracting or collaboration is common. The environmental responsibility is not well defined. If manufacturers were to pass the risky part of their business, e.g, the pollutive part of the production, outside of Japan, they have to be stopped.

Technologies

Japan can contribute through existing technologies that can be of use in environmental protection. For those large national projects such as prevention of CO_2 from power plants, substitution of CFC, electric cars, bio-degradable plastics and so on, the technology should not be used as a means of business domination. There would be a need to structure the grant of such know-how in an 'environmental' manner.

Let us take a look at a case in the film industry to conclude the chapter.

In 1986, Fuji Film launched the first disposable camera on the Japanese market. In 1990, Fuji introduced a semi-recycling system for it, which consisted of simply breaking down the camera into its components which were then disposed of separately. The only part that was re-used was the flash bulb. Fuji seems to be determined to seek better solutions as long as they are still cost effective.

Kodak followed the Fuji example, and they were even later than Fuji in launching their semi-recycling system. The European player AGFA doesn't claim to be environmental and is therefore not a player in this market.

As the system brings back the whole camera to suppliers for development, the manufacturers should have been prepared for volume of waste from non-film parts, which unfortunately was not the case. Despite criticisms regarding the wastefulness of the disposable camera being heard from the beginning, it took many years for the manufacturers to act on them.

And what we see today in this market is one successful FUJI, who took the lion's share and the environmental consciousness reputation, KODAK the follower and no AGFA. . .

'To many it will always seem better to have measurable progress towards the wrong goals than unmeasurable (and hence uncertain) progress towards the right ones.'

John K. Galbraith

7 ENVIRONMENTAL MANAGEMENT AND INVESTMENT DECISIONS

by Dominik Koechlin and Kaspar Müller

Suppose pollution prevention equipment would add another £3 million to an investment in a new factory that costs £20 million. Assume the new equipment could prevent soil pollution that would have to be cleaned up in ten years' time at a cost of £10 million pounds. If these figures are considered in a classic investment appraisal as used in most companies, the conclusion would have to be that it is uneconomical to invest in pollution prevention. This is reason enough to take a closer look at the way in which companies plan their investments and at the implications of this being done in a way which is not coherent with an environmental strategy.

The financial world, meaning the investors putting their money into stocks and bonds of companies all over the world, is showing a growing interest in environmental issues. This is partly due to the fact that if a company fails to take environmental issues seriously it runs the risk of being held liable for the environmental consequences of its production processes and products. Moreover, if a company does not recognize, and make use of 'green' opportunities it might not be such a good investment after all.

This chapter does not aim to discuss the international and macroeconomic dimension of environmental issues, nor the viewpoint of an investor in the capital markets. It wants to focus on the impact a classic management tool, discounted cash flow analysis, has on the environmental performance of a company.

INTEREST RATES AND RISK

Interest rates play a key role in investment analysis. The general level of interest rates in an economy varies. With interest being the price for capital, it is determined by supply and demand – like almost everything else in a market economy. The willingness of individuals and institutions to supply capital depends on their preference for future over present consumption. If they forgo present consumption and lend their money to others, they will do so at a price: the interest rate. The level of interest demanded by the suppliers of capital depends on the level of risk in the use of their capital. Because a company always runs a more or less substantial risk of defaulting it will have to pay a higher price for capital than the government. The rate at which the government borrows money is called the 'risk free' rate, because nobody expects governments to go out of business. The risk free rate is the basis from which the risk premium a company has to pay its capital providers can be calculated. The demand for capital is dependent on investment opportunities. A well managed company will only look for capital if it has ideas about where it can earn more than its capital costs.

Other factors influencing interest rates are inflation rates and monetary policies. An interesting aspect of the inflation rate is that if it is low, the probability that the expectations of borrowers and lenders can be met is higher, because interest rates are less likely to fluctuate. This makes the future more predictable, which increases long-term thinking. High inflation rates on the other hand increase the uncertainty as to how interest rates will fluctuate and therefore reduces the willingness to invest. The rate of inflation is relevant to the economy as a whole and especially to environmental projects as it determines the time horizon of a company's investment projects. Effective environmental management practices often mean forgoing short-term earnings for the benefit of a long-term sustainability of the company's competitive position.

In order to earn money in the future companies have to invest in the present. There is always a time gap between the production of a good and the cash inflow from its sale. For services this gap might be smaller but the fact that the production of the service or the good cannot be payed with the proceeds it earns remains the same. If a company does not have the means to generate enough cash for its planned investments, it has to apply for a bank loan or look for investors in the capital markets. Investors and banks are risk takers and because a company poses a greater risk than the government they will charge the company a higher price than the riskless interest rate.

The place where this price is set, where people and institutions with spare capital and willing to take risks and companies in need of financing meet, is the capital markets. The riskier the company is perceived to be, the higher the premium over the risk-free interest rate it has to pay.

When managers evaluate an investment opportunity they will first have to ask themselves how risky the project is. Risk is, however, very subjective, depending very much on where the observer stands. There are nevertheless 'objective' ways of pricing risks. The most common way is by comparing a project with alternative investments in the capital markets. As mentioned, investors demand a reward for investing. Different securities offer different levels of return. In efficient markets these returns are the price the issuers of the securities have to pay the investors for taking the risk of investing. They are therefore also a good measure for the price of other risks. One has to bear in mind that a company could also, with the same level of risk, choose to invest its money in the capital markets, instead of investing it in a projects of its own.

The concept of discounting

When assessing the risk of a planned project it is helpful to look at similar projects in the capital market. How much interest would £1 earn when, instead of being put into a project within the company, it would be invested in the capital markets? To make the comparison meaningful one would have to look at investments with the same risk level as the company's project. The interest rate that results from this comparison is called the opportunity cost of capital or discount rate.

Because costs and benefits of a project occur at different times, they are difficult to weigh against each other. By using the discount rate found in the capital markets, one can qualify the effect of time on value. The method by which this is done is called *discounted cash flow analysis*. It enables the company to compare money earned in the future with the value of money earned today. How much more is £1 earned today worth compared to £1 earned in two years' time? On top of establishing the appropriate discount rate a company has to estimate its expected cash flow. How much cash does the project need to get started, how much to run, and how much will it bring in and when? It is often possible to predict the initial cash outlays (e.g. for machinery) early in the planning phase. For the cash inflows, more difficult projections of expected sales and possible margins etc. have to be made. These cash inflows, together with the initial cash outlays, adjusted over time with the discount rate lead to the *net present value*, or NPV. Discounted at a rate of 10 per cent £1 received or payed next year is today only worth $£1/1.1 = £0,91$, £1 in two years has a present value of $£1/(1.1)(1.1) = £0.83$ etc. Is an investment of

£7 that would guarantee £1 income each year for the next 10 years sensible? The NPV calculation shows the answer:

$$-£7 + \frac{1}{(1.1)} + \frac{1}{(1.1)^2} + \ldots \frac{1}{(1.1)^n} = -0.9.$$

The figure is negative so the investment would not be worth while. It is important to note that at a discount rate of 10 per cent £1 in ten years' time is in today's money only worth 38 pence. Managers should basically stick to the rule only to proceed with investments that have a positive NPV. But of course these calculations leave plenty of room for potential errors, either by taking a false discount rate or by overestimating future cash flows.

A useful way of checking how realistic a positive NPV is, is to look at the project for competitive advantages. What makes us think that people will buy our planned product rather than those of our competitors? Do we offer any unique features at an attractive price? Do we have a unique selling proposition as the marketing people would say? Only if a positive NPV of a project can be justified with special competitive attributes of the project the calculations should be trusted.

Pitfalls

Of course even the biggest admirers of discounted cash flow analysis admit that it has its perils. When putting values on future events one always runs the risk of forgetting that these values are based on assumptions and should therefore be treated with caution. When looking for the appropriate interest rate for discounting future cash flows many companies use their weighted average cost of capital, meaning the average interest rate they have to pay their share- and debtholders. If the project for which the projections of cash flows are made is more risky than the company's normal business – which can be the case when companies try to diversify into green market niches – then cash flow forecasts should be discounted at a higher rate to reflect the additional risk.

DISCOUNTED CASH FLOW ANALYSIS AND THE CONCEPT OF SUSTAINABLE DEVELOPMENT

The notion of discounting future earnings to get a present value is also used in the stock markets. Modern finance theory suggests that the price of a stock is nothing else than the present value of the expected discounted earnings streams. The prices of the stocks vary because of the varying expectations. For environmental management there is an interesting link to the concept of sustainable development. If our planet is to be able to absorb the pollution of its entire world population, then it seems quite clear that the growth rates of the industrial economies will have to be moderate in favour of more growth for the developing world. It simply cannot sustain developing and developed world growing at high rates. Knowing this, many of our assets such as shares of companies are worth less than we think, because they are nothing more than the discounted, expected future cash flows. If people have to revise their expectations about the growth of the future cash flows then they have to reassess the value of many of their assets. If the concept of sustainable development means less growth than has been anticipated by, e.g. the stock markets, sustainable growth does not only mean that our notion of growth will have to change in the future, but that we have to give up asset value today!

The payback period

Every investment has to pay back its initial costs within a specified number of years. Such an investment appraisal method is very simple and many companies use it.

The payback period is often the same for all investment proposals, regardless of the risk and structure of the expected cash flows. An objective criterion as to which payback period is to be used does not exist and the period used remains arbitrary. Most companies, depending on the industry they do their business in, use a payback period of 4–6 years. The biggest drawbacks of a company setting its own payback period as a bench mark for investments are that the time value of money and the risk are neglected. Furthermore, the gains of many environmentally orientated projects, such as entry into new green markets or the introduction of new pollution prevention programmes, only materialize after a number of years, often *after* the end of the payback period. If the payback method is used they will not enter into the calculations. A fixed payback period as a criterion for a company's investments is therefore seldom compatible with a green strategy.

Discounting and the issue of time

We stated earlier that interest and discount rates make a statement about time preferences. High discount rates reflect high risks. The higher the discount rate the more weight is given to cash flows occurring in the short term and less to the more distant cash flows. A low discount rate indicates that the future value is not considered to be very different from today's and that potential risks are therefore low.

The impact of a low discount rate for environmental management would be that cash flows in the more distant future would gain in weight, which would help the company to pursue an environmentally compatible strategy.

It is interesting to know that the basic idea behind discount rates, i.e. to give something in the future less value than today because of uncertainty, is implicitly used whenever things are compared over time.

A study done by 'Resources for the Future', Washington D.C., confronted people with the choice between a pollution abatement programme that would save a hundred lives now and one that would save two hundred lives fifty years from now. The authors point out that with the increase in time the uncertainty of a benefit or cost increases and that value, not only in monetary terms but also in many other, decreases with time. Because of the unpredictability of the future, the more time passes, the less likely it is that a benefit will materialize. This notion is expressed by the implicit discount rate most people use in their assessment of time-related events. Another interesting finding was that some people in the survey preferred the present-orientated programme, no matter how many lives were promised to be saved in the future.

The authors of the study think the reason for this is the belief that technical improvement will enable to save these lives in the future anyway. This unshaken confidence in technical progress, the belief that there is a technical solution to every environmental problem is still very common.

A look at the issue of global warming or the depletion of the ozone layer shows that the problems cannot be solved by new technology alone, but that patterns of behaviour will have to change. One of the reasons why technical thinking still dominates environmental management is that in most companies the people responsible for environmental performance have a technical background. Whilst this was reasonable in the early days of environmental management, when managing environmental issues meant installing 'end-of-the-pipe' equipment and dealing with regulators, today's requirements are different. Many of the technical staff are ill equipped to face the strategic challenges of environmental management, and companies will have to consider how to integrate strategic environmental management into their organisations.

It seems quite obvious that good environmental management involves long-term thinking. Long-term thinking, however, is exactly what discounted cash flow analysis, the way it is used in most companies, does not allow for. From the viewpoint of when a decision is taken, environmental liabilities most often occur in the (distant) future. It is therefore understandable that managers do not take them into account in their cash flow projections.

Necessary framework

What managers consider when putting together the numbers and the time horizon for evaluating a project is very much dependent on the framework within which the company operates. Because even if the legal system can cope with a long time horizon and hold a company liable after 20 or more years, the costs for the clean up have to be very high to have influence on projects and net present value calculations 50 years before they materialize. For example, clean up costs of 50 million pounds expected in 50 years' time have, discounted at a rate of 10 per cent, a present value of just £426,000. They are therefore not likely to influence the cash flow projections of a major project.

An increasing enforcement of the *polluter pays principle* (ppp) will make companies more accountable for their impact on the environment. It aims, strictly speaking, at internalizing the external environmental costs a company generates. According to the ppp a company should bear the full price of the environmental resources it uses. If the company is not forced to pay that price, environmental aspects will have a hard time influencing its cash flow projections.

With a strict integration of the ppp into environmental legislation the price of a good or service should fully reflect the natural resources such as air, water and land used. As early as the 1970s the OECD proposed that a less strict form of the ppp shall be introduced in the environmental legislation of its member states. In the OECD version the implementation of the ppp should ensure that a company bears the cost of its pollution abatement equipment and that subsidies should be the exception. The more pragmatic approach of the OECD relates to the problem of assessing the monetary values of the (still free) resources used and damage done by a polluter. Most countries therefore concentrate on allocating the cost of the required pollution control equipment to the polluters. There is however a tendency, especially in the environmental legislation of the EC, to move towards a stricter ppp and make polluters pay also for the damage caused by their products. This big step towards integrating environmental costs into prices is accompanied by the planned introduction in the EC of so called 'economic instruments' such as a carbon tax or tradable emission permits. Once these are introduced, it will be in the interest of every company to pay as little as possible, in other words to outperform its industry in environmental management.

The reform of civil liability rules in many European countries will be an additional incentive for companies to think about environmental management systems and look differently at environmental investment proposals.

Making it easier to take companies to court on the grounds of the damaging effect their products and processes have on the environment has a preventive effect, even without the huge amounts of compensation awarded in the US. Only the lawyers involved seem to benefit from these large sums of money, not the environment, because once paid out in compensation, this money is no longer available for e.g. clean ups. Environmental liability rules have to be designed very carefully to encourage companies to invest in a more environmentally conscious way without increasing their risks to such an extent that they will not invest at all. The build up of the economy in the former East Germany has suffered a lot because of potential investors' fear of having to pay for the clean up of sites polluted during the last fifty years.

A better integration of the polluter pays principle and stricter environmental liability rules will alter the way cash flows related to environmental issues enter into investment appraisals. Environmental aspects will be easier to quantify for those doing the analysis and more environmental investments will save money immediately and therefore remain undisputed.

The loss of an opportunity

A different and often underestimated risk of not integrating environmental aspects into investment decisions is that of lost opportunities. Who would dare to quantify the competitive fall back in ten years' time, because of poor environmental performance?

It is very difficult to let potential benefits of good environmental performance influence the discounted cash flow analysis. Environmental management often means dealing with a large time gap between spending the money and reaping the benefits. If a company starts to invest in an integrated environmental management programme ranging from new production technology to green products and environmental perform-ance-linked executive compensation schemes etc. it can take years until the benefits show in the financial results. Imagine the effect this long time horizon has on a manager responsible for the cash outlays but long gone when the benefits come to light.

This raises the interesting question as to what time horizons companies think in. Maybe one has to differentiate between the various interest groups within a company. It is fair to say that managers, because of the need to show results in order to get promoted, often have a shorter time horizon than the shareholders of the company. But even the owners of the company can be a very diverse group with each very different ideas on what time horizon is relevant for a company's strategy.

Better image, more credibility, and better relationships with cus-tomers, future employees, public authorities and other stakeholders are difficult to quantify. They affect different aspects of the business such as the time it takes to get the permits for a new production site or the amount of cash needed for a new green marketing campaign. They are so called 'soft factors' which many managers find difficult to grasp and which they therefore tend to neglect. But with the rising public awareness for the dimension of environmental problems and the increasing possibilities for gaining competitive advantage through good environmental manage-ment this attitude could prove to be very costly.

The way out

Discounted cash flow analysis is too established to be discarded and it could be argued that there are no alternatives in sight for evaluating the financial impact of a company's projects. One could argue, that the only way to integrate environmental costs or benefits into a discounted cash flow analysis would be to alter the discount rate. A lower discount rate would flatten the differences across time and therefore increase the importance of cash flows some years down the line. But by doing so, the whole concept of risk, which is based on a comparison of a project's risk to a similar risk in the capital markets, would be discarded and the little reliability financial theory and forecasting were able to develop would be gone. One of the best referees of the success of a company's strategy, the capital market, would partly be lost. We will have to find solutions which ideally should link the financial aspects of an investment with its strategic implications.

Finance theory has long been familiar with valuing possible events in the future by giving the right to act in a certain way in the future a value. For instance, an option in the financial markets gives the holder the right to buy or sell an asset at a specified price at some time in the future. The factors affecting an option's price are the price of the underlying stock, the exercise price, the time to maturity as well as the riskiness of the stock and the risk-free interest rate.

Different models for calculating the expected market value of an option have been developed, the Black-Scholes formula being the most successful. Option pricing theory models the time series interaction between investments, while discounted cash flow analysis looks at the financial implications of isolated investments. If it looks at a company as a whole, at sums of investments, the option theory gives certain investments a special value because of their relationship with other investments. Projects with a strong environmental component, i.e. the launch of a green product line or the introduction of a integrated environmental management programme for a company clearly have this element. Most of these projects are of a strategic nature because of their long duration and the impact they have as to where the company is heading.

Stock options were created because of investors' desire to safeguard themselves against risks. By using options investors can make sure that they will benefit from a rise in the stockmarkets or be hedged against a fall of the markets, without having to buy the stocks immediately. Complicated models have enabled sophisticated investors to construct portfolios with this insurance component and exactly the risk return characteristics they desire. The value of an option is mainly determined by the volatility of the underlying stock. The higher the volatility, the higher the risk, but because of the upside potential, the higher also the value of the option.

From the options of the financial markets an analogy can be drawn to the options a company has to invest in real assets. Discounted cash flow analysis gives the value of a potential investment in today's money, but unfortunately it is unable to take into account all elements of an investment's value and possibly of great importance to a company. These aspects can be regarded as the options a company has. Most management decisions aren't irrevocable. Managers usually have the flexibility to adopt to changing circumstances even after a project is started. This flexibility to revise a project and either defer its completion, abandon or expand it, is not captured by discounted cash flow analysis. This is especially important for environmental management. Imagine a company getting rid off the CFCs in its products in the 1970s when the discussions about their effect on the ozone layer first started. Surely such a renunciation in those days needed some investment. But to belong to the first suppliers of for example CFC-free deodorant sprays was likely to result in an increased market share once the international debate on the ozone layer got going.

Because of the increasing knowledge about environmental degradation new issues with a huge effect on an industry can emerge very quickly. The capacity to adapt quickly to new circumstances is therefore clearly very valuable. It also enables the company to get involved in a large number of projects which create opportunities to undertake further investments in the future.

This interdependence between investments can be of great strategic value. If these strategic aspects of an investment decision are regarded as being very important, they might even justify investing in a project with negative NPV.

The option value of an investment is especially critical for environmental management. Just as in financial markets, the value of the strategic option increases with the riskiness of the underlying cash flows. With stricter legislation and increasing risk, investing more to prevent environmental liability has an option value. It entails the option to stay out of the court rooms and public debate and to create a positive green image. As a growing number of environmental issues will force the legislators to react, the strategic value of doing more than required by the authorities is increasing and the option value will be higher than the additional investment in pollution prevention equipment.

Creating in-house expertise in environmental technology and environmental management carries the possibility of starting new lines of business. More and more chemical companies are starting subsidiaries or profit centres that market environmental technology. However, this option is only open to those companies that have gathered engineering know-how in the most advanced environmental technologies. Companies that have always aimed for minimum legal compliance in their environmental management have passed up on this opportunity.

For some chemical companies, such as Sandoz, the value of good environmental performance only became really clear after a major accident severely polluted the Rhine. Today Sandoz has a successful subsidiary for environmental technology. So it is not always the farsightedness of management that creates green opportunities. Sometimes the environment has to give a 'hint' of its potential for the development of a company.

Even more attractive is the call option embedded in green product lines. Starting early with environmentally sound products enables a company to set the standards in its industry while its slower competitors will have a tough time trying to catch up. This is an especially important aspect as long as most countries define their pollution standards with the requirement for companies to use 'the best available technology'. Increasingly, the standards for the environmental performance of products are set by looking at the best performer in the industry. Being an environmental innovator and investing in the option of remaining one can therefore make a competitive advantage more sustainable.

CONCLUSION

Environmental management has a great deal to do with the time horizon a company thinks in. A closer look at discounted cash flow analysis shows that companies use a management tool that tends to undervalue the long-term and strategic implications of an investment decision. The strategy of a company is implemented by the investments the company undertakes, but in most companies finance and strategic planning are still regarded as two completely different disciplines. For environmental management it is vital that the two can be brought together. Only then will it be possible to let the strategic dimension of environmental aspects, of which more and more companies are becoming aware, have an influence on the way a company goes about its daily business.

Integrating the ideas behind the option pricing theory into investment appraisal systems could be a first step in the right direction. Admittedly, whilst the underlying logic of applying option theory to strategic environmental management is relatively straightforward, it remains very difficult to actually place a monetary value on the options embedded in environmental management. Because of the difficulties arising from the lack of market information on strategic alternatives as well as from incomplete information on other inputs, option pricing should be used with caution. Often projects are tailored very specifically to the abilities and the needs of a company and cannot easily be sold. The marketability of the underlying assets being a precondition for option pricing models, the agenda for further research seems set.

Nevertheless, using option pricing theory for evaluating strategic decisions has already taken place. Especially in the oil and mining industries, where there is accurate information on the underlying assets, more and more companies are applying option valuation techniques to help them evaluate strategic alternatives. In the oil business, option theory can help determine the value of a potential oil field, without having to make a forecast on future oil prices. The option pricing models only require the potential price range of for example the oil price to value the option. Oil companies can therefore regard the purchase of an oil field as an option they will execute only when the oil price reaches a certain level. Determining the price range and the variability of the price is all the option pricing models ask for.

For environmental management this is good news. Managers are used to relying on numbers when taking a decision. The option theory can provide them with a mathematical model that captures the strategic value of a project. In some cases it might even be possible to come out with quite exact figures. But even if the option of staying in business through state of the art environmental management is, with today's models, still very difficult to quantify. Much more important is the notion that especially environmentally orientated projects could have an option value that goes beyond a mere NPV calculation. The value of these options will increase as environmental degradation and its public perception continues. Companies that keep the environmental options in mind will be better environmental performers. And that will certainly be a prerequisite for a successful business.

'Money is a capitalist tool for achieving environmental and social goals. It is up to us to use it.'

Carlos Joly

8 GREEN FUNDS, OR JUST GREEDY?

by Carlos Joly

INVESTMENT PERFORMANCE

The sales argument for environmental mutual funds, also known as green funds, consists of three claims:

1. green funds perform as well as general equity funds;
2. green funds do environmental good; and
3. green funds are, from an ethical point of view, better than funds that don't have environmental criteria as part of their investment philosophy.

Given the number of green funds that have been launched in the past three years, there is enough information to begin to draw some conclusions. What is really behind these claims? Are they valid? This chapter marshalls some of the relevant data from the US, the UK and Scandinavia. It draws on the author's personal experience as manager and marketer of two environmental funds, in addition to managing money market and bond funds.

For readers who like conclusions served first, let me summarize: I will argue that green funds need not yield lower returns and in some cases yield significantly higher returns; that they do contribute, even if indirectly, to making the world environmentally better; and can in some cases be said to be ethical. But the extent to which the latter statement is true will depend largely on whether they apply more broadly defined ethical selection criteria in addition to environmental criteria.

Green fund performance

Let's begin with the claim that green fund investment performance is consistent with or better than the performance of the stock market as a whole and of equity funds in general. Let's postpone for a moment the question as to what a green share is or how it ought to be defined and let's for now simply say that green funds are funds that call themselves green. (We'll get back to this. I'm not trying to duck the issue.)

The most comprehensive stock index covering environmental equities in the United States is tracked by First Analysis Corporation. It is calculated from the capitalization-weighted prices of about 70 publicly-traded companies, with data going back to 1984.

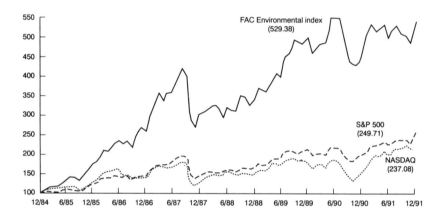

Figure 8.1   First Analysis Corporation Environmental Index, December 1984 through December 1991 – monthly

At first glance it is rather evident that equities represented by the index have outperformed the market. Two interesting facts emerge: green equities sell at a premium to the market – what I have previously called 'the green premium' – and the green premium grows larger in bull markets and gets smaller in bear markets.

The first point is illustrated in the following table:

Country	Company	Company P/E	Market P/E	Green Premium
USA	Waste Mgmt	21	12	1.75
Holland	Grontmy N.V.	15	10	1.5
Norway	Tomra	13	11	1.6
France	Generale des Eaux	18	13	1.4

Table 8.1   The green premium (company P/E divided by market P/E)

The second point is illustrated in the following table:

Country	Company	1.1.88	1.1.89	1.1.90	1.1.91	1.1.92
USA	Waste Mgmt	1.26	1.94	2.12	1.45	1.30
Norway	Tomra	1.21	1.35	1.71	1.32	2.01
Holland	Grontmy	0.58	0.66	1.57	na	0.90
France	Gen. des Eaux	1.86	1.56	2.07	2.05	1.43

Table 8.2 The green premium trend (company P/E divided by market P/E)

A closer look reveals that certain periods during the past six years exhibit dramatic underperformance, whereas others show a dramatic over-performance. Now look at a the more detailed picture: the index week-to-week in 1991.

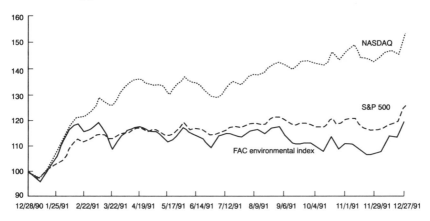

Figure 8.2 Environmental Index, 28 December 1987 through 27 December 1991 – weekly

We see here that even though in the longer term environmental equities have outperformed the general market, in 1991 and also in 1992 this sector has underperformed. Why the periods of overperformance and underperformance?

Over- and underperformance
There are several explanations. The first one relates to the fact that from the mid-eighties onwards, investors thought of pollution control stocks as high-growth stocks and were therefore willing to pay high price-to-

earnings multiples. High-growth expectations had been priced into the valuations and the premium over average market pricing grew through 1990. With such large built-in gains, investors opted to liquidate a portion of the green stocks in their portfolios, when reducing their total equity exposure after the Gulf War of 1990 and then as the recession deepened in 1991 and 1992. In times of uncertainty, investors tend to realize gains wherever they are able to.

The other reason has to do with the growing recognition during 1991 that pollution control stocks, previously thought of as recession-resistant, turned out not to be so. In times of declining consumer and industrial sales and orders, industry and government postpone investment in capital goods, including pollution control and recycling equipment. Though some investments are of course not postponable due to regulatory deadlines, in other cases government enforcement becomes more lenient. The total volumes of industrial waste being processed by pollution control companies and pollution containment investments relating to production processes have measurably declined in these tough times. Pollution control equities are therefore now viewed as being more cyclical in nature, given that their earnings have declined significantly in the current recessionary economy.

Why is the sector lagging behind the market's rise in the US in the first months of 1992? Why has sustained demand for green shares not emerged so far this year? The main reason is that most investors are on the sidelines awaiting confirmation whether the much desired economic recovery in the United States is actually on its way.

Another reason has less to do with economic fundamentals than the stock market's intrinsic behaviour. The past two years have seen a very large outflow of initial public offerings of small new pollution control companies with ambitious control growth plans. Wall Street and London investment bankers and brokers have aggressively promoted these new stocks. In many cases, these issues have proved disappointing in the short term. Managements have been immature or profligate and financial results have not matched investor expectations. In notable cases, the investor response has been unforgiving and severe, with big blocks of shares being dumped by disillusioned institutional investors. Prices in some cases have consequently dropped by up to 50 per cent. This kind of shock is enough to make investors take a wait-and-see attitude.

In all fairness, though, we should remember that pollution control stocks have not been alone in experiencing volatility – biotechnology, computers, chemicals, real estate, oil drilling, to name a few sectors, have also been through their respective wringers.

In my opinion, this is a natural evolutionary development which will not affect the long-term attractiveness of pollution control stocks. The outperformance seen in the mid-eighties will most likely resume and be in evidence by the mid-nineties. Necessary investments in pollution control, recycling, clean-up and prevention can be postponed and kept on industry's and municipalities' back burner for a few intervening years, but not much longer. The need is too great, the voting public's concern is too deep to ignore and environmental law is already in place. Politicians can muddle on for a while until they hit upon programmes and financing mechanisms that do the job, but they cannot ignore the public's genuine interest in the problems. Enforcement will pick up.

From the previous graphs and numbers one can well draw the following investment corollaries:

- Bear market bottoms are the best time to buy green shares, which is true of most shares and, though not a startling discovery, nonetheless reminds us that the best timing requires the most courage; (on the other hand, let no one be confused into thinking courage alone guarantees good performance);
- Green shares tend to outperform in sustained bull markets, which is true and significant;
- Green shares tend to underperform in bear markets, which reflects investor sell-off of high-growth stocks in times of uncertainty;
- And last, but perhaps most significantly in the long run, relative to other equity sectors green shares are extremely attractive for the investor interested in long-term capital gains.

An indication that the timing may now be right can be found in a study showing that pollution control stocks in the United States have outperformed the stock market by, on average, over 50 per cent in each of the last four post-recessionary bull markets since World War II.

If we believe we are at the time of writing (March 1992) in an 'after-bear-market' climb during a recession that may slowly end in 1993, and observe further that pollution control stocks have not yet rebounded to the extent the broader market has, we could well draw the conclusion that now is the time to commit fresh money to green funds. I am among those who believe this to be true.

Environmental mutual funds in the US, the UK and Scandinavia have, by and large, performed in line with their markets, generally doing somewhat better in bull markets and somewhat worse in bear markets. It is important to realize, however, that most green funds were launched after the stock market crash of October 1987 and that their performance has been significantly influenced by the erratic performance of the markets since then.

The following six charts show two global environmental funds versus the Morgan Stanley World Capital Index, two United States environmental funds versus the Dow Jones Index, and two European environmental funds versus their respective country indices (one is focused in Norway, the other focused in the UK).

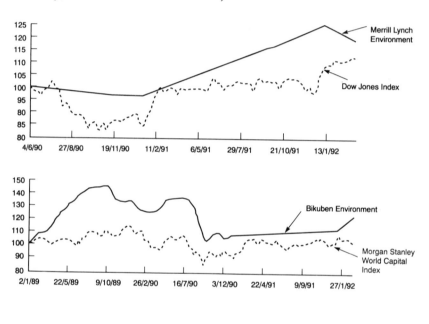

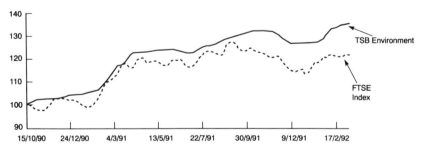

Figure 8.3

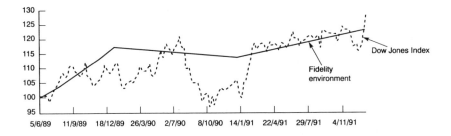

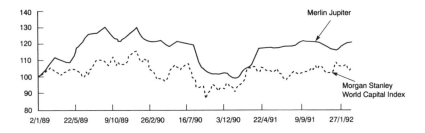

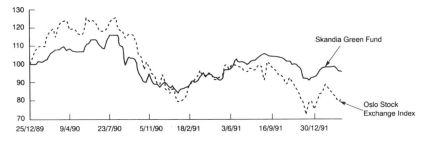

Figure 8.3 continued

CONCLUSION

The most significant common denominator is that over the longer term the performance of the green funds is turning out to be generally better than the performance of the general market indices. This suggests that in the long term, by which I mean the decade of the nineties, green funds will do as well as the general market indeces. With new revaluation of green stocks to more reasonable P/E levels, green funds once again will have an opportunity to outperform the general market.

The investment philosophy of environment funds is predicated on the proposition that society is moving in the direction of more environmentally-suitable products and processes. Environmental legislation, consumer pressure and the desire for sustainable development are long-term forces that will not disappear. This is not a fad. The social and economic fundamentals are in place for superior performance in green funds once the current uncertainties of the stock markets subside.

The fund I manage, Skandia Green Norway (Aksjefondet Skandia Grønt Norge), invests primarily in Norway. By the end of its first year of operation, 1990, when the Gulf War took place, it had outperformed the Oslo stock market. The Oslo Stock Exchange Index, fell −2 per cent. In 1991 our performance was up 9 per cent after management fee, compared to a further 10 per cent fall for the Oslo Stock Exchange Index and an across-the-board decline in the value of all other Norwegian equity funds. In the case of this fund it is correct to say the green investment strategy has worked well financially and environmentally.

I expect by the mid-nineties country green funds will be within the top quartile of all equity funds in their respective countries. I also expect the global equity funds to match the performance of the Morgan Stanley World Capital Index, which tracks stock markets worldwide on a capitalization-weighted basis.

WHAT IS A GREEN COMPANY?

Deciding whether a product is green is a rather complicated matter of methodology and fact-finding. What is more important? The product's ingredients, the way it is made, the use it is put to, or what kind of waste it makes? How far backwards or forward in the materials and production chain is it appropriate to go? Despite the complexity of the issues at hand, eco-labelling systems like Germany's Blue Angel show that it is possible to put together workable classifications for many consumer product categories, such as detergents, paper, electrical appliances, paint, and so forth.

But deciding whether *a company* is green gets considerably more complicated insofar as not only must one evaluate products, but also know something about production processes, management policies and practices, size of the company's environmental business as a percentage of the total, expected growth in this area, other areas of the company's business which may contradict environmental purposes, and so forth.

A good example of a typical problem is the well-known industrial giant, Asea Brown Boveri (ABB), which employs over 200,000 people worldwide. It owns Flacht, Norsk Viftefabbrikk and other acknowledged leading environmental control companies. It is also major supplier to mass transit systems via its locomotive business and is big in water, gas and wind power generation and transmission. But it is also commited to atomic power plant construction and engineering. This aspect of its business disqualifies it from our green fund. (Other green funds do include ABB in their portfolios but we are in principle opposed to nuclear power primarily because we do not believe the radioactive waste disposal problem is solved.)

There is no generally accepted ranking scheme concerning the environmental worth of companies. There are no generally accepted environmental auditing principles. Many private and governmental groups in North America and Europe are doing serious work in this field; but so far it has not passed beyond the R&D stage. Therefore, in the absence of a rating system or agency for environmental quality (comparable to rating agencies for debt issuers), the only way to proceed when defining green equities is by doing one's own research and using one's own judgement. This is what you pay a green fund manager to do, in addition to money management.

A green fund can chose to rely on consulting companies to do the job, or selected environmentalists. But the truth of the matter is that nobody can honestly claim to have a reliable ranking system for companies on an international basis.

It is therefore necessary to look at how a green equity is defined in practice by concerned investors. Three kinds of definition seem to prevail, each followed by different constituencies, each yielding its particular and, not surprisingly, somewhat overlapping sets of companies.

Core Definition

The first definition, which I call the core definition, defines a green company as a company whose business is pollution control. The company primarily makes money by making, selling, installing or operating air, water and soil pollution control equipment or services in industrial and governmental installations. Under this definition, no social or otherwise

ethical criteria are considered. Concievably, therefore, a pollution control company thus defined could be in violation of regulations or in
contravention of ethical business practices. For example, Waste Management, Inc., the US's largest company in its field, has been repeatedly
accused of circumventing Environmental Protection Agency regulations
and is involved in a number of environmentalist-initiated lawsuits. (That
a company is the subject of law suits does not prove it is guilty. But it is
reason for researching it more deeply.)

It is also worth observing, as the case of ABB shows, that application
of this definition will not necessarily yield uncontroversial judgements.
Well-meaning, well-informed people can differ as to which technologies are indeed environmental control technologies or whether they
are environmentally beneficial. And this is understandable. Environmental problems are not easy, they draw on many different areas of
scientific and technical expertise, and are often freighted with a great
deal of emotionalism. Witness media coverage of water dam construction, tropical forest use, oil spills, rare birds and baby seals, to
name but a few well-publicized issues. The degree of media attention
some issues get can be rather disproportional to their present and
potential danger.

The kinds of businesses included in the core definition are solid and
toxic waste management (landfills, e.g. American Waste; waste-to-
energy incineration systems, e.g. Wheelabrator), air pollution control
devices (catalytic converters, e.g. NGK Insulators), filtration and sewage
systems for water pollution control (e.g. Generale des Eaux, Ebara),
catastrophy prevention (navigation systems and fire control systems, e.g.
Bird Technology and Autronica), environmental engineering (e.g.
Harding), pollution measuring and monitoring devices (e.g. Horiba),
used oil (e.g. Safety Kleen) and used tyre recycling (e.g. Bandag), plastic
recycling (e.g. Wellman), chemicals recycling and treatement (e.g.
TetraTechnologies).

By extension, cleaner forms of energy (natural gas, wind power, hydro-
electric and geothermal), mass transit (locomotives and railroads) come
in under this definition.

The core definition is the one being used by most financial analysts and
brokers who cover the sector. It is how Wall Street and London brokers
view the sector. It is also in use by various green funds, principally those
launched by big banks and big brokerage firms. Examples are Bikkuben
Miljø (Copenhagen), Merrill Lynch Environment (New York) and
Fidelity Select Environment (Boston).

Expanded Definition

In addition to the positive screening criteria built into the core definition, the expanded definition applies negative screening criteria concerning unacceptable social and ethical policies and practice. The expanded definition incorporates evaluation criteria having to do with such things as the company's employee policies, hiring and compensation practices, relations with certain countries (South Africa being a case in point when sanctions were in place), and the company's compliance with environmental regulations and good environmental practice.

The expanded definition can best be used to exclude companies that come in under the core definition but don't meet ethical guidelines. It is an ethical screen. But the fact that many green funds don't have such an ethical screening procedure results in the ironic fact that green funds classed under the category of 'ethical funds' by mutual funds rating services such as Lipper (and newspapers that rely on them) can in point of fact be investing in unethical companies. As previously mentioned Waste Management, Inc,. which is the biggest core definition company of them all, is an example of a company that has been questioned, in the United States, on social and ethical grounds.

Sustainable Development Definition

The third definition I call the sustainable development definition. This concept is, as far as I know, not widely in use among any of the environmental funds, although it is occasionally applied by The Skandia Green Norway fund, Merlin Jupiter, and Merrill Lynch Eco-Logical. It incorporates the notion that a company may be green even though it has nothing to do with making and selling pollution control equipment and services per se. An example would be The Body Shop. Some analysts would also include Wal-Mart in this category. I am proposing that investors, insurers and bankers make use of this concept when making capital decisions, and prioritize sustainable development companies over companies that do not otherwise show environmentally responsible conduct. This concept is being discussed at the United Nations Globe 92 Conference in Vancouver (March, 92) and at the International Chamber of Commerce Session of the Earth Summit (United Nations Conference on Environment and Development) in Rio (June, 92).

Which kinds of companies would qualify under a sustainable development definition? Companies that have incorporated into their production processes and materials environmental protection measures that set them demonstrably in front of companies they compete with in their own field. An example is the Norwegian company Håg, a privately-held company we have invested in, which makes ergonomic office chairs and is market leader in Scandinavia. Ergonomic furniture is in itself not a green product, even though it is user-friendly. But the way Håg makes its office furniture and chairs is environmentally responsible: energy-efficiency at the plant, no use of CFC gases in the foam-making process, no use of woods from areas that don't have good forestry practices, recycling of enamels in the laquering process, and so forth. In addition, the company has gotten through a period of financial difficulty without laying off workers, has unusually low employee turnover and sickness rates, and has supported young local artists and designers for years. The aspects are particularly relevant given that the company is the biggest employer in a small town located in what used to be an active coal-mining area.

By extension, it ought to eventually be acceptable to include the environmentally best chemical company, the environmentally best steel company, the environmentally best cement maker, the environmentally best hotel company, the environmentally best shipping company, the environmentally best cruise line, etc. in a green fund that uses the sustainable development definition.

But there are two very real problems with this. The first is the complexity of the evaluative process and the fact that fund managers usually do not have the resources to do this. The second is that public opinion will have trouble accepting a chemical company or a steel company within a green fund. The irony is that a big steel or chemical company that could meet the sustainable development definition might well be far more ethical in its business behaviour and may have far more impact on the global environment than a small uncontroversial core definition green company. An example might be the chemicals giant Dupont which, as a matter of policy, is committed to good environmental practice and has a self-imposed requirement to implement the best environmental technology in its plants in third world countries. Monsanto also deserves a mention, since it has voluntarily pledged to reduce worldwide emmissions of 307 hazardous chemicals by 90 per cent by the end of 1992.

Seen strictly from an environmental point of view, if a steel producer or a plastic producer could demonstrate it was, say, 30 per cent better than its competitors on energy efficiency, recycling and re-use of end-user product, reduction of air and water pollution, and had a credible environmental auditing system in place, then why shouldn't it be in a green fund's portfolio? But a green fund that included such a company would run into a severe image problem. Just imagine the newspaper headlines!: 'Green fund pure rubbish!', or 'Greens plastic fantastic!'

The two environmental funds I manage – Skandia Global Environment (Aksjefondet MiljøInvest) and Skandia Green Norway fund (Skandia Grønt Norge) have adapted the following selection criteria for the portfolios:

1. The company must meet the core definition, as outlined above.
2. In the case of large multinationals with a multiplicity of products or businesses, at least one third of sales or earnings must come from core definition activities and the remainder must be environmentally neutral.
3. If evidence arises that the company violates good social and environmental practices (i.e. fails to meet the expanded definition, as outlined above or fails government environment agency reviews, etc.), it will be sold and excluded from the portfolio.
4. On rare and uncontroversial occasions, a Sustainable Growth Definition will apply.
5. Excluded from the fund are companies engaged in nuclear power generation, weapons manufacture, tobacco and automobile manufacture.

As should be rather obvious, implementing these guidelines requires more work than goes into managing the usual stock portfolio.

Andreas Føllesdal, a philosopher who directs the Norwegian Centre for Values Research, has two interesting observations on the above. He has drawn a diagram of my definitions, which might serve to clarify them. It looks as follows:

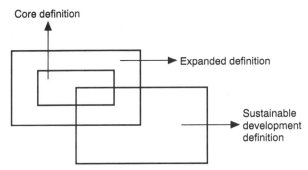

Figure 8.4

He also cites John Rawles' distinction between ideal and non-ideal ethical theory as helping to account for why investing in the environmentally best car company *might* be appropriate for a green fund. In an ideal world, there would not be any car companies. In the real world, there are. The important question is how we improve our present non-ideal world. One way might be to adopt a non-ideal investment policy that allows investment in 'second-best' technologies, if they are an inevitable and in practice necessary step in the right direction. (Once the ideal world is reached, one would conceivably not have to worry about ethical investment policy, as all available investment options would presumably be good. This is not an issue I expect to face in my investment life time.)

DO GREEN FUNDS DO ENVIRONMENTAL GOOD?

Let us now address our second question.

Radical environmentalists and deep ecologists tend to be suspicious of green funds. They suppose that if the aim is to make money, then the environment will not get first priority. This point of view is based partly on a misunderstanding as to how capital markets work and of the role of capital formation in the economy, partly on a confused ideology that assumes idealistic goals must be gained only through not-for-profit activity, and partly on a healthy suspicion of investment salespeople.

Environmentalists rightly think: if green funds don't do environmental good, what good are they? This is a good question and deserves a serious answer. In turn, one would hope those raising the question are open to an answer that may not conform entirely to their ideological inclinations.

What is the point of green investing? Green investing has two purposes. For the individual saver, it is to make his or her money grow more than it would in the bank. A green fund should have this as a necessary goal, otherwise it is just better to make a donation to an environmental organization and leave the rest of the money in the bank or in a money market fund.

The other purpose is to have the money put to better use than it would be in the bank or in normal equity funds. In the bank, our savings are put to all kinds of uses: loans to companies that make good products and bad, loans for road and bridge building, for automobiles, for homes, for medical equipment, for education; but also for nuclear energy plants, for weapons manufacturers, for tobacco companies, etc. The point is we do not know where our money goes or what it is used for. Moreover, it is safe to say part of it goes to economic activities you and I may not be in agreement with. In the bank or in a traditional equity fund we are recycling money into the economy indiscriminately. The advantage of a green fund is that we can decide which economic activities our money is used for.

Green funds and ethical funds provide you as an individual with decision-making authority over uses for your money which otherwise you do not have (unless you are very rich and own a company you can re-direct to do what you think is right).

But why does buying shares do any environmental good?

The following figure shows the role of equity capital in green capitalism.

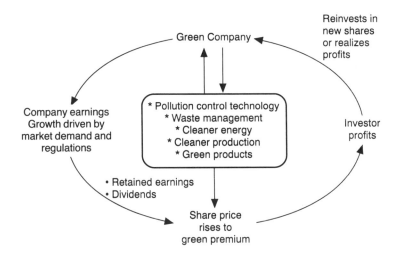

Figure 8.5 Green capitalism – capital for sustainable development

The diagram illustrates the economic dynamics of price changes in a green company's stock. When the stock price rises it can raise new capital more cheaply, by issuing new shares. The capital that is brought into the firm can be used for expansion and growth. This is particularly true of small- and medium-sized companies. They typically do not have access to bond markets and their rate of potential growth may be limited by their bank lines. Investing in green companies therefore contributes to the growth of the pollution control industry. As share prices rise, the investor profits and can chose to cash in or keep riding a good investment. The profit goal and the pollution control goal are part of the same process of economic activity. Capital flows and work gets done. Money gets recycled into that side of the economy one wants to see flourish.

Most people recognize that if pollution clean-up, control and prevention are to occur it is going to take a lot of work, hundreds of thousands of man-hours and a lot of money. It is not a job that can be done by non-profit foundations or voluntary organizations. Non-profit organizations can do a good job of calling attention to environmental issues, but the solutions have to be implemented by business. The implementation has to be part of the day-to-day business of the economy, and we have to make it part of business-as-usual. To object to the profit motive in environmental work is not only to object to the way the economy works but also to object to the very possibility of economic environmentalism in our generation.

One can of course object to how the economy works, but this then becomes another kind of discussion. It becomes a discussion about utopia, or about what kind of economic system might conceivably be more equitable, fair and effective than the one we have today in North America, Western Europe, Japan, etc. But finding Utopia is harder than finding green companies. Even if one were to assume, for purposes of discussion, that at some time in the next 50 – 100 years the world will find its way to a post-consumist, post-capitalist form of social and economic organization, environmental clean up and prevention has to be done right now within the existing structure of finance, economics, and work.

That is why buying green shares does environmental good. It incentivizes the greening of industry. And it increases the ability to raise new capital for R&D, marketing and expansion of pollution control technologies.

THE ETHICS OF PROFITS. ARE GREEN FUNDS ETHICAL?

There's quite a lot of confused thinking about the ethical questions raised in connection with money. I have chosen to contest views put forth by *The Herald Tribune* in its Money Section because they provide a representative sample of common misconceptions and because they've been put forth repeatedly.

Here are some of the questions raised, the answers provided and my critique of their views:

Is the profit motive truly compatible with ethics, or ecology, or indeed anything except itself?

This question is certainly worth asking, but the paper mistakenly suggests the answer is 'no' and says a company's environmental quality is wholly unrelated to its financial and investment quality. On the back of this error rides a false dilemma: either clean air or quick money.

This is nonsense. A polluting company is liable for environmental liabilities. In the US, under the Superfund legislation, liability is retroactive to before passage of the legislation. This can and does have severe consequences to the income statement and the balance sheet. Financial analysts and insurers are getting more and more sophisticated at assessing, pricing and discounting environmental risk. If a company is party to a pollution event which becomes known in the market, its share price suffers. Think of the effect on earnings when a plant loses its operating license for non-compliance with environmental regulations. Think of the effect on your own wealth when the building you just bought is found to have asbestos insulation. Or when the shopping centre you've invested in turns out to have toxic waste buried under it.

Furthermore, the Securities and Exchange Commission requires that companies who are a principal responsible party to a pollution event must quantify their liability in the financial statements. If a company fails to disclose pollution liabilities it should have disclosed and you as the investor are misled and lose money as a result, you can sue the company and its management.

The reverse side of the coin is that companies with green products do have competitive sales advantages, as a consequence of consumer preference for environmentally better products. Green companies do command a green stock price premium (as demonstrated above, pp. 132, 133. Investors believe that companies with good environmental practices are also likely to have good management, although this is not always the case. Nonetheless, companies who have invested earlier than their competitors in environmentally sound production processes and prevention have often been spared from very expensive end-of-the pipeline remedial action later.

Profits are but a convenient and generally accepted measure of a company's performance in using human resources, material goods, infrastructure, and financial capital. But it is a somewhat arbitrary measure, insofar as investors could conceivably agree to use changes in the company's asset value instead of profits as the telling measure. The accounting profession might one day rule that environmental parameters must become part of the balance sheet of companies; environmental conservation would be reflected as an asset and pollution risks as liabilities. A company could therefore be showing short term profits at the same time as it showed degradation of its net asset value because of environmental liabilities incurred to its balance sheet. Vice-versa, it could show short term losses at the same time as it showed increase in net asset value due to revaluation of environmental assets. Preservation of nature would thereby explicitly become part of the preservation and growth of capital.

Can there really be such a thing as a morally 'good' or 'bad' investment? Does the subjective intention of the investor really affect the – supposedly objective – moral quality of the act?

The question is valid. But the answer – *money is outside morality. It is amoral* – is , again, nonsense. Let me explain why I believe it to be wrong. Intentionality has of course a role in ethical judgement. If a crook intends to cheat you but screws up in the attempt, you are not cheated, no damage has in fact been done, but the crook is no less a crook. If a drunken driver crashes into you without intending to, his unintentionality doesn't do him or you any good. On the other hand, good intentions are no guarantee of good consequences. The road of human disasters is paved with good intentions. Wars, marriages, failed political systems bear sufficient witness.

The Herald Tribune's problem is in forgetting to make the distinction between moral desires and moral behaviour. Moral desire becomes efficacious when moral behaviour is the result. A morally good investment, in both senses of the term, is one that in fact succeeds in accomplishing the good purpose it is intended to accomplish. The fact that some people, perhaps most people, make investments without thinking about the moral consequences of their investment does not invalidate those that do. I would argue that people who intend to do moral good when they invest are, from a moral point of view, more praiseworthy than those that don't. I would also argue they stand as fair a chance of making money as index fund investors do. (See pp. 132/133.)

One could of course ask, what about accidental good results? Are you a moral hero if you save a life without actually meaning to? Say, for example, you are a nurse on night duty and forget to give a hospitalized child a prescribed medication. But it turns out the patient is allergic to the medication and would have died if she got it. The outcome is certainly felicitous. The child's parents love you for your mistake. But, morally speaking, you have done nothing commendable.

The same applies if you invest in a green company just to make money. Nothing wrong with that. And certainly better for the environment than if you put your money into a high-sulphur coal plant. You may well make a felicitous profit in the green company and that will enhance your net financial worth but it will neither add nor substract to your net moral worth.

What about knowledge or lack of knowledge about a company's policies and record? How accountable is an investor for the actions of a company he or she owns shares in? Let's consider an extreme case of accountability, a violent crime. Society does rightfully penalize people who commit crimes, however unwittingly. 'I didn't know what I was doing' may get you out of jail if you're a serial killer but it will not keep you out of a mental institution. Even if you engage an agent to do the killing for you, the agency aspect of the act gives no absolution to either the agent or the principal. Surely, one will say, investing is different and one cannot be held accountable for criminal or unethical behaviour done by a company one own's shares in.

But this is not necessarily so. One needs to consider who the shareholder is and how systematic the company's behaviour is. Is the subject a typical small investor who simply follows a stockbroker's tips? Or is it a professional investor who manages a pension fund, a bank's portfolio, or a mutual fund? The degree of accountability and the degree of reprehensibility have a lot to do with the professionalism of the investor. Investing without caring about what you invest in may be reprehensible depending on whether you are a professional investor or not.

Professional investors who invest in companies without any concern at all as to what these companies do to the general public and to the environment ought to be held accountable. 'I was only investing in a quoted company and didn't know what they were doing' may not put you in jail. But it arguably does make you, as a professional investor charged with a fiduciary responsibility for other people's money, morally accountable. I would propose that fiduciary responsibility is not divorced from moral accountability.

An institutional investor has the time and resources to find out about a company's policies and practice as well as its financial condition. I would argue the professional investor has an obligation to do so because a company's social and environmental qualities are material to its investment quality. Even though the concept of responsibility for knowing what a company does socially and environmentally is not part of the consciousness of most professional investors, it ought to be. Some companies as a matter of (undocumented) policy do decide to behave unethically. What they do shows what they believe in. A professional investor ought to make it his business to find out. Otherwise his ignorance is willful or negligent and therefore culpable; and once the evidence is in he or she has no excuse for not acting on the information.

The goal of maximizing profits does not override ethical goals. If investing is immune from moral judgement, what's wrong about investing in the cocaine trade? Nothing in the stock market can give you such high returns. 'No fiduciary obligation can demand that one maximize returns by unethical investing.' Money is as tied to morality as guns are tied to killings. Most Americans want to reduce the public's access to guns in order to reduce killings and street violence, despite the gun lobby's facetious argument that 'guns don't kill, people do'. Likewise, people who think like me want to reduce the viability of morally unworthy companies by limiting their access to capital. We believe that money is unethical when it is put to unethical uses, ethical when it is put to ethical uses. We believe, to paraphrase Forbes, that money is a capitalist tool for achieving ethical goals, as well as financial goals, and that ethical funds are a mechanism for making business more ethically conscious.

Consider the following investment strategy.

Imagine an anti-smoking group plans to encourage non-smokers to sell short Phillip Morris stock. They stake their own money on the play. They call a press conference and get TV coverage. They give fair warning to pension funds who hold the stock that they better get out sooner rather than later. Suppose the strategy works, that Phillip Morris stock falls as a consequence. Is this morally good or bad investment strategy? I'd say it's good investment strategy, in both the moral and financial senses of the word.

Consider a company that as a matter of policy decides not only to adhere to environmental regulations rather than fight them but decides to be one step ahead, even if it costs more up front. They are willing to investment spend on greener production processes. (Perhaps the case of Dupont, Monsanto or Ciba Geigy.) Are they being unfair to shareholders? Not if the company manages to publicize the fact – as they should – thereby creating competitive marketing advantages for its products and drawing attention to its stock, conceivably leading to its revaluation as a green company (sustainable development definition) and a higher multiple. The green premium can be thought of as an economic reward for corporate activity that satisfies green goals in an efficient way. Environmental good and investor profits can go hand in hand.

How comfortable should investors feel when they discover they hold stock in the same companies as Saddam Hussein? . . . What is the moral significance? . . . Ethical screening is no more than a neat piece of marketing.

This is a confused question matched by a rather dumb answer. Wouldn't you rather Kuwait put its money in environmental technology and green industries than in weapon manufacture? Wouldn't you rather drug money stopped getting ploughed back into more drugs? (Of course, there ought to be no drug trade to begin with!) That dirty money may like to ride along with clean money does not make a clean investment dirty. Nor ought it cast suspicion on ethical investors, be it their intentions or their profits.

Moral Principles

When thinking about ethics and investing it is relevant to think about the principle of internal consistency and the principle of proportionality. If you are an ethically-inclined investor and your portfolio consists of a fund that invests in the market index (the good, the bad and the ugly, indiscriminately) as well as an ethical fund, you are being inconsistent. You are not necessarily doing anything immoral. But you are not being consistent, ethically speaking. Sometimes we can't be consistent even if we'd like to. I have bank deposits even though I don't know where the money ultimately goes. But prudence and a certain degree of risk-aversion lead me not to have all my money in green stocks. There are no green banks or green bank deposits where I bank; so I have no choice.

By the principle of proportionality I mean the following: If you are a typical small individual investor, you can't be expected to know that much about the companies in which you own shares directly or about companies in which you are indirectly invested through a pension fund or mutual fund. But if you are an institutional investor you have a greater degree of accountability. Portfolio size and the fiduciary aspect create proportionately larger accountability.

We all need to become more intelligent about the relative moral merits of different investment strategies. This is a difficult area and very little has been written and researched in it. Investors and business schools could profitably devote more time to this field.

CONCLUSIONS

A morally motivated investor will be able to find investment funds that screen out companies that do things he or she wants to avoid and include companies doing things he or she wants to promote. And doing so need not imply giving up the possibility of making acceptable returns on investment. It might even increase the probability.

People and companies who invest only with the goal of maximizing profit without paying attention to environmental concerns may well find themselves surprised by pollution time-bombs hidden in the balance sheets of companies they've invested in. Hard-headed short-term thinking can boomerang.

The profit motive does not stand in the way of capitalism's evolution in an ethical direction. It can and ought to be used as an incentive. To paraphrase Forbes, money is a capitalist tool for achieving social and ethical goals.

As John Kenneth Galbraith has said:

'We can have the social control that establishes the necessary framework for economic development and that erases or segregates industrial squalor and preserves and even enhances beauty. Economic development enables us to pay the price; it is one of the advantages of development. It cannot be supposed that we have development in order to make our surroundings more hideous and our culture more meretricious.'

Putting your money where your heart is might be the brainiest investment of all.

References

Føllesdal, Letter to C. Jolly 13 April 1992

Joly C., 'The Green Premium and the Polluter Discount', The Greening of Enterprise, ICC Publication 487 E, June 1990, Paris

Joly C., 'Environmental Investing: What is the Point', *21st International Management Symposium*, University of St. Gallen, Switzerland

Lehman Shearson – inc. Garzarelli E., 'Industry Stock Market Performance

After Bear Market Bottoms During Recessions', Dec. 1990.

The Herald Tribune, 'When ethics make way for cash returns' (Dec 8, 1990, p 18); 'Good, Bad? Or is money just ugly?' (Nov 30, 1991, p 15); 'Moral man in amoral markets?' (April 13, 1991, p 15,).

De George, 'Corporate Responsibility, the Social Audit, and Ethical Investing', *Business Ethics*, Macmillan, N.Y.

'Most of today's decision makers will be dead before the planet suffers the full consequences of acid rain, global warming, ozone depletion, widespread desertification and species loss. Most of today's young voters will be alive.'

The World Commission on Environment and Development, 1987

9 THE GREEN ORGANIZATION

by Richard Ford

'GREEN ORGANIZATIONS' SHOULD BE THE RULE, NOT THE EXCEPTION

If being 'green' means, as it surely must, using natural resources and energy with care, minimizing waste, and thereby not deliberately jeopardizing the long-term future of planet Earth, then in theory no organization should be ungreen.

After all, the economic system as a whole is concerned with the rationing of scarce resources, and the competitive organization has evolved as the most efficient economic mechanism for supplying products and services into the economic system. So organizations should presumably be concerned with managing all the world's resources considerately and wastelessly. Ergo green.

In other words, viewed from a classical economic perspective, all organizations ought self-evidently to be green. In practice, however, this is clearly not the case. The phrase 'green organization' is readily understood as referring to a special kind of company – one which has an above-average appreciation of the pressures being placed on the environment, as well as specific plans and procedures to minimize its own harmful impact on the environment.

In fact, the ways in which companies respond to the environmental challenge vary substantially, and the phrase 'green organization' is meaningful precisely because so few companies aspire to or achieve this sort of status. In fact, if all companies are, in economic terms, focused on the management of scarce resources, very few demonstrate this in their environmental policies and conduct.

Why not? Three reasons seem to be particularly pertinent: the rise of the 'non-economic' organization; the time scale of investment and payback; and the insufficiency of government safeguards. We will look at each of these in turn.

The rise of the 'non-economic' organization

As noted above, economics seeks to ration scarcity as efficiently as possible. However, in this section we suggest that the economically most efficient form of organization is one which is in practice rare. The upshot of this is that waste and inefficiency may to a certain extent be institutionalized, especially in large companies.

Classical economics relies on the principle of perfect competition, in which products are standardized and barriers to entry and exit are low, with the result that new entrants quickly move into new markets where they see opportunities for profits. Likewise, companies can get out of unprofitable markets painlessly.

Under such conditions, there will be a large number of players, competition will be extremely fierce, and profitability will always be marginal and therefore determined by the ability to minimize waste in the use of all resources, whether physical, human or financial.

Now, perfect competition is a useful model, and there are some industries and some countries with versions of perfect competition. But competition which is 'perfect' for the economic system as a whole is not at all perfect for participants in the market. Companies will seek to avoid perfect competition by 'de-standardizing' products and by erecting barriers to entry. They will search for 'rents' of all sorts – innovations and new technologies, exclusive agreements and licences, branded properties, relationships up and down the supply chain, and so on – which are all completely legitimate but which minimize the danger of being caught in the cleft stick of perfect competition.

Moreover, where markets are perfect but important (or, in the language of Brussels and Washington, 'strategic'), governments generally step in to prevent the full workings of perfect competition – witness most agricultural and mining industries in the developed world, where producers are guaranteed a minimum price for the produce, in order to stop them leaving the market altogether.

The very largest companies often use a combination of rents and political influence to avoid the full rigours of competition. Their market power makes it possible for them to weave webs of relationships and cross-subsidies which can undermine even the most efficient of their smaller competitors. At the same time, they can demonstrate their importance to government, in terms of jobs, taxes or exports, and thereby forestall government interference. The idea that 'What is good for General Motors is good for America' is economic nonsense, but it sounds like a truism to politicians faced with an uncertain alternative.

All of these methods of evading perfect competition have the effect of creating organizations which are not economically optimal. This in turn means that these organizations are not as concerned with the management of scarce resources as they would be under a more competitive regime. They have a greater tolerance for waste and inefficiency than companies operating in more competitive environments.

Competition is thus a pre-requisite for being green, although many organizations suggest, in their communications with government and the media, that they can only be truly green if they are allowed to forego the rigours of competition. We will examine such arguments later in this chapter, and will seek to demonstrate that they are bunkum.

The timescale of investment and payback

Managers frequently suggest that 'green' initiatives take longer to implement than other managerial decisions, and therefore put them low on their list of priorities. They tend to argue that they are 'too busy to be green', and that the time-scales and rates of return they require for investments do not allow them the luxury of being green.

In other words, managers assume that green investments are long-term, while measures of corporate performance are short-term.

But green investments are not necessarily any more 'long-term' than any other investments. Numerous studies have shown that such initiatives as waste-reduction and energy-efficiency programmes can pay back their investment very rapidly. The fact that world-threatening environmental issues, such as global warming and the extinction of species, are long-term and uncertain, does not mean that it is impossible for companies to be profitably green in the short run. Green investments can often be shown to be justified, by using exactly the same rate of return criteria that are applied to other corporate activities.

So there are numerous green profit opportunities to which companies turn a blind eye. This tendency can be exacerbated by having a managerial fixation with making profits this quarter rather than increasing the overall value of the enterprise. The need for 'instant profits' can often be a disincentive to making new (and green) investments which would raise the value of a company to its shareholders by considerably more than the amount invested. If managers wear short-term blinkers, they are even less likely to see the potential for profitable green initiatives.

The insufficiency of government safeguards

But perhaps the biggest reason why companies are not overly concerned with the management of scarce environmental resources, is that these environmental resources are often not priced in a way that encourages efficiency and conservation. There are two reasons for this: many aspects of the environment such as clean air, water supplies, natural habitats, non-extinct species, and so on are 'public goods' for which the free market is not able to provide clear price signals; and governments often fail in their duty to ensure that these environmental public goods are priced in a way that encourages their wise and prudent use.

In fact, all governments encourage the inefficient use of environmental resources through, for example, water, energy and agricultural policies which subsidize the use of resources, not their conservation. In this way, tax payers allow companies to use natural resources wastefully, and thus to harm the environment.

The motives for such policies are, naturally enough, political. Governments subsidize the things which they see as the most basic, in order to keep their electorates satisfied. Moreover, many countries' governments appear to be willing to beggar their neighbours environmentally, by encouraging their own industries to expand through underpriced resources, in ways which cause global or regional environmental damage – a most brutal and short-sighted form of mercantilism.

So long as individual governments continue to place political advantage over sound environmental economics, and in the absence of strong transnational forms of government to limit excesses, environmental price signals will remain confused. Managers will therefore be unable to make decisions which simultaneously maximize the value of their companies to shareholders and minimize the harmful effects of their activities on the environment. They must decide on the trade-off between these two goals.

This trade-off is, in effect, one of the key challenges of green management. Perverse government policies make it legitimate for managers to decide how green their organizations want and can afford to be.

The good and bad justifications for organizational greenness

Companies respond in very different ways to the environmental challenge. The main reason for this is that organizations vary in how they perceive the advantages and disadvantages of being green. In this section, we examine the pros and cons of having an organization which is considered to be green.

The terms 'green' and 'ungreen' are not used judgmentally here. We assume throughout this chapter that all companies follow the law to the letter and obey all government regulations regarding the environment. But, for the reasons adduced above, government regulations are not always environmentally sensible, so it is possible for 'green' companies to pay more attention to the environment than they are obliged to by the law.

This is not to say that 'green' companies are any more moral or societally advantageous than 'ungreen' ones. It is at least arguable that, by concentrating their efforts on keeping in line with, but not going beyond, government environmental regulations, ungreen companies are able to devote themselves to the business efficiency which is, after all, their economic *raison d'être*.

Nevertheless, there is a strong sense among most ordinary people that 'green' companies are better in virtually all respects than 'ungreen' ones. This may be based to some extent on popular misconceptions about capitalism – for example, most people would be alarmed to realize that it is the social and economic *duty* of competitive companies to maximize their profits. But there is no doubt that this moral sense of green superiority accounts for the fact that there are more reasons for an organization to be green than to be ungreen. The main organizational justifications for being green appear to be as follows.

People prefer to work for green companies

There is clear evidence that companies which are perceived as being green find it significantly easier to recruit and keep hold of good employees than those perceived as ungreen. This is partly explained by socio-economic factors – the work force is younger than the population as a whole, and younger people are more likely to be environmentally aware than older people. Besides, among graduates and others with above-average qualifications, the environment is particularly important, and the commitment of potential employers to green issues is crucial to the decision to join one company rather than another.

In other words, the more desirable the employee, the more likely that concern for the environment will be a motivating job factor. This means that companies which need highly skilled employees also need a relatively good reputation for being green. It also means that companies which are attempting to upgrade the skills base of their work force need at the same time to upgrade their environmental consciousness and policies.

Especially given that the greatest benefits now increasingly accrue to companies whose employees are quality-conscious, creative and adept at problem-solving, at all organizational levels.

Obviously, the importance of being green wanes under conditions of economic recession and high unemployment, when job-seekers will be less willing to turn down a job, no matter how a potential employer treats the environment. However, it would be a mistake totally to dismiss the effect of being green even in a recession. Unemployment tends to be concentrated among older and less skilled people. A demand remains, even in the deepest troughs, for brilliant, and often environmentally concerned, young people. Besides, recessions invariably end, and companies whose reputation for being green has been tainted during the downturn will find it harder to recruit and hold on to workers in the upturn.

All employees will be concerned with perceptions of the company they work for, in the immediate community. So if a company has a poor environmental record in the vicinity of its site, this will poison the peer group of its own employees, whose commitment to the company will consequently be reduced, regardless of the pay and perquisites being offered.

Being green is a sign of care and consideration

This is related to the previous point, but it has wider organizational implications. If a company can demonstrate that it cares about the environment, then its employees, and the other people who depend upon it, are likely to feel more confident that it will care about them. If a company publicly commits itself to be green, it signals that it will be run in a way which takes into account other interests apart from those of its directors. It will, in effect, be democratic rather than autocratic.

In fact, all the empirical evidence suggests that no company can combine a demonstrable commitment to the environment with a dictatorial management style. Green organizations do not operate in an atmosphere of management certainties – they are 'learning' organizations, tolerant and flexible, and these qualities feed through their entire structure. Moreover, they rely on a sense of shared company goals throughout the work force, which are based on something more intangible, social and 'moral' than profits alone.

Worker contentment, commitment and solidarity are hallmarks of the green organization. The philosophy of being green underpins the way that managers treat the work force. In fact, it often removes the distinction between managers and workers altogether, since all see themselves as equal compatriots sharing in a mission to carry forward the goals of the company. In this sense, a green philosophy can be seen as the natural counterpart of the quality movement, whose stated objective is to instill everywhere the appreciation and procedures for quality verification, but whose deeper aim is to empower workers to take control of their own processes, and thereby to make large companies function with the same single-minded determination to meet customer needs as small ones.

Green is not grasping

Being perceived as green helps a company demonstrate to all sorts of interested parties that it is not interested in making large or otherwise 'unacceptable' profits. 'Profit' remains, if not a dirty word, then at least a highly ambivalent one throughout the developed world. As noted above, the idea that profit is not only acceptable under conditions of open competition, but is also the moral duty of business people, is still subject to scepticism and downright antagonism among a broad swathe of the population.

Making and announcing large profits can leave a company open to attack from politicians, regulators, consumer groups, trades unions and many others. But a strong stated commitment to the environment can make a company's profits seem much cleaner, much more deserved, because they come as a result of green objectives, not as an end in themselves.

In other words, among audiences who are uneasy with the notion of making money, corporate environmentalism can be a means of *atoning* for profits. This is a particularly important function in countries like the United Kingdom, with profound middle-class antipathy towards business and making money. Where capitalism, with its talk of competition and profit, seems harsh and selfish, being publicly green can allay the fears and misgivings of an educated, cogent and influential part of the population.

Being green assists co-operation

If the previous reason for being green was, in economic terms, bad, this one is even worse. The argument is frequently heard, that setting environmental standards and minimizing the environmental impact of products and processes requires the co-operation of all the companies in a given industry. But, obviously enough, co-operation is the opposite of competition, and study after study has shown that competition is vital to the upgrading of products and processes, and to making the most of society's scarce resources.

Companies like to co-operate on new products and processes. That way they can reduce the danger of producing things which are inferior to those of their competitors, thus guaranteeing their profitability. Through technical co-operation, established companies can also 'raise the drawbridge' to potential competitors who are not involved in the co-operative agreement.

Technical co-operation, even if lionized by the term 'green', is anti-competitive, and is therefore not in the interest of society as a whole, nor in the long-term interest of the companies involved. Yet the arguments in favour of co-operation seem thoroughly sensible and persuasive: without co-operation, companies will waste resources making products which are ungreen and which no one will want to buy; far better then to ensure that all companies in the industry are being as green as they can while satisfying customer demand; co-operation is therefore essential if everyone is to be rowing in the same direction.

The problem is, that it is only through competition that customer demand can properly be fulfilled. Co-operating groups of companies presume to know what customers will want, and how much they will pay to be green.

If standards are to work, then they must be set by governments, with the full force of law. They must be non-negotiable. It is right that companies should be involved in green standard-setting but, once standards are set, co-operation has to end, because the essence of capitalism is competition within a legal and regulatory framework.

GREEN MANAGERS AS UNELECTED CHAMPIONS OF THE ENVIRONMENT

The final justification for being green is connected with business people's perceptions of themselves and of their reasons for being in business. It is well known that managers tend to 'satisfice' rather than maximize profits. In other words, they work hard enough to achieve satisfactory business results, but that corporate goals and objectives are often less important than personal ones. This is in stark contrast to the economist's traditional conception of the manager as profit-maximizer.

The difference between the manager in economic theory and in reality can in part be attributed to the companies' financial and organizational

structures. Economic theory assumes that managers work for themselves, that they are their own shareholders; in reality, most managers are
the agents of outside shareholders and do not have a large financial stake
in their companies. Even private companies have elaborate
organizations, so that individual managers do not make decisions as if
they were the actual owners of their companies. The small, wholly
entrepreneurial company is rare indeed.

Moreover, even where managers are incentivized in a way which
makes corporate goals fully congruent with their own personal ones,
there are indications that they do not necessarily maximize profits. The
rewards of being in business are not simply financial, and many managers
pursue courses of action which are designed to improve their social,
political and moral standing in the general community. In other words,
managers are often willing to place kudos and visibility above the profitability of their enterprises, even when they have a direct stake in those
enterprises. This seems to reflect increasing financial self-confidence,
either as companies themselves grow bigger and stronger, or as the
general population gets richer and the possibility of business failure
becomes less fearful.

Many companies' green strategies and policies are often driven by
these undesirable aspects of managerial behaviour – the fact that many
managers concentrate on 'non-profit' goals. Managers in many cases
want to be seen to be green because this brings them a social status which
they believe they could not aspire to just by being in business. Anti-
business attitudes are pronounced in Europe and the USA. There is in
many countries an ignorance about how the economic system works,
coupled with ingrained pessimism about the lot of 'ordinary folk'. These
lead to a strong popular view that the interests of businesses are inimical
to the interests of society as a whole, that the pursuit of profit is necessarily bad, and that private investment is always less socially beneficial
than public investment.

In other words, business people know that the rest of the population
doesn't really understand, trust or even like them. Under these circumstances, there is a strong temptation to use environmental issues to show
that they have social responsibility and trustworthiness – qualities which
they feel are otherwise denied to them. Because the need to be green is
something which is taken for granted throughout western society; it is,
indeed, a political 'hygiene factor', which nobody running for high office
can afford not to support.

Thus, much of the stress which business people claim to place on green issues stems from nothing so much as a personal need to gain respect from the rest of society. In a world where people often lack a basic knowledge of capitalism and where the profit prerogative sounds selfish, managers often feel that they can gain status by invoking their commitment to the environment.

Unfortunately, this commitment is often shallow, superficial and hypocritical. It does not take into account the contradictions and trade-offs inherent in making companies more environmentally responsible. As such, it mirrors the sort of environmentalism typical of ordinary people in the developed world, who consider themselves green but are unwilling to make economic or lifestyle sacrifices to prove it.

Moreover, the tendency of managers to claim a commitment to the environment in order to improve their social standing is subversive in two ways. First, managers substitute 'competition to be virtuous' for the more traditional forms of competition – by price, product, service, and so forth, and thus become diverted from their social justification and duty of making profits in competitive markets. And second, they seek to use their economic power to set the environmental agenda, and thus to take on the role and responsibilities of elected governments.

TOWARDS A TYPOLOGY OF GREEN ORGANIZATIONS

Given the variety of impulses, some laudable, others less so, which managers have for 'being green', it is not surprising that there are a number of different ways for companies to be green. In the final section of this chapter, we characterize some of the various types of 'green organization'.

It is possible to imagine the ways in which different companies cope with environmental pressures as lying along a spectrum of environmental activity. At the far left of the spectrum are those companies who have never thought about the environment in any way; at the far right are those companies for whom improving the environment is the sole justification for being in business:

Environment		Environment
= Non-existent	⟵――――――――――――――――⟶	= Sole goal

In reality, such extremes would almost never be encountered. But the spectrum can help to define companies in terms of their level of environmental awareness and activity. Furthest to the left of this spectrum are those companies which are inactive with regard to the environment; they merely ignore all currents of green opinion. Next to these are those companies which are reactive; they respond to clear changes in market tastes or government legislation, but do nothing to shape these changes.

Over towards the right of this spectrum are companies which are proactive about the environment; they try to anticipate market or legislative changes. And furthest to the right are companies which are environmentally hyperactive; they seek to provoke changes. These various shades of organizational green lie like this on the spectrum:

Environment is non-existent			Environment = sole goal
Inactive	**Reactive**	**Proactive**	**Hyperactive**
Ignore	**Respond**	**Anticipate**	**Provoke**

In the remainder of this chapter, we analyse in greater detail the attitudes and behaviour of environmentally inactive, reactive, proactive and hyperactive companies in each case using suitable mnemonics.

Inactive companies: Ostriches

Environmentally inactive or 'Ostrich' companies appear to put their heads in the sand, and ignore the whole issue of the impact of their business on the environment. In general, this is because they have had no specific green pressures on their business, either from consumers, intermediaries or government regulators.

In the absence of external threats to the way they do business, the directors of Ostrich companies have tended to see the environment as a low priority, especially in the context of broad and breath taking changes in technology, in cost-structures, and in consumer demands for quality. The climate for business has never been more volatile, and as change continues to accelerate, companies whose priority is simple survival do not see green issues as pressing or even interesting.

It is important to recognize that these Ostrich companies are not in any way acting illegally or immorally. They are often small, customer-driven, in highly competitive industries, and with a justifiable hatred of overheads. Their directors do not believe that it is responsible for them to devote money and energy to environmental objectives which have not been laid down for them, either formally by the government or informally by the market place. They strive to keep their heads below the environmental parapet.

Reactive companies: Chicken Lickens

Chicken Licken lived in terror of the sky falling down on him, until one day that is precisely what happened. Reactive or 'Chicken Licken' companies have suddenly found that unexpected environmental pressures have wrought or are threatening massive changes in the way they do business. Thus they have started to address environmental issues, not through their own volition but under pressure from their customers or from government. They are essentially 'Ostrich' companies for whom the environmental parapet has somehow been lowered, and who therefore find themselves staring at a totally unexpected calamity.

Chicken Licken companies are completely non-strategic in their approach to the environment. They see each piece of new legislation and each change in their customers' requirements as an ad hoc problem, and they do not attempt to forecast the course of future customer requirements or government interventions, much less influence them. This clearly leaves them vulnerable to the attempts of their more proactive competitors to change the time-honoured 'rules of the game'.

On the other hand, it is at least arguable that there are benefits to Chicken Lickens' reactive approach. They do not invest heavily in environmental expertise unless and until they self-evidently have to. They do not back new green technologies before they are forced to, so they never back the wrong horse, which can provide an important operating economy when green guidelines and technology are both changing rapidly, and when the solution which is technically most effective may not necessarily be adopted by regulators or customers. And they do not lobby for the universal adoption of their own green strategy, which can also reduce their costs.

Indeed, the reluctance of reactive companies to invest speculatively (that is, ahead of regulations or market changes) in green systems, products and processes can keep costs down and can also provide the sort of flexibility which is particularly valuable in times of economic downturn.

Nevertheless, these possible benefits are outweighed by drawbacks. In particular, the Chicken Licken approach to the environment is taken *faute de mieux*, as a reaction to someone else's green agenda, not as part of their own. Reactive companies find themselves being hustled into changes they did not want to make. They fail to discern changes in their market or regulatory relationships, and thereby fall behind their competitors and lose money and goodwill by having hastily to reconfigure the ways they do business.

Chicken Licken companies, like their Ostrich cousins, are fundamentally 'ungreen'. They do not recognize that the environment is of great and growing importance to other people – heir customers, their customers' customers, the government's electorate. They are insensitive and arrogant towards change and the opportunities change can bring. Moreover, this insensitivity and arrogance carries through to their treatment of employees, their attitudes to the communities in which they operate, and every other element of the philosophy and policies whereby they do business.

This means that Chicken Licken companies tend to be badly managed: the absence of vision which bedevils their environmental strategies (which are non-strategies) also blights their market analysis, their setting of objectives, their quality programmes, and everything else they do. A company's directors might themselves choose not to care about the environment – that is, after all, their personal prerogative. But if they are unaware or unconcerned that other people *do* care about the environment, *that* is bad management, because it means that they are unable to understand, much less to control, factors that critically affect their business[1].

Proactive companies: Green Hornets

Environmentally proactive companies, or 'Green Hornets', seek to anticipate and act on future changes in customer requirements and government regulations, so that they keep stinging their more inactive and reactive competitors. Green Hornets have made a strategic commitment to stay abreast and ahead of environmental change. They are driven by dominant personalities, who appear to have a personal stake in corporate green policies. So their interest in green issues comes from the top of the company, and they have senior executives responsible for

[1] But note that companies are not badly managed because they are ungreen; being ungreen is one of many effects of being badly managed. On the other hand, being green does not automatically mean that a company is well managed, as we discuss later.

environmental policy. They recognize that their heads are well above the environmental parapet, and ensure that their position on environmental issues is defensible at all times. They would not pursue profits where these would lead to what they considered to be unacceptable environmental consequences, even if they were not strictly breaking the law. At the same time, they are happy with the conventional mechanisms for judging company success, such as profits and stockmarket capitalization.

Green Hornets consider certain issues as critically important to their environmentalism: for example, the health and welfare of their staff and communities; the cradle-to-grave environmental impact of their own and their suppliers' products and processes; and the maintenance of high, 'first world' standards in their third world operations.

Moreover, they are keen to grasp tomorrow's environmental issues today. They believe that the environment will be the most fertile area for building and maintaining competitive advantage at the end of the twentieth century and the beginning of the twenty first. In this respect, Green Hornet companies are visionary. At the same time, their visions of the future are grounded in a solid understanding of the present. They are unremittingly pragmatic and in the mainstream of capitalism. This combination of the visionary and the pragmatic provides them with their particular strength.

Hyperactive companies: Robin Hoods

Hyperactive companies, or 'Robin Hoods', have their own system of environmental morality which transcends government and customer requirements. They tend to ignore future changes to laws or markets, on the assumption that their own environmental standards will naturally be superior to those laid down in the statute book or the market place. They are more fervent about environmental issues than proactive companies, and have faith that their species of green thinking will one day prevail in the business world.

Robin Hood companies are propelled forward by very strong-willed and environmentally committed leaders, with whom they are largely identified. Leader and companies alike see themselves as pace-setters, and are adroit at positioning themselves as utterly non-traditional, radically different to other companies. They try to distance themselves from 'normal' business practice. Their business objectives are framed in moral, social and environmental terms, and profit or returns to shareholders is considered to be at best inconsequential and at worst outrageous[2].

Robin Hood companies go further than Green Hornets by getting vocally involved in environmental issues unrelated to their own particular business. They are trenchant, for example, about the need for a more equitable distribution of wealth and incomes, and are happy to criticize the environmental standards of companies in industries completely unconnected with their own. In effect, hyperactive green companies are outward-looking and evangelical, whereas proactive green companies are more inward-looking and pragmatic.

Robin Hood companies sublimate profits to their own sense of environmental morality. This is extraordinary and highly controversial, in that it flies in the face of the economic axiom that in a competitive market, companies that maximize their profits also maximize their benefit to society. On the contrary, hyperactive green organizations seem to be suggesting that they maximize their benefit to society, by pursuing environmental benefits not profits.

Moreover, for the most hyperactive green organizations, the lack of a profit perspective is just the most visible element of an overall business philosophy which is radically different to that of the 'textbook' capitalist company. Their objectives are not growth, market share or profits, but the maintenance and communication of what amounts to a system of beliefs and ethics; their attitudes to workers are those of a community of like-minded individuals; and they see profit as a means of sustaining the values of the company, not a goal in itself. In other words, Robin Hood companies seem to be more like profit-generating charities than conventional companies.

Battle-hardened old-school executives are often tempted to attack the 'hippy' attitudes of environmentally hyperactive, Robin Hood companies, many of which indeed had their genesis in the late sixties and the early seventies, the dawning of the 'Age of Aquarius'. But many large, quoted companies have now adopted some of the trappings of the Robin Hood company: a 'mission statement' or over-riding vision for the company based on shared values; a distancing of the company away from profit for its own sake; 'enlightened' attitudes (at least in the annual report and other corporate communications) towards workers, society, the environment, and so forth. Clearly, the approach of the Robin Hood company has been influential.

---

[2] Which is not to say that hyperactive green organisations are unprofitable. But profit is never pursued for its sake.

Nevertheless, Robin Hood companies are fundamentally anti-capitalistic, denying as they do the primacy of the profit motive or the role of the stockmarket. They are also arrogant, in that they go beyond what is required of them by government regulations or customer requirements in the belief that they know better than the government or their customers. They stimulate and provoke all companies to take more cognizance of environmental and other moral issues than they, but implicit in their approach to business at all times is a profound distaste for capitalism and a holier-than-thou attitude to all other companies, not merely their direct competitors. Hyperactive green companies in the economic system are like the pieces of grit in oysters which stimulate the production of pearls; but they are not necessarily pearls themselves.

'Teach your children what we teach our children: The earth is our mother. What happens to the earth, happens also to the sons of the earth.'

Chief Seattle, Chief of the Duwamish, in a speech to the President of the United States, Franklin Pierce, 1855

by Piroschka Dossi

THE FEMALE GODDESS

The earliest gods were goddesses: Isis in Egypt; Ishtar in Mesopotamia; Kali in India; Gaia, the earth goddess, in Greece. These archaic deities were rulers over life and death. Both their nurturing motherliness and bloodthirsty destructiveness were aspects of the eternal cycle of life: of becoming and passing, of creation and destruction, of birth and death. The inscription of these eternal truths in the collective consciousness has almost been erased. Old, age, illness and even death are considered to be mere construction defects in the order of things which have to be eradicated. The dark side of the eternal laws does not match the worldly religion of a puritan working ethic which assumes that mankind can dominate matter through mere productiveness. Nature itself produces increasing counter evidence: acid rain, polluted rivers, the ozone hole, contaminated oceans, extinction of species. According to *National Geographic* every year 14 million children under the age of five die of the consequences of pollution. A further three million are already damaged as a study of the United Nations Environment Programme indicates. By exploiting Mother Earth, we are destroying our own future. Now the goddess Gaia is waking up from her thousand years' sleep.

A MALE WORLD

Our world – the world of rational decisions, technical progress, labour division and industrial production – is a world shaped by male values and visions. It has favoured rational knowledge over intuitive wisdom, science over religion, competition over cooperation. Its social and political structures are based on abstraction and quantification. Money is its ultimate symbol.

The birth of our western civilization was prepared by the rise of dualistic philosophy. It crystallized in the 17th century in the thinking of René Descartes. His view of reality was based on a fundamental split into two separate realms: that of mind and that of matter. Descartes' famous statement *'cogito ergo sum* – I think therefore I am' has led us to equate our identity with our minds instead of with our whole being. The so-called Cartesian division prepared the path for the mechanistic world view and created the realm of rational knowledge which measures and quantifies, classifies and analyses.

The heart – originally considered to be the seat of true wisdom – was replaced by the head. Emotion, intuition and instinct – characteristics traditionally attributed to women – were systematically devalued. Serious scientists spent their lifetimes developing theories to prove the inferiority of women and the defectiveness of female essence. The discrimination of the female principle consequently led to the exclusion of women from knowledge, autonomy, societal influence and power and the reflection of their values in the outer world. Until the turn of this century women were not allowed into universities. They had no right to vote and were not even allowed to dispose of their own money. Even a progressive thinker like Freud was convinced that women were ultimately incapable of making ethical judgements. The ethic that ultimately shaped our society was a male ethic.

Where there is light, there is also shadow. The male world view has created formerly inconceivable progress in science and technology with a global economic system as its material manifestation. But the principle of separation has also created alienation: from our feelings, from our intuition, from our human essence. It has alienated us from work, from our fellow human beings, from our environment, from nature. The economic and political conflicts caused by an unjust distribution of resources and the environmental crisis are the destructive consequences of this one-sided development which our civilization now has to face.

An ancient Chinese proverb states that the yang, the male principle, having reached its climax, retreats in favour of the yin, its female counterpart. Today, we are witnessing a comparable change in our value system. It becomes apparent in the rising acceptance of ecology, the growing interest in spirituality, the rediscovery of holistic approaches. Also in the economic environment there is a shifting in values: from admiration of big monolithic organizations to ideas such as small is beautiful, from excessive consumption to voluntary modesty, from material to ethic issues. They are all manifestations of a self-regulating trend which has excessively favoured masculine values at the expense of their female counterparts.

FEMALE ETHIC

For ages men have both condemned and adored women as enigmatic creatures governed by some strange and incomprehensible logic. Women in turn have been much more pragmatic about themselves. 'It is obvious', wrote novelist Virginia Woolf in 1929, 'that the values of women differ from the values that have been made by the other sex'. In fact women experience life differently from men. In the words of Carol Gilligan, Harvard scholar and forerunner in the research on the dynamic of male and female identity formation, women speak in a different voice.

Indeed women have something to tell. Their view of reality is more empathetic and intuitive than the one of men. Men and women seem to have a different way of relating themselves to the world. Of crucial importance in female existence is the sense of relationship. Where the basic masculine sense of self is separate, the basic female sense of self is connected to the world. Where the male ethic is centred around hierarchy and competition, the female ethic is centred around connection and care.

One of the fundamental reasons that prevents women from ever becoming as separate as men lies in the fact that they are mothered by their own sex. They develop a pattern of relation that allows them to experience themselves connected or even continuous with others. In early infancy all children form a symbiotic relation with their mother. But as soon as they start to develop an independent sense of self, girls and boys find themselves in different situations: girls do not have to separate as completely and irrevocably from their mother as boys must in order to develop an own gender identity. Little girls simply adopt it from their mother. For little boys the task is much harder. They have to break the early union with their mother and seek a new and unfamiliar male identity.

This basic divergence leads to essential differences in perceptions and values. Women consider people as interdependent. Men regard them as self-reliant. Women emphasize care. Men value freedom. Women view actions and events as interrelated while men tend to see them as isolated.

Societies being dominated by men consider male standards as normative. Female values are not simply accepted as reflections of a different reality but judged as somehow defective: based on emotion rather than reason, on intuition rather than logic. But female ethic – a supposedly irrational and illogical form of thought – actually has a clear logic and rationality and reflects central facts about life. Being connected, women are much more in touch with reality – which is nothing but the connection and interdependence of its innumerable parts.

Women have access to a way of relating self and other that is more cooperative and less hierarchical, more caring and less exploitive. In contrast to men they place morality and self together. If they bring such knowledge into positions of social power, Carol Gilligan concludes, they may bring about important social change. Their ethic of care is comparable to what Ghandi called *satyagraha* – the power of the soul. It was often misinterpreted as passive resistance or as non-violence, which is just one of its characteristics. Actually, *satyagraha* takes its gentle power from two seemingly opposing attitudes: autonomy and compassion.

The message of a female ethic is to use power not to dominate but to take care of the world. Actually, women are much more active in fighting for human issues than men. They fight emphatically for peace and humanism, against war, violence, and oppression. In 1980 the gender gap became statistically relevant in the US with women voting on the more liberal side. Now in Europe the driving force behind ecological movements are people below 25 and women. The feminist movement has become a major force in questioning the traditional values of our society. Their ideas have influenced public opinion and political programmes and last, but not least, the status of women in society. Their goal is not simply equality but the improvement of an imperfect world. Women do not want to exchange places with men, as Gloria Steinem once wrote, they want better places in a better world.

Women in a male world

The German poet Rainer Maria Rilke predicted in his visionary book *Letters to a Young Poet* a phase of female imitation of male virtues and vices. But the male disguise, he wrote, 'would only be a transitory one. It will enable women to free themselves both from false femininity and male influence and to finally unfold their powerful female essence.'

Rilke was right. Not long ago the key to success for a woman in business was to act and think like a man. A woman who wanted to make it had to be tough, aggressive and domineering. The price for entering male domains was the sacrifice of femininity. But times are changing. As more women enter the business world, they feel less pressured to act like male alter egos. The need to hide female characteristics vanishes with growing self-confidence and acceptance. Now that women have put a foot in the door they are not longer keen on any breakthrough to the top – especially if it would mean managing a polluting company or producing weapons for some questionable war. Women are starting to rediscover their own values, and with it they are starting to change the rules of the game.

A new female style of management is emerging: less rigid and hierarchical, more caring and empathetic than the traditional male approach. Emphasis is put on consensus instead of hierarchy, on cooperating instead of competing, on sharing information instead of withholding information. Ironically, this approach was considered a distinct disadvantage in business until it began to be defined as the key factor of Japanese success.

Power and love can be reconciled. James MacGregor Burns, historian and Pulitzer Prize winner, describes it as a male misunderstanding to define leadership in the sense of command and control whereas the true purpose of leadership lies in sensing and mobilizing human potential. A true leader does not use his power for personal objectives but knows how to sense and transform the needs of his followers. 'When we realize the true essence of leadership', Burns says, 'men will more easily accept women as leaders and change their own leadership style'.

The idea is not a new one. In the East, where the female principle is an inherent part of culture, the gentle leadership style has a philosophical tradition. Lao Tse writes in the Tao te Ching, a thousand year old book of wisdom: 'If you want to govern people, you must place yourself below them. If you want to lead the people, you must learn to follow them. The Master is above the people, and no one feels oppressed. He goes ahead of the people, and no one feels manipulated. Because he competes with no one, no one can compete with him'.

Women are becoming change agents and role models. Work demographics show that the emerging female management style is gaining influence. Not only because of the simple fact that more women will achieve positions in the upper echelons of management but mainly because their flexible and mediating approach will be indispensable in coping with the increasingly complex problems of a global economy. In a living system all phenomena are interconnected and interdependent. They form an integrated whole which cannot be reduced to its parts. Unrestricted economic growth is just one example. It creates profits but drives at the same time ecological destruction and financial indebtedness.

Such problems will not be solved by a mere competitive struggle for benefits as the detriments cannot be externalized. Economic growth will have to be assessed within the context of global sustainability. Responsible management will therefore require the ability to understand the organizing principles of a living system – ultimately to see the world n terms of relationships. The integrative force of female ethic will become equally vital in dealing with the different cultural ground rules of an increasingly heterogenous work force and the existential challenge of a pressurizing ecological crisis. 'If *satyagraha* is to be the mode of the future', Ghandi once said, 'then the future belongs to women'.

A female vision

Still women in elite positions are not abundant. Not many of them have climbed the ladder high enough to put their mark on corporate culture. In the top ranks of corporate management fewer than one half of 1 per cent are female. Up to now the emergence of a distinct female style has not yet transformed many workplaces. Most working environments are still dominated by the hierarchical style of the common corporate culture.

Anita Roddick, founder of the most successful British cosmetics chain, is one of those few women who realized their vision in large scale. Her company is not just a successful profit generating machine but an intriguing social experiment. Her goal is nothing less than to rewrite the book of business. Principles such as respect and care, humanity and creativity appear in her business philosophy as well as profits and productiveness. She is forging a union between ethic values and traditional business practice. Her holistic approach reconciles two seemingly apart worlds: money and morality.

The basic ideas are just as astonishing as straightforward. Anita Roddick has replaced the traditional concept of triggering consumption with advertising pressure and creation of artificial needs. Her company is not just a dream machine like any other cosmetics company. She does not promote the illusive ideal of eternal youth or perfect beauty. She even does without the glossy fictions of advertising. Quite the reverse, she promotes the satisfaction of real needs: she simply offers skin and hair care. Along the lines of this philosophy of appropriate consumption are the simple packaging of her products and the refill and recycling services in her shops.

She has dropped the concept of manipulation and exploitation of nature in favour of a careful use of resources. Her much more organic approach requires that all ingredients are obtained as close to source as possible and from sources that are both renewable and sustainable. Ingredients of vegetable are preferred above those of mineral origin. Ingredients of animal origin are rejected as well as any kind of animal testing which has been replaced by a computerized testing system.

Principles of care and respect complement the traditional business practice emphasizing efficiency and profit. She cooperates only with people or organizations that adhere to non-exploitative labour methods. Investment projects in developing countries are accompanied by anthropologists who facilitate a careful integration into existing social and cultural structures. All projects for the Third World are designed as self perpetuating trade links enabling whole communities formerly dependent on foreign aid to regain their economic autonomy.

The Nepalese paper project is one of the local long term investments in the Third World. Nepal is one the ten poorest countries in the world. Its fragile agricultural basis is endangered by growing deforestation. The chopping down of trees has removed the protector from the top soil which is now washed away from the foot hills of the Himalayas to the Ganges delta. After the government put a stop to lumbering, whole villages living on paper making went out of work. Anita Roddick and Mara Amats, a paper making expert, went to Nepal to examine the opportunity to start up a project. Meanwhile a small paper making factory has been built and is in full operation. The use of alternative ingredients like banana leaves and water hyacinth revives the ancient craft of paper making, expands its perspectives, creates work for local people and helps to slow down deforestation. Moreover it is profitable. The hand made paper from the Himalayas sells for a premium in industrial countries.

The corporate mission is communicated through the shops. They are not just a place for selling and buying. Similar to traditional market places they serve as areas of communication where both material and immaterial values are exchanged. These so called arenas of education are regularly dedicated to social and environmental issues thus creating a direct involvement of customers.

The magic word is connection. For Anita Roddick it is more than just collecting signatures to stop the burning of the Amazon rain forest or donating an aeroplane to the Kayapo indians. Her goal is to create a global community. The common bond is the belief that business should do more than produce goods, create jobs and make money. 'Business is the most powerful force in society today', she writes in her autobio-graphy, 'and it ought to be harnessed to effect social change and to improve the quality of life in those societies around the world where basic needs are not being met'. By focusing on this mutual desire to contribute to a better world Anita Roddick transcends the traditional polarisation between producer and consumer. She unites them in favour of a common goal.

Her concept of 'enlightened capitalism' matches an increasing awareness in both consumers and investors about their own influence and responsibility. They realize that it makes a difference from which company they buy or in which they invest. They judge a company not just by its products or profits but by the people and the ethic behind it.

In contrast to most business men the unconventional beauty-queen is counting on the belief in a better world as the most forceful motivation in people. She does not rely on material greed as the so called invisible hand regulating individual decisions in favour of the common good as once postulated by Adam Smith. Actually every system is a feed-back machine teaching its members to play according to its parameters. A free market economy reinforces a specific side of human potential: egoism, competition and achievement. Anita Roddick in turn addresses a kinder side: care, responsibility and contribution.

Anita Roddick defines business – for most professionals mere trade – as art. It starts where vision, spirit, values and ideals come into play. When the language of curves and figures, of budgets and cash flows starts to dominate a company, she says, the spell is broken. A magic adventure turns into the dead science of money making.

Body Shop is managed by a woman. The strategy is formulated by women. The image is created by women. The product development is controlled by women. Of course this makes a difference. Women do not have sacred cows, Anita Roddick says, they have a more playful approach to business. What terrifies most corporate executives is an integral part of her formula: anarchy. Anarchy is irritation and irritation is a source of energy and creativity. Tap the energy of an anarchist, she advises, and he will be the one to push your company ahead.

Another part of her secret is to have fun and not to take business too seriously. It may sound superficial but points to a deeper truth: many people have forgotten that business is just a means to an end – and not an end in itself. We live in a global economy, Anita Roddick argues, and as global citizens we have a global responsibility – not just for products and profits but for our planet. The ethical credo of the company is established in the Body Shop Charter: We will demonstrate our care for the world in which we live by respecting our fellow human beings, by not harming animals, by working to conserve our planet.

This brings us back to the basis of culture. The bible says: 'In the beginning was the word'. Words contain meaning and their meaning is determined by cultural values. We have reached a point where this basis of our value system has to be reexamined. We have to reevaluate our values. Is affluence the same as welfare? Is quantity of consumption the same as quality of life? Is money the same as value? Is economic non-productiveness the same as uselessness? We have to look at problems from new perspectives. We have to transform our parameters. And as any true transformation it has to take place not only in the head but also in the heart.

HEAD MEETS HEART

'In the history of human thinking', the Nobel prize winner Werner Heisenberg wrote, 'the most fruitful developments take place at those points where two different lines of thought meet'. This is where we find ourselves today. Women hold up one half of the sky, a Chinese proverb says. Now they are reconquering their half of the earth too. Of course it has been a long road. Women had to learn from men. Now men can learn from women – from their greater connectedness, their greater sensitivity, their greater intuition for future orientation, their greater patience and their greater ability to care.

The future lies in the hands of those who are capable of giving the next generation substantial reasons to live and to hope. This and nothing less is the challenge of our time. The answer is not a choice between two separate ways but their synthesis. It is the reconciliation of head and heart, of thinking and feeling, of logic and intuition, of male and female. In Plato's 'Timaeus' each human being is the result of a bisection and therefore bound to desire and pursue the reunification with its missing half. In Egyptian mythology Isis wandered through the universe to find her male counterpart Osiris. The holy wedding – the fusion of the opposites – created the world. Similarly the overemphasized and over-burdened male principle in our culture – and especially in business culture – needs to be complemented by its female counterpart. The reconciliation of masculine and feminine sides in human nature and society is a recon-nection: to our heart as our human essence and to nature as our ultimate source. 'Just realize where you come from', Lao Tse says, 'this is the essence of wisdom'.

References

Capra F., *The Tao of Physics*, Fontana Paperbacks, 1989
Gilligan C., *In a Different Voice*, Harvard University Press, 1982
Chodorow N., *The Reproduction of Mothering: Psychoanalysis and the Sociology of Gender*, University of California Press, 1978
Rubin L.B., *Just Friends: The Role of Friendship in our Lives*, Harper & Rowe Publishers, New York, 1986
Time, Special Issue, Fall 1990

'There is nothing more difficult to take in hand, more perilous to conduct, or more uncertain of success than to take a lead in the introduction of a new order of things, because the innovation has for enemies all those who have done well under the old conditions and lukewarm defenders in those who may do well under new.'

Machiavelli

11 ENVIRONMENTAL MANAGEMENT: THE RELATIONSHIP BETWEEN PRESSURE GROUPS AND INDUSTRY – A RADICAL REDESIGN

by Douglas Mulhall

The key to environmentally sound industry is radical redesign of products and processes. The way to achieve this is to combine the holistic approach of environmental pressure groups with the inventiveness of industry. This chapter shows why and how such an alliance could occur.

INTRODUCTION

Has the newly discovered environmental awareness in industry translated into production changes which put companies on the right track? The answer is: in a few cases, yes, but in many cases industry is headed on another wrong and ultimately unprofitable track instead of clearly identifying sustainable development pathways.

After twenty years, despite resounding growth and influence on public awareness, the impact of environmental pressure groups on reducing overall rates of ecological destruction is zero. While 'environmental management' has emerged in government cabinets and corporate offices, the world is in more ecological trouble now than ever. More than three quarters of all new pollution is being created in developing and newly industrialized nations by governments and multinational corporations. As poor nations strive to improve their living standards and pay off their debt to rich nations, they are accelerating the depletion of their natural resources. These resources are being sucked up by the industrial world at an accelerating rate, and spewed out as waste.

In Eastern Europe and the former Soviet Union, environmental consciousness emerged in the first blush of freedom and thousands of environmental organisations sprang up. However, these groups are now virtually powerless against the onslaught of consumerism. Western companies, despite warnings from the environment ministries, are increasingly free to dump environmentally unsound products into Eastern Europe to meet consumer demand.

This is apparent in the five new lands of Germany, where development is pursuing the same environmentally destructive path as in western Europe. Massive road building plans have been approved. The openly stated aim is to create another mega-automobile market, and so the status quo continues. Western industries claim that the new products they bring to eastern Europe are less polluting than the old Communist ones. Herein lies the fatal flaw.

'Less polluting' simply means a slower rate of destruction. Even if western products are twice or three times less polluting than old Socialist products, this comes nowhere near the changes needed to achieve sustainable development. Instead it develops infrastructures which move industry in the same old wrong direction.

The environmental movement knows this, but is reacting in a schizophrenic way. On one hand they see their influence growing, and changes beginning to happen, so they support industrial sectors which show signs of changing. On the other side, there is a feeling it may be too little too late, that the changes are confined to non-critical sectors, and that radical action may be required. This is leading environmentalism into another phase, commonly referred to as Deep Ecology.

The driving belief behind Deep Ecology is that all human activities which are bad for the environment must cease immediately and be replaced by other processes, no matter what the short-term economic cost, because the option is catastrophe. This is a vast oversimplification of the term, and there are those who would argue it is not so. However, regardless of what the philosophy says, the 'stop it now' sentiment is being used by a growing group of activists as a rallying cry. This movement finds itself at the same stage of growth and influence as the Greenpeace of the 1970's, but rather than taking 20 years to mature, it could progress much faster.

Opposite the Deep Ecologists, inside government and industry, sit the Eco-Stalinists. These people comprise a dangerous minority among business people. They still believe environmentalists are wild-eyed hippies. The Stalinists, are a dying breed. However, history demonstrates that the last lunge of a dying breed can be fatal. Eco-Stalinists include senior corporate managers who perceive ecologists as economic threats, and politicians who see environmentalists as scape goats to blame for economic problems created by years of neglectful public policies. Eco-Stalinists had remarkable success at the Earth Summit, scuttling most of the meaningful treaties which were designed to herald a new era.

Environmentalists are partly, but not largely, to blame for the emergence of this group. During the late eighties, some managers in corporations began to convince their boards to start a dialogue with the movement by releasing more information about the company's impact on the environment.

Unfortunately, elements within the environmental movement who hold a strong distrust of the corporations and their motives, seized upon this new information to demonstrate how nasty these polluters really were. Environmentalists shot the messengers, and progressive managers lost face with their colleagues, because their companies were singled out for blame.

This allowed the Eco-Stalinists to say inside their own organization 'we told you so', re-enforcing the corporate position for secrecy and creating a dangerous gap between the environmental movement and business which risks destroying chances for environmentally sound management.

How is this dilemma to be solved?

The first step in the right direction is to stop using the term 'Environmental Manager'. For centuries human beings have tried to 'manage' nature. The term environmental management is a misguided continuation of the age-old philosophy that somehow humans can conquer and tame natural forces. Experience shows that while it is possible and desirable to benefit from nature's resources our primitive attempts to reformulate billions of years of evolution have repeatedly led to catastrophe.

Industrial processes need to be redesigned in ways which allow the natural environment to sustain itself. This change in outlook is a key to survival. Once a company adopts this philosophy, it can start along the road to prosperity and get the edge on less prepared competitors. Environmental pressure groups and institutes are the repositories of this philosophy, and so they have a lot to offer companies.

REASONS FOR THE RISE OF ENVIRONMENTAL GROUPS

It may seem redundant to ask why environmental groups have become so powerful or why they could play a central role in industrial re-design. However, the reasons are deeper than many people realize. It is essential that these factors be understood by managers preparing for an environmental future, and by environmentalists trying to move from raising awareness to practical solutions.

Five factors have led to the rise of environmentalism:

- impact of environmental degradation on people's daily lives,
- science,
- waste management costs,
- instant media, and
- alienation from nature.

Impact on people's daily lives

The direct impact of environmental degradation on people's daily lives is a driving force behind the growth of the environmental movement. For example, in many parts of Europe, car drivers have nowhere to drive. Most major roads are constantly blocked by traffic jams. The fact that people cannot get anywhere anymore is achieving what the human death toll from accidents failed to do: force a fundamental reconsideration of transport strategy.

The lifting of EC trade barriers will see a dramatic increase in traffic. The focal geographic point for this is the mountain passes of Switzerland separating north and south. In this region truck traffic stops for days at a time. Traffic gridlock is neutralizing the advantages of freer trade. Furthermore, fumes from engines are poisoning trees on steep mountain slopes, causing die-off, which in turn destabilizes the soil. The result has been an increase in avalanches, even more traffic delays and a rise in cost to prevent them. These developments affect the wages of millions of people who earn their living from the road transportation industry and have aroused the fear of millions of Swiss.

In other industries thousands of case histories have emerged which chronicle economic and personal disaster: poisoning from toxic dumps across North America and Europe; emergence of allergies among a high percentage of children living in south Germany; increases in deforestation-related flood fatalities in Asia. These events are creating a statistically significant segment of the population who have been personally hit by environmentally related events. The case of Dow Corning and breast implants, referred to later in this chapter, is an example. It is this economic and health impact which drives environmentalism. Media coverage, which frustrated businesses wrongly target as the villain, only reflects this personal reality.

Science

The miniaturization revolution in scientific measurement created sophisticated techniques which uncovered dangerous substances where previously none were thought to exist. This was magnified by concurrent discoveries that even pico-particles can significantly affect the health of living organisms. The trend is towards finding more harmful interactions among man-made products. Asbestos, CFCs, silicon implants, DDT and aromatics are just a few examples which, at their inception, were thought to be harmless, but after years of experience proved to have serious environmental or health drawbacks.

Science has also unwittingly strengthened environmental groups through its educational failures both in its own field and in the political arena. Few elected members of any government would be able to describe the environmental implications of emerging industrial technologies. Few scientists have gone into politics, and those who did lacked interdisciplinary training. This resulted in 'linear leaders' – such as Margaret Thatcher.

Mrs. Thatcher, a scientist, was truly ignorant about the economic implications of turning over nuclear power to private industry. In the midst of selling off its energy industry, the government discovered that the enormous costs of nuclear liability and waste disposal meant investors would not buy it. In other words, the market had to tell the government what everyone else knew all along – nuclear power could not pay for itself. This resulted in the government taking an embarrassing turnabout and carving the entire nuclear industry out of its privatisation strategy. As a result, Mrs. Thatcher gave away the profitable part of the energy industry, and kept the loser. The world was then treated to the unusual sight of outraged conservatives lobbying for an end to the British nuclear program. This struggle continues under John Major today and is a huge thorn in the government's economic recovery programme.

Similar contradictions throughout America and Europe have caused many voters to correctly conclude that their leaders are environmentally illiterate, and this has translated into support for green pressure groups.

Cost and liability of waste management technology

The continued artificially low prices of commodities in relation to their true economic and environmental costs has led the industrialized world to suck up resources at an accelerating rate and spew them out as waste at the other end. The cost of managing this waste threatens our infrastructures with bankruptcy. Yet waste management continues to be the preferred environmental 'solution'.

It takes 26 tonnes of waste to produce one tonne of car. By the end of this decade, some of the richest companies in the world will be waste management companies. Spending by states in the US for hazardous waste dump cleanup increased by 68 per cent from 1989 to 1990. A recent EPA study indicates industry spending will increase by another 60 percent to $195 billion by the year 2000.

Who pays these waste managers? Companies do, from their profits. The more they pay for waste management, the less they have to invest in development of new products.

In Germany industries must pay more than two hundred dollars a tonne for incineration and other forms of waste disposal. Given that Europe produces more than two billion tonnes of waste annually, one can appreciate the cost implication as such levies spread across the EC.

In government it's the same. In 1991 European environment ministers approved a plan to upgrade municipal waste water treatment which will cost EC municipalities more than $55 billion to implement. All of these real costs are causing the taxpayer alarm. They point to the failure of governments to cope.

Aside from the costs of actually handling waste, a far greater monster is environmental liability. Many managers still have the fatally mistaken idea that remaining ignorant of an environmental impact will relieve them from liability if they get sued. This is not only wrong – it can also destroy a company. Three environmental liabilities – legal, image, and boycott – can kill a company or bring down a government.

One company which recently suffered all three is Dow Corning, a company producing breast implants. In a stunning reversal of fortunes this company, which in 1990 was doing a roaring business in silicon breast implants, was forced out of the business after revelations of the implants causing suspected immune deficiency syndromes and other health problems. It is possible that with all the pending lawsuits, the company could surpass its insurance claim limits. Whether Dow knew about the problem beforehand is irrelevant. As soon as the health impacts became known, demand for the product simply evaporated, and people started calling their lawyers.

Many managers would not see this as an environmental problem, and this is a dangerous mistake. The definition of environmental pressure groups is broadening into key areas such as health. Dow Corning was undertaking the most risky of all environmental experiments: putting synthetic substances into living beings. This made environmental activists out of millions of affected women, and so the definition of 'environmental pressure groups' is expanding.

The health backlash is also hitting governments. This year the EC abandoned its office headquarters at a cost of $170 million due to asbestos contamination. Today, governments would rather take this type of loss than face lawsuits from employees who are increasingly aware of the risks.

Anyone who thinks they can get away more cheaply in developing nations need only look to the recent explosion in a Mexican city. Here gas fumes accumulated in sewers caused an explosion which resulted in immediate imprisonment of numerous government officials, and promises of lengthy trials.

Legal liability is becoming such a large issue that special newsletters such as the *Hazardous Waste News* are published monthly on the topic. In the United States, the number of cases referred by the USEPA to the Justice Department for prosecution tripled from one hundred in 1982 to 350 in 1989. Additionally, hundreds of consent decrees have been agreed out of court. Texas Eastern Corporation agreed in 1988 to pay half a billion dollars to clean up PCBs dumped along its pipeline system over the years.

The Sandoz spill into the Rhine river in 1986 resulted not only in enormous cleanup costs for the company, but has also affected its operations internationally. When the company applied to build a plant in Ireland, local authorities demanded zero discharge from the factory.

A recent study by the General Accounting Office in the United States found that the average payment among the insurers questioned has risen from $15,600 in 1985 to $65,400 in 1989. The GAO only surveyed 13 major insurers, but even among this group the number of pollution claims was fifty thousand, with two thousand pending lawsuits. Bankers who lend money to polluters are being held liable for actions of borrowers. The US District Court for Rhode Island has allowed a case to proceed against a credit union that lent mortgage money to a landowner accused of polluting a river with raw sewage. The claim is that by lending the money, the credit union aided the crime.

Consumer boycotts of companies and governments for various reasons including environment have become so common that there is now a magazine called the *Boycott News* which chronicles these events.

One of the most effective boycotts recently was the 1990 Greenpeace led boycott of Icelandic fish in retaliation for Iceland's continued whaling. This is estimated to have cost Iceland $50–75 million.

In terms of image, here is one chilling example for any PR manager: in 1990 Phillip Morris fell from number 2 to 79 in Fortune Magazine's Most Admired Companies. While this has had no short-term impact on profits, it makes the job of attracting qualified people more difficult. One executive participating in the poll said, 'I downgraded companies with political action committees, products that kill and companies insensitive to green issues'.

There are signs that this attitude is extending to shareholders. A recent survey of 246 shareholders of 100 shares or more, in 50 states, published in the *New York Times* rated environmental cleanup and product safety ahead of higher dividends. This is an unprecedented occurrence.

The growth of environmental auditing is primarily driven by fears over liability. The *Financial Times* recently explained the reason for the spread of environmental auditing this way: 'First anti-pollution legislation is set to become even tighter. Second, the cost of dumping rather than recycling waste is rapidly increasing. Third, the insurance companies and shareholders are more nervous about the huge liabilities caused by environmental disasters.'

The Instant Media

The briefness of this section by no means indicates its level of importance. The massive impact of instant media in accelerating the message of gross environmental incompetence by our leaders can be summarized in three letters: CNN. It means that a company's reputation can be destroyed globally in one day.

Alienation from Nature

The earth is a closed system, except for energy from the sun, which nature uses to create biological complex systems for stability. Conversely, humans use energy to create systems which destabilize natural complexity, and this is the difference between design by nature and humans.

For example, nature has developed a system which allows marine organisms to deposit billions of tonnes of excrement and by-products into the oceans, forming part of the system which keeps those oceans alive.

Human beings have developed systems which extract elements from below the earth's surface and deposit these along with excrement into the oceans, creating enormous pollution.

This chasm between human and natural design is creating a spiritual crisis, exacerbated by the visual, physical and emotional effects of that pollution. People simply do not feel part of nature anymore.

What environmentalism offers, and what business leaders for so long ignored, is a return to wholeness of the human spirit – a return to nature.

This return to nature should not be confused with the commonly misconceived image of radicals rejecting modern progress. For example, the environmental movement strongly and unanimously supports research into rainforests which has uncovered sophisticated natural medicines which are accepted by even the most conservative of physicians. The key difference is that this science uses human knowledge to learn from billions of years of natural evolution.

Unfortunately, most government environmental regulation and legislation of the past generation has ignored this path, and instead tried to put the genie back in the bottle after it was unleashed.

Almost everyone now agrees that end-of-pipe controls on chemicals have failed. While they have pushed companies towards pollution prevention due to sheer costs of non-compliance, legislation is incapable of keeping up with the tremendous increase in the number and volume of chemicals. In early 1992, for example, European Community regulators confirmed their inability to stem the rise in water pollution through end-of-pipe controls, twelve years after a stringent drinking water directive was put into place.

A generation of regulatory experience has shown beyond any doubt that it is impractical to regulate the planetary ecosystem, as thousands of unenforced laws pile up.

As a result, pressure is emerging by the public for politicians and companies to change their spiritual attitudes rather than just comply with laws, and in this regard pressure groups are getting a lot of support when they begin to challenge the basic values of business.

That challenge has manifested itself in ways destined to change business forever. The underlying factors supporting environmental pressure group growth would still be present even if those groups disappeared tomorrow. 'Business as usual' is finished. The changes will extend to financially sensitive areas of liability, international trade and design of products.

IMPACTS OF PRESSURE GROUPS ON GLOBAL TREATIES

The environmental movement has played a key role in strengthening the role of international environmental conventions. This began with the International Whaling Commission when environmental groups convinced non-whaling nations to join the commission and vote against whaling. It soon extended to the Commission for International Trade in Endangered Species (CITES) which regulates the global wildlife trade, and which recently banned the ivory trade to try and save the elephant.

The 'big-time' turning point for environmentalism in international economic affairs came in the late 1980s when the London Dumping Convention banned first the dumping of nuclear waste into the world's oceans, then banned incineration of waste by ships traveling at sea.

These events had a huge impact on the waste and nuclear industries especially in Europe, because they forced governments and industry to start dealing with a backlog of waste which they could no longer drop in the ocean. Around this time came the Montreal Protocol on CFCs and a host of other developments at international level, led by environmental interest groups.

In response to revelations by environmental groups about industrial world waste going to Third World nations, the governments of Africa recently started an association to co-operate on stopping waste trade, and real inroads have been made into stopping it through co-operation with NGOs.

The free trade agreement between the US and Mexico will likely include new environmental regulations to deal with the infamous Maquiladora industries – foreign companies which moved just across the US border into Mexico, then sent enormous amounts of pollution back to the US via the Rio Grande. Much of this has been documented and drawn to media attention by environmental pressure groups.

The General Agreement on Trade and Tariffs (GATT) is also a battle-ground. Under pressure from groups to enforce its own legislation, the United States government banned all imports of yellow fin tuna from Mexico due to coincidental dolphin kills. Mexico claimed this was unfair competition under GATT. The issue is, at time of writing, going back and forth, but in any case has thrown a major stick into GATT negotiations, and has raised the question of where free trade stops and environmental protection starts.

New working relationships?

In response to these pressures, business has increasingly been approaching environmental pressure groups to try and find mutually acceptable solutions.

If you were a supplier to a major company which has taken this route, then you would be wise to become involved, or risk losing your business. Below is one example of what happens to third party companies when their client company gets serious about finding an environmentally sound product, and the suppliers fall asleep at the wheel.

Under pressure from millions of children (i.e. customers) who were criticizing the company for its ozone-destroying packaging, McDonalds made the smart move to engage a team of experts from the Environmental Defense Fund to examine their entire packaging line. Among this packaging was the polystyrene 'clamshell', which the plastics industry had targeted for a multi-million dollar recycling plant.

Due to a series of hasty decisions, combined with an underestimation of the power of environmentalism, suppliers to McDonalds spent millions of dollars developing a polystyrene recycling operation which lacked the support of the environmental community. As a shock to its suppliers, McDonalds switched to a form of paper packaging. Plastics recyclers were left holding the clamshell and a factory with little to recycle.

The story points out what happens when one company in an industry – a very big company – decides to go it alone and its suppliers decide on a 'business as usual' tack instead.

The McDonalds experiment also points to a much greater problem mentioned earlier – lack of an integrated approach to environmental solutions, and this is covered in more detail later on in this chapter.

Government and business – replacing pressure groups?

With environmental awareness getting around like religion, will traditional sectors such as government and business usurp the role of the environmental movement? This is unlikely in the short term, given the high level of public mistrust of government and corporate performance in this area, and the dismal inability of government to act. However, institutions are taking advocacy positions which were once the exclusive purvey of environmental groups.

Take for example procurement of goods and services: in 1986 the German Federal Ministry on Environment published a handbook on environmental protection in government purchasing for office equipment, which was a first step towards environmental criteria. The German town of Erlangen decided in 1985 to give ecologically sound products preference in government purchasing. In its environmental report of 1989 the municipality outlines criteria for environmentally responsible procurement for offices and use of cleaning agents in municipal buildings. Erlangen also decided in 1990 to require environmentally sound methods for structural engineering.

Recent EC and OECD moves towards economic incentive instruments, show that many positions being advocated by environmental groups are on the road to adoption.

Several international business groups have emerged to deal with the environment. These include the International Network of Environmental Managers (INEM), the Environment Bureau of the International Chamber of Commerce (ICC) and most recently the Business Council on Sustainable Development.

This latter group, led by Swiss businessman Stephan Schmidheiny, developed the business strategy for the UN Conference in Brazil in 1992. The BCSD consists of more than forty chief executives of multinational corporations – some of the world's worst polluters and perhaps most anxious environmental reformers. Mr. Schmidheiny is to be highly congratulated for his stand against subsidies as a main cause of environmental degradation, and his urging of companies to wean themselves from such government-induced spoon feeding.

Unfortunately, Mr. Schmidheiny's recently published and highly publicized book *Changing Course*, makes the key error of mixing environmentally sustainable activities such as vegetable oil-based leather tanning, with dangerous stop-gap measures such as new gasoline additives which prolong the necessary move towards zero emission vehicles by making investments in the wrong technologies. By trying to walk the line with its own constituency, including companies which depend on subsidies to survive, the BCSD has difficulty providing clear vision of the basic changes required for industry to become sustainable.

My advice for any company wishing to 'change course' is that they look at such books as worthy attempts, but also recognize that Eco-Stalinists still play a large hand in such works, sending them off the mark.

In another well-intentioned but misguided development, some companies have gotten on board the right train, then stood still at the station due to internal conflicts. Here is one example.

For years the most common packaging used for personal care products

– including health care products – has been plastic, and today our shampoo bottles live five times longer than we do. Several years ago International Chemicals Incorporated (ICI) invented a truly biodegradable plastic – Biopol – which decomposes into non-toxic elements when exposed to bacteria (as opposed to false biodegradable plastics which simply degrade into dust-size particles of plastic). This material is synthesized by microorganisms from glucose made of sugar beets or cereals. Aside from some optional additives which can be replaced, Biopol is completely biodegradable in a compost, as opposed to the 'false' biodegradable plastics made of starch and plastic. A comparison with other packaging plastics, e.g. PVC, show that the traditional materials have far more additives with considerable environmental impacts.

In theory Biopol should be taking the market by storm. However, ICI also produces PVC which is used in containers at a high profit margin. This, according to their own PR people, has produced a conflict of interest. The result is that ICI has found itself in conflict with clients who by all measures should be allies.

A few years ago, the Wella company, one of the world's largest hair care products companies, asked ICI for a batch of Biopol for its shampoo bottles. It was only through long and tense negotiations that this happened at all. Even so, Biopol is seeing only limited applications compared to its potential. The initial price quoted by ICI to Wella was said to be up to ten times the price for a normal plastic container, and ICI said this was due to research, development and material costs. Wella paid the premium, and in 1990 Biopol bottles appeared on German store shelves – three years after negotiations began – and even then in very small quantities.

Today, ICI continues to advertise Biopol, and continues to resist aggressively marketing it to customers.

This is a good demonstration of how vested interests are slowing the emergence of environmentally sound products and why environmental pressure groups need to work with companies to get these items to market.

Had a European government for example offered ICI a tax break based on environmental savings, and at the same time a penalty for selling less environmentally sound products when an alternative existed, we would probably see Biopol on every store shelf in the western world today.

FINDING A SOLUTION

As repeated often in this chapter, one of the key mistakes of industrial society has been to isolate its professional disciplines from each other. I am constantly amazed at the lack of interdisciplinary co-operation within major scientific and business institutions. Engineers in electronics companies often have no idea of what chemicals go into their products, aside from the ones which have necessary electromagnetic properties. We recently had an executive from a world-class electronics company come to us with a list of 36 hazardous chemicals in their television sets. We had to tell him that his TV was constructed from several thousand hazardous chemicals. He left our office in shock, but much to his credit came back asking us to analyse their product.

Industrial methods of making, marketing and using products are so out of balance with natural processes that it is clear we need to redesign everything, and while it is important to clean up the mess we made, the urgent task is to redesign products, processes and marketing to be compatible with nature.

The people who have the capability to start this – even though they may not know it – are the product designers; the architects, engineers and chemists who design what we use. These people are in scientific institutions and corporations – not the environmental movement.

A crisis has emerged within the environmental movement because most lack these designers holding the solutions. They exist at MIT, SONY, Ciba Geigy, and other establishment institutions. As our society moves from awareness to action, environmentalists find that to take the next step they lack the skills. There are some brilliant designers in the movement, but they are definitely in the minority, and pale in numbers beside those in companies and institutes.

On the other side, companies and educational institutions who employ the designers are sadly uneducated about the changes needed to redirect these people's talents.

The key to solving this problem is to bring the ecological way of thinking from the environmental movement together with the genius of designers who unwittingly control the future of our global environment. This has to be done in developing and newly industrialized nations, rather than just the industrial nations, and so the link between the environmental movement and business becomes doubly important. This is what the United Nations Conference on Environment and Development (UNCED) tried to start at the Earth Summit meeting in Rio, and fell far short of achieving. Maurice Strong, Secretary General of UNCED, summarized the aim:

> '. . . Particular responsibility rests on those who shape economic policy and carry it out, as well as those who provide the scientific and technical guidance to policy and decision-makers. What we need is far greater partnership amongst these various sectors. They have too long functioned in isolation from each other. One of the aims of the Earth Summit is to bring them together.'

The extent to which this coming together is required goes far beyond traditional thinking. It is not being addressed adequately by organizations such as the Business Council on Sustainable Development or by the environmental movement. It is beginning to be addressed by some institutions such as MIT and the Technical University of Denmark, plus a new group of small institutes such as the Environmental Protection Encouragement Agency (EPEA) in Hamburg, William McDonough Architects in New York, the Center for Resource Management and Rocky Mountain Institute both in Colorado, and the Right Livelihood Foundation in London.

The key to environmentally sound solutions is integration of professional disciplines; basic science, social science, economics, theology, and sheer imagination. This integration needs to be applied at the very beginning and throughout the product design and manufacturing process, to take account of nature's needs.

Unfortunately, this coming 'together', faces one vicious reality – governments are incapable of moving fast enough to do anything. In the United States, it took thirteen years to negotiate a Clean Air Act, and it will take another five years to implement. At the international level, the Law of the Sea, negotiated more than 12 years ago, has yet to be ratified by many countries. Implementation is questionable.

So, no matter what has been agreed, governments will be too slow to implement. In the short years left before global disruption strikes a crippling blow to humanity, the only organisations with the capability to move quickly enough are the multi-nationals. Even they can only be effective if they find new ways to co-operate with government and NGOs. It is here that the real breakthrough is needed, and where environmental groups have a responsibility to start working together with business.

Happily, I can report that several major multinational companies have taken up this challenge, and this trend is accelerating rapidly as the smart money goes into ecology. Unhappily, I am prevented from saying who these companies are because trade secrets and competition are keeping a lid on information about new developments.

For this reason alone, a greater vehicle to multiply solutions and freely dispense information about them is needed to win this race for planetary survival. Business, government and the environmental movement need a compelling global focus as a catalyst. Several months before the Earth Summit, our institute, in an article published by German and Brazilian newspapers, proposed a World Exposition of Environmental Solutions to be this catalyst. This possibility is EXPO 2000. The World's Fair in 2000 is scheduled to take place in Hannover, Germany.

World Expositions have traditionally been expensive temporary showpieces which celebrate techno-achievement and give everyone a good time at taxpayer expense. Events such as Sevilla 92 in Spain, have been environmental disasters, using ecologically unsound material and high energy-consuming methods. This was graphically proven when the flagship pavilion at EXPO 92 burned down prior to opening, releasing clouds of toxic vapors from supposedly fireproof building materials.

World Expositions are the biggest business and governmental events of their kind and represent an opportunity to demonstrate effective global environmental solutions. At the turn of the millennium, it is time to transform these expositions into something which has lasting impact.

One way to do this is to use EXPO 2000 as a Centre for Global Environment and Development. Such a centre could provide the global focus and practical impetus for environmental pressure groups and international business to collaborate in an unprecedented way to help solve environmental problems. This could help define new political, social and economic models for environmentally sustainable development and avoid extremes of environmentalism and industrialism.

Most investment for the World Exposition would go into long-term, global demonstration projects to help define a new development agenda. During the next eight years, projects would take shape around the world, then be exhibited at EXPO 2000, as a practical step from the Earth Summit.

EXPO 2000 is concretely taking this direction. Fair organizers recently adopted the revolutionary 'Hannover Principles of Design', a series of principles developed by William McDonough Architects and EPEA, which outline ecological principles for construction of all EXPO exhibits. The principles have also been adopted by US institutes of architecture and are the first internationally recognized ecological design principles to be applied on such a scale.

Other examples will surely follow. But the point is this: global scale projects must be identified where corporations, governments, scientific institutions and environmentalists could start to learn to work together to reverse an otherwise instoppable slide towards Armageddon.

It is up to the environmentalists and the companies to find ways to redesign everything from cars to catalysts that human design emulates natural design.

This is feasible. In some cases it is already underway. However, the methodology is a complex work outside this essay, which our institute and others are developing. Governments might help, but they have shown themselves incapable of leading.

Whether business and environmental groups co-operate or annihilate each other depends on how quickly they recognize the only road to survival is co-operation.

'Voluntary acceptance of responsibility is the price of freedom'

Gotlieb Duttwiler, founder of the largest Swiss retailing group, 1953

12 THOUGHTS ABOUT THE CHANGEABILITY OF CORPORATE CULTURES

by Tilman Peter Oehl

A CHANGING CORPORATE WORLD

In theory

When comparing annual reports of major corporations in Europe and the United States with those of some ten years ago, a few interesting changes in the appearance as well as the topics covered can be noted. Not only are they now largely printed on recycled paper or at least non-chlorine bleached papers, but they also unanimously agree upon the global responsibility of industry for the welfare of mankind and the protection of our environment.

They are often used to point out the company's environmental achievements of the last few years. Impressive charts are used to illustrate the increase of 'green' investments or the reduction in pollution the company has managed to achieve. In some cases they serve as a mouth piece for the company's opinion on controversial environmental issues – mostly stressing the controversy of the issue as explanation why the company hasn't jumped on that particular band wagon! – or, even more extreme, to publish a company's environmental objectives and code of ethics.

The green issue which, ten years ago, was not even recognized as an issue, has reached the boardroom and there is not one top executive who has not prepared a speech outlining the company's genuine concern for and commitment to the environment. No company can afford to ignore the environmental problems it may be causing and all are keen to show that they are doing their utmost to come up with a solution.

If a questionnaire were to be sent out to the CEOs of the top hundred multi-nationals in which they were asked:

- Should we reduce waste?
- Should we reduce CO_2-emissions?

- Should we save the rain forests?
- Do you like clean rivers, unpolluted beaches, fresh air and unpolluted soil?
- Do you want to eat healthy food?

the answer would be a resounding 'yes' to all of the above.

However, although concern about the environment has reached the top level, little of this is apparent in the day-to-day management of many companies. Environmental accidents are seen as disruptions to the production and selling of products which hinder economic growth and which require nothing more than some mopping up. Once taken care of, they can be forgotten about and it is again 'business as usual'. They are not seen as opportunities from which the company – and the environment – could benefit longer term by introducing more environmentally friendly processes and stricter safety guidelines to avoid reoccurrence.

The 'caring' attitude does not limit itself to the environment. Another issue which has become fashionable in the last decade is that of the human factor in organizational development. Great efforts are made to improve the social skills of management in order to maintain the happiness of the crew. As they say at McDonalds: 'Happy people sell more hamburgers'. It is getting increasingly more difficult to make the people happy, but companies seem to be giving it their all: the amount of literature on the subject has increased drastically, seminars on how people interact with one another are being hosted or attended, managers are being sent on courses to improve their social competence, the Japanese example is studied, competences are decentralized, quality circles are put into place, everything thinkable is being tried.

The execution

The theory in both areas is discussed at length and well documented. The fact that, in practice, there is precious little to show for it is blamed on the failure to implement that theory properly, not on a deficiency in the theory itself.

An interesting observation in the current discussion between the green movement and the increasing number of scientists, publicists and some far-sighted entrepreneurs on one side and the majority of executives on the other side is that the overall goal to preserve this planet as home for mankind is the same. However, each side thinks that the other side goes about reaching that goal in the wrong way. It must be very difficult to reach a common goal if the parties concerned move in different directions!

Part of the problem lies in the fact that the green movement has not really presented its case in a way that everyone could agree to it. It's not so simple to change the course of a supertanker at full speed. It takes a lot of effort and hard work to even decide on that new course.

On the other hand, industry by and large has not yet accepted that the current ecological and social state of the earth, is not the result of an accident, but of industrialization. There is a growing awareness that things cannot stay the way they are, but very few executives seem to read that as a call to change the direction in which their company is going. They do not seem to understand that 'business as usual' will lead to 'no more business at all'.

Of course, the 'mopping up' process has to take place. Regulations and voluntary improvements to control pollution, reduce the waste stream, protect nature's reservations, give us a little bit more time to think about future.

And thought is certainly required, not so much for nature's sake as our own! The environmental crisis is not a crisis of nature: nature needs no protection, nature will handle the case and write off the human experiment as a negative example of evolution. Nature has got plenty of time to start all over again. The environmental crisis is one of human making and the question is can we overcome it? We don't seem to have much choice in the matter. If mankind wants to survive, we have to.

A CHANGING GEO-POLITICAL WORLD: *GÖTTERDÄMMERUNG* OF THE EMPIRES

Not only the corporate world is subject to a great number of changes. School children of the 21st century will have their work cut out if they want to study all the historical turnarounds that occurred in the late 1980s and the early 1990s. Nobody knows today what will be the set-up of the world ten years from now, but it is quite clear that the time of the big empires is over.

The desire of the individual to have at least the chance to live its own life in personal freedom and the possibility of individual choice have been stronger than tanks and troops. The tragedy that is taking place now in the chaos following the break up of the old USSR should remind us that the threat is not over now.

The attitude of the West seems to be one of an interested but uninvolved spectator. It is even felt in some quarters that in wanting to catch up with the Western world the East is only getting its due for hanging on to Communism for such a long time. This attitude is more than a bit naive because there is no reason to think or even hope that the shock waves of these series of earth quakes will not reach us. In fact, they already have.

Our only advantage over the East is that our system of the balance of powers worked better and the concept of private initiative is stronger than the concept of collectivism. The symptoms that have led to the downfall of the collective system can equally be found in our society, especially in governments and big companies.

Then there remains the still unresolved relationship between the industrialized world and the Third World.

Moreover, we have enough explosive potential within our societies, that we have no reasons to be complacent. Or haven't you heard about unemployment, new poverty, the drug war, to name just a few of the problems?

The present situation cannot be managed by governments and international institutions alone. Individuals not only have to make their voice be heard, they also have to take responsibility for their share of the action. Almost every adult individual is organized in an economic entity that interacts with the society in one way or the other, namely the corporations. These are therefore the ideal place to start.

The new role of the corporation – corporate citizenship

Contrary to all rules of discourse, I am starting this section with some conclusions: corporations will only be able to maintain their present role in the future if they not only fulfil the material needs of their people, but also reflect the ambitions, emotions, likes and dislikes of their employees. They will only manage to attract the growing number of skilled people they need for maintaining their operations if their case is legitimate – which is totally different from being legal.

The legitimation bench marks are:

- social acceptance of the products
- acceptable organisational culture and development
- environmental acceptable products and procedures

Although this book discusses the ecological implications of management, the environmental aspects cannot be singled out. To change the packaging of the product to a more environmentally friendly one is one thing, to abandon a product, because its production is not sustainable is another story.

The crux is, that in order to fulfil the many tasks the Western world has, the profits of corporations are badly needed. We need short-term profits to repair the social and environmental damages short-term-profit-thinking has caused. But if corporations do not want to leave the field to populistic politicians, they have to gain legitimation and credibility.

Corporate citizenship should not be confused with corporate identity.

The difference is that corporate identity only reflects the outer surface of the organisation, while corporate citizenship reflects the identity of the corporation as an organism of different members.

Corporate identity can be maintained by standards and policies that are implemented by order of the management. Corporate citizenship can only be maintained by horizontal acceptance of basic principles of the internal and external relation of the company. Corporate identity is a marketing tool, corporate citizenship is a model of behaviour of its members.

A corporation that regards itself as a corporate citizen is necessarily more political. It cannot remain neutral if something goes wrong in a society its success is based on.

Corporate citizenship is based on the understanding of the members of the corporate organism, that in order to maintain business in the future, the society that forms the markets has to be kept in order. Since this balance is volatile the corporate citizen has to accept its share of responsibility for the function of the society in which it lives.

This can call for a global approach, if one looks to the global challenges, but it could also require action at a very local level.

The corporate citizen goes beyond merely complying to safety standards set by the home authorities. It recognizes the implications that this short-sighted attitude might have for geographically adjacent markets, and that an unbalanced situation in these markets could cause problems on its own turf too.

The reluctance to invest in countries of the former East, including the old GDR, is understandable if one knows the obstacles investors have to overcome there. But can we afford not to?

If no efforts are made to repair the environmental and economical damage of decades of communist mismanagement, we will soon feel the effects of the so called 'ecomigration'. People of the old communist countries are understandably not keen to stay in economically poor and ecologically unhealthy areas if they can't see any real improvement taking place soon. Now that the borders have opened there is nothing stopping them from moving westward to try and get a slice of our cake. Wouldn't it be far better if we brought some of our cake to them?

We often read in editorials that the West has to be prepared to share its wealth, that a new ethical and altruistic type of manager is needed, to meet the challenges of the future. Easily said! Everybody seems ready to come, if all the others are too!

How to become a corporate citizen

Becoming a corporate citizen need not affect our competitiveness and our standards of living. But how to go about becoming one? How to convince the shop floor manager of the need to become one?

It is very unlikely that the average manager will change the way in which he does his job, if he cannot be convinced that he will perform better if he accepts his role as corporate citizen. He must be persuaded to come away from his tried and trusted routine of not looking further than his own business.

For obvious reasons companies which come under heavy criticism for their environmental performance, tend to develop a sensitivity for the complexity of the relations between a company and its 'ecosystem' rather quicker than those companies who are not yet seen to be causing any damage to the environment. The realization that it is more economic to pro-actively solve a problem the company faces than to bulldozer it, will lead to a more strategic approach to dealing with a crisis.

An example of severe problems caused by misunderstanding public emotions and underestimation of the decisiveness of politicians who want to be reelected, is the decline of PVC as a packaging material, particularly in Germany.

You do not need a crystal ball to be able to predict that PVC will disappear from the packaging market, although it is a superb and extremely useful material. What is the reason then? PVC, mixed with poly-olefines, is in practice almost impossible to recycle. Plastics altogether are under suspicion for being the cause of all kinds of environmental damages.

Since plastics are used more and more it is obviously impossible to get rid of them altogether. PVC was accused of being responsible for the emissions of dioxin from incineration plants, and now serves as scapegoat for the chloride-industry in total.

The PVC manufacturers got together and tried to improve its image. Good and valid arguments were being used and a lot of money was spent on a campaign to advertise the advantages of PVC, but the campaign remained half-hearted. The main argument that PVC does not contribute to the production of dioxins if burned properly was easily countered with the argument that incineration plants do not always function properly.

If we test PVC against our legitimation benchmarks the following emerges:

- it is not socially acceptable because of the hazards in its production and disposal
- the organisational cultures of the producers have been unable to react properly
- measures to make its use environmentally acceptable have not been taken.

So PVC as packaging is virtually dead. What could have been done?

1. The producers should have accepted the significance of public concerns regarding their product, even if scientific evidence indicated that these concerns were unfounded.
2. Technologies should have been developed or accelerated, to keep PVC away from landfills and incinerators.
3. Recycling of all PVC products should have been promoted by voluntary take-back facilities.
4. The responsibility of the producer to organize and finance these efforts should have been accepted.

This has not been the case. PVC is still very difficult to sort from among the normal mixture of refuse and therefore ends up in the remains of refuse that are incinerated. The major users of packaging have consequently ruled out the use of PVC because it does not help to reach the recycling goals set by German and future European packaging regulations.

This means that PVC producers are faced with severe losses and huge investments to convert their production lines to other products. The substitution of PVC in the packaging market will cause a big increase in the demand for other plastics. The increase in demand for these other plastics will result in an increase in their price, which then becomes equal to that of other, socially more acceptable materials. This means that the price barrier between PVC and those materials has come down.

The failure to see the consequences of acting as a corporate citizen will result in an overall increase in prices for packaging and a loss of legitimation for the plastic producers in total.

The same reluctance to accept customers' objections to some kinds of products can be found in many industries today, i.e. the producers of disposable packaging. It is predicted that they will lose substantial markets, where the use of reusable packaging is technically possible, as long as the producers (and the users) do not really look for ways to make disposables as good as reusables in the public eye.

Corporate citizenship is the ultimate form of the use of synegoisms. That means, that I can reach my goals easier, if I can help others effectively to reach their egoistic goals. The use of synegoisms, which are the only not destructive forms of egoism, necessarily have as a precondition the ability to have a better understanding of the complexity of industrial and social relations. To know which goals the others are chasing – and as a corporate citizen I need them to be successful at achieving these goals – means to understand their work and their role inside the corporations and the society.

That means that a manager who wants to be successful in the long run, has to look beyond his area of competence. This is a very common insight, but in everyday life inside companies there are precious few signs of this actually happening. Much energy is wasted in departmental empire building. Information is used as an instrument to keep as much power as possible.

Similar to ordinary citizens, the corporate citizen knows that he depends on the function of society. He knows, that the factors deciding between recession and boom are mostly psychological.

To keep people happy means not to give them more and more, but to give them the right thing at the right moment. If that is a sound environment, cultural diversity, good education for their children, public security, interesting jobs, the corporate citizen has to accept his share of action to reach those goals. If his products fit into the structure of needs, fulfil a legitimate function within the society, he will not have problems to market them.

The increase in production of goods which do not pass the legitimation bench marks is a waste of time and resources. For production – and quantity-orientated managers this may be a hard to understand approach. But there have to be ways to make the same amount of, or even more, profit by adopting a function-orientated approach based on quality rather than pumping increasing quantities of goods in the market.

Car manufacturers are next in line to learn that lesson the hard way. Their success is based on the fulfilment of two functions: the function of providing individual mobility at any required moment, and the function of status symbol. However, the traffic situation, in particular in metropolitan areas, leads to a situation where it becomes ridiculous to sit in a traffic jam for hours or drive at an average speed of 10 mph in a car that is able to reach 160 mph. By losing its function of providing individual mobility, it also starts loosing its function as status symbol. That is why the new Mercedes S-class is frequently considered a dinosaur.

But what is the solution to all this?

THE SEVENTH GENERATION PRINCIPLE – OLD METHODS TO COME TO NEW DECISIONS

The joint chiefs of the Cherokee nation had a rule in their constitution: they had to consider the consequences of any decisions they made for the nation as a whole, seven generations hence. Not that the Cherokees trusted their chiefs to be able to look into the future. They were, quite on the contrary, well aware of the human tendency to look at the past. The Seventh Generation Rule served to remind leaders of the consequences that any decision made today might have for future generations and that they owed these future generations, as well as the present, a decent living environment.

It is a great shame that this rule was not incorporated into the American constitution, because the constitution of the Cherokee nation served as a blueprint for the Union.

Due to the lack of written interpretation of this rule, we have to define it to our needs to find out whether we can apply it to our own situation.

Sunday speeches are full of commitments of politicians and industry leaders for future generations. But their actual performance witnesses more of their willingness to leave their kids the challenge to solve our man-made problems than to pave the way for the future.

The Seventh Generation Rule has its modern expression in the term 'sustainability' although this term has some different aspects.

'Sustainability' means that we only may use natural resources in a way to leave future generations the possibility to exploit the wealth of the planet in the same way we do.

The Seventh Generation Rule looks to man, nature and society as one, inseparable entity. Cultural changes influence the individual to the same degree as the development of the individual influences the culture he/she lives in. These changes also affect economical behaviour and values, so that we have a network of interactions between all kinds of human life and its consequences for our natural and social surroundings.

It is quite clear, that under the Seventh Generation Rule we would not have spent so much resources to increase our dependence from nuclear power, while neglecting the development of regenerative energy sources. Not taking into account the present threat of a GAU (*grösster annehmbare Unfall* – greatest thinkable accident) especially in older plants, we leave the disposal problems to the next generations, plus the care they will have to take with the removal of old plants. The time frame during which control over nuclear waste and abandoned plants has to be maintained properly is about 10 000 years.

The German Minister for the Environment, Mr. Töpfer, recently estimated that the inevitable closing down of the Greifswald nuclear power plant in the former GDR (which is of same type as the Chernobyl reactor) will cost 4 to 5 billion D Marks. A further 14 nuclear power plants of the same type will require similar treatment.

This example shows very clearly the economic consequences of the development of overly complex technologies, not even taking into account the famous *Restrisiko or 'remaining risk'*.

The 'can do' philosophy that ruled the technological development in the last decades and fuelled the ambitions of generations of managers led to a degree of technological complexity in industry and society. This makes our everyday life highly vulnerable to disruptions and breakdowns.

The security of nuclear power plants depends on the reliability of computer systems running highly complex software programs. Anyone working with computers knows that the default risk increases with the complexity of the program. Why should those monitoring systems be excluded from that rule?

The *Restrisiko* of a nuclear power plant cannot be calculated. Therefore, applying the Seventh Generation Rule, the farewell to nuclear power is inevitable.

Is the reintroduction of the Seventh Generation Rule utopistic?

Books on how people should act to reenter paradise fill libraries. Looking to reality such books are only frustrating. It is cold comfort, when

Herbert Marcuse stated, that, if practice does not comply with theory, the worse it is for practice.

Is the Seventh Generation Rule another unpractical theory? Not at all. John Naisbitt's Megatrends are an example of how tools to predict future changes are developed. Many institutions earn their living thinking about the future. The only thing that is not yet widely recognized is that predictability is limited, that we cannot see around the corner. Most people, like most corporate managers, would like an insurance for the risks of the future, but the degree of certainty in relation to the future is obviously very limited.

Most people have a more or less clear idea of how the world they want to live in should look like. The only obstacle they have to overcome is, that they don't dare to act on this ideal image because they think the status quo is irreversible.

Our recent history shows that is not true. Things can be changed and individuals can make that change happen. Institutions and hierarchies lose their meaning, if they are passed by individuals.

People who are committed to their companies, regardless on which level of the traditional hierarchy, should try to find allies who help them make the company into a company they can like rather than let the company turn them into uniform employees.

Top executives would be astonished if they were to step down a few levels and encourage the line or staff managers to open their drawers. They would find treasures of long-term concepts, ideas for improvements, new products, which did not pass the corporate filters.

Internal corporate communications should be developed to a point where communication is a true interactive process, where the messages and feed backs are truly understood by the respective senders/receivers.

The cost of corporate citizenship

Social- and ecobalances are fashionable items and much money will be spent to develop them. This would be money well spent, if a corporate calculation incorporates as a standard, social, cultural and ecological cost of production into the price of a product, which should account for disposal, recycling and other measures to make the production, sale and use of that product 'sustainable'. To do that voluntarily would be the most interesting challenge and opportunity. But the biggest danger for environment and social development, the Wall Street Analysts, will prevent most top executives from jumping so far.

The sheer size of existing and future problems will force governments however to structure taxes, fees and other regulations in such a way that those creating the problems will have to bear the cost of solving them. Privatizing profits and socializing cost will no longer be accepted.

It is clear that the customer will be the one who ends up paying. Who else has the money? The only thing that changes is that the responsibility of the producer will be extended to the period of use and the disposal or reprocessing of the product after its time of use.

The packaging law and similar regulations in Germany, the product and services liability regulations of the EC Commission are examples that a global approach to the problems is needed.

The common excuse for not applying the Seventh Generation Rule, which should really exist in the genetic code of almost everyone, is that the shareholders expect their return in increasing proportions every quarter. The illusion of immediate wealth without hard work, the driving force of the Reaganomics boom has broken down, not only in the US, but also in Japan. The tempting vision of becoming a millionaire overnight still has some attraction, but it is evident that the damages this 'can do' ideology has caused will take a long time to repair.

THE 'MASTERS OF THE UNIVERSE' HAVE HAD THEIR *GÖTTERDÄMMERUNG* TOO.

There is no doubt that the time is right to convince the majority of share holders, that long term profits are better than higher taxes, disposal fees, public cost of repairing the damaged environment.

It is only a matter of evaluating the risks of being the first to leave the fortress. For companies as well as national economies the chances of winning are better than ever.

The Jiu-Jitsu-Principle or how to use threats as a source of energy

Frederik Vester, a well-known German professor of bio cybernetics formulated the Jiu-Jiutsu principle which is taken from the Far Eastern art of self-defence: unlike the Western type boxer, who has to use energy first to block the power of the attack of his opponent and then again to place his punch, the Jiu-Jitsu-fighter uses the energy of his opponent to overwhelm him. The bamboo vs oak analogy follows the same logic. The oak stands firm against the storm until it breaks down. The bamboo bows down almost flat to evade the power of the storm, but it stands up again when the storm is over.

These analogies can help us to develop a way to react to challenges and threats, whether it be criticism, competition or political changes.

We first need to analyze our own position, strengths and weaknesses and the position we would like to have after the attack is over.

Sometimes it is sufficient to use the energy of the attack to make our opponent off his feet or at least make him lose his balance.

A typical example of this can be found in the reactions to environmental crises following accidents in production or transportation, from Chernobyl to Exxon Valdez. Acknowledging the problem and admitting the failure of until now functioning security measurements, and the openness to reasonable changes, inviting the opponent to help with better solutions absorbs the position of the opponent and forces him to either work with you in solving the problem or, if he is unwilling to do this, admit to his aim of wanting to hurt you, instead of helping to solve a problem or limit damages.

Only if you admit to (and know) your weakness and vulnerability, you can successfully overcome an opponent who has more power than you.

Try it!

The same method of letting your problems work for you can be applied to the development of technical solutions or marketing problems.

If, for example, a company is faced with a certain amount of environmentalist criticism, it can be the proper way to apply the Jiu-Jitsu Principle to form a committee with the environmentalists to solve the reason of the complaints. That is how McDonalds solved its problems with the EDF (Environmental Defense Fund) in the U.S. The result was that McDonalds was at least recognized as a company who takes its responsibility seriously and is open to discussion on changes.

THE GERMAN DUAL WASTE COLLECTION SYSTEM – RIGHT APPROACH WITH WRONG GOALS?

A very interesting playground for the application of the approach described above can presently be seen in Germany – the development of the so-called Dual Waste Collection System represented by the 'green dot'.

The history

Germany, heavily populated, is running out of landfill space. Incineration plants, the preferred solution of government, local authorities, and industry, could not be built because of massive protest from environmentalists and neighbours. The NIMBY principle is popular in Germany too.

Community authorities and politicians which, for a long time, neglected the obvious need for a solution have all of a sudden found the source for all the trouble: disposable packaging. Undeserved or not, it seemed that everybody jumped on the bandwagon that reduction, reuse and recycling of disposable packaging would solve the waste problem. The argument that, at the end of the line, there would still be waste, was met with the counter argument that everybody has to take his turn in providing a solution. The packaging industry remained passive (and by and large still is). Plastic and paper producers took a defensive position, not accepting responsibility for the use of their product.

Mr Töpfer, the German environmental minister gave strong signals to industry and trade that he would force a reduction in the amount of waste going to landfills and incineration.

The first target was the PET disposable soft drink bottle which was introduced by Coca Cola to replace the glass returnable 1 litre bottle. Töpfer claims that the introduction of the PET bottle was a breach of the voluntary agreement with the soft-drink industry not to increase the proportion of disposable drink packaging.

Despite heavy PR endeavours by Coca Cola to set up a system for the collection and recycling of PET bottles, the ministry could not be convinced, that this would lead to less waste. It claimed that the switch to PET disposable bottles would be a wrong signal to the public and counterproductive to the reuse, reduce, recycle-policy.

As first step the minister imposed a 0,5 DM deposit on each bottle. The PET disposable was dead and Coca Cola faced a severe loss in converting the production capacities and the bottle to a reusable one.

Once on track, the ministry announced the plan for a packaging regulation which comprises:
- a take back obligation for trade and industry for all packaging
- and an obligation to collect and recycle up to 80 per cent of all kinds of packaging outside public waste treatment installations.

Trade and industry have been 'invited' to come up with proposals on how they would organize such a 'Dual System' of Packaging Waste Collection.

McDonalds Germany was one of the first to come up with a proposal to manage its own waste and managed to reduce the level of 'McDonalds waste' reaching landfills and incineration plants to almost zero.

Since McDonalds waste was only a drop in the ocean the ministry could not be convinced to refrain from its plan to exclude packaging from the municipal waste stream. In June 1991 a packaging decree which imposed the above mentioned regulations on producers and users of packaging was therefore issued. Trade and industry have until 1995 to avoid the penalties laid down in the law, if they are able to set up a nationwide private collection scheme which is able to collect 80 per cent of all packaging waste from private households *and* to recycle 80 per cent of all packaging collected.

To fulfil that task the producers of raw packaging materials, plastics and paper producers, the packaging industry, trade companies and waste treatment companies formed the Duales System Deutschland GmbH, which has as its goal the distribution of special waste bins to all households in Germany (approx. 34 million). These bins are collected on a regular basis by a separate organisation and transported to separation plants where the different packaging materials are (still) manually separated into recyclable fractions. These fractions are guaranteed to be taken back by the producing industry and recycled.

To finance the gigantic new organisation, those wanting to participate in the scheme have to obtain a license to use the so-called '*Grüner Punkt*' which is a sign that the packaging can be placed in the separate bins and sorted out for recycling.

Today almost all available products have a 'green dot', but only very little is recycled as yet. The leverage point Mr Töpfer used, was to put the burden of having to take back non-recyclable packaging on the individual store. Therefore, in order not to be converted into landfills, the trade chains put pressure on producers for solutions.

If the scheme fails to reach its goals by 1995, the take back obligation will be reinstated and a mandatory deposit on all packaging will be the next sanction. The scheme's main goal is therefore to avoid the take back obligation and the deposit regulation.

Since the cost of the 'Grüner Punkt' is calculated in the price, the competitive status quo has remained unchanged. The only difference to the world before is, that the waste collection, separation and recycling industry is booming as never before.

Public reaction

From the beginning this scheme has faced severe criticism from many sides. It was claimed that, whereas the main goal of the waste policy was to reuse and reduce of the use of material, this scheme was based on recycling.

Since recycling of post consumer waste hardly existed, much money has to be spent to build up an infrastructure of recycling plants without a solution for the marketing of those recycled materials. No sufficient and efficient separation technology exists especially to separate mixed plastic waste into single fractions and from organic contaminants. This is more so true for compounded material i.e. paper + plastics + aluminium etc.

Most critics blame the scheme as a big bluff to increase the use of disposables instead of reusables and a way to increase the pressure to built new incineration plants after the experiment has failed. The chance to develop a circle economy which uses less (virgin) natural resources has not been grasped. Manufacturers of packaging have no interest in converting their product-orientated thinking into the fulfilment of a function in the circle of sales and transportation of the packed products.

Conclusion

The criticism is basically justified. The majority of the collected waste will end up in landfills and incineration plants after a very expensive intermediate treatment, because the technologies to separate and recycle have yet to be developed.

Under the strategy outlined in this chapter the scheme would be a perfect tool to really gain credibility in the public eye, but chances are that this unique chance for industry to reach a status of corporate citizenship and respect through long-term thinking according to the Seventh Generation rule will pass unused.

The dominant fear of changing the current way in which business is conducted has prevented companies to understand the opportunities they were being offered. Once more the legislator had to impose rules to industry and the reaction came too late, too half-hearted to really begin a new era of distribution of goods and services. On the raw materials side the focus is still more on quantities than on reusability and separability.

With few exceptions like the Tengelmann TMS-System, which aims to replace corrugated cartons as transport packaging with reusable plastic containers, little has come on the market to pave the way for a cradle-to-cradle logistic system.

The take back obligation has been viewed as a threat to trade, whereas it is an opportunity to increase the frequency of a customer's visits and the possibility to tighten the relations with the customer at the individual location. The same is true for the deposit.

Instead of demonstrating caring consciousness of the individual company, the solution was delegated to an anonymous organisation with an increasingly doubtful reputation. The value of a trademark or sign such as the 'green dot' is beginning to be diluted by inflationary use on packaging that will never be recycled. Credibility of trade and industry in total is at risk.

The basic concept that those who create a problem are responsible to solve it is no doubt correct, but if the solution just postpones and defers the problems, the public reaction is predictable.

But there is still time to differentiate a company's profile from the mass.

It is possible to build true circular systems where, from the raw material through the distribution line, the marketing approach to the customers, the redistribution for reuse and recycling and the incorporation of recycled raw material into the new product, everything is in line.

The marketing battle of the future will be won on the field of redistribution. Nobody in industry is delegating his marketing to institutions, so why should that approach work in the area of redistribution?

Strong organisations do not need protective fences or, putting it the other way round, protective fences weaken the competitiveness of a company and industry as whole. The application of the Jiu-Jitsu-Principle therefore demands the company to build-up a profile that it is part of the solution and not part of the problem.

To challenge their own staff to come up with innovative solutions that increase the value of the products and services the company provides to its customers can create a quantum leap in motivation and, as result of that, in profitability. Using less resources, less energy, less packaging, reducing distribution cost, using the effectiveness of smaller operative units, is worth thinking about, not only from the ecological, but also from the organizational development standpoint.

The challenges of the future cannot be met by window dressing: the real challenges, ecological and social, require genuine solutions.

REAL CHALLENGES – REAL SOLUTIONS

At a time when the world economy is in decline(1991–92) voices are getting louder again, that environmental laws could overburden the strength of the Western economy, especially in Central Europe.

For more than just the obvious reason that ecology needs a functioning economy because no one can spend money they do not have, this argument has to be taken serious. It unveils the tremendous demand for new entrepreneurs. There are only very few left who can not only think, but act with long-term vision.

The average top executive is a more or less excellent administrator of the money of others. His ratings are based on his present results, not on the long-term existence of his company, which necessarily implies the solution of environmental problems.

There are many signs that those managers who left their fortress of 'business as usual' have moved back inside the walls, because priorities have changed. Nobody should blame them for wanting to steer their company through rough seas. It is likely, that through increased efforts, cost – and job-cutting etc the lost positions in the markets can be recovered, but it is also very likely, that the cycles of recovery and crisis accelerate with increasing efforts to hang on to the old way of doing business. The speed with which ups and downs follow each other refrain the manager from reflecting on his vision. Day-to-day business absorbs him totally.

Many Western managers do not realize that they are basically about to run into the same problems their former Soviet manager-colleagues have today. These have to find new products, new ways to distribute those products, have to learn new methods of managing, have to really make decisions – something they have never had to do before.

The problem is that the East is about to get the same standard McKinsey-company treatment that is one of the best tools to maintain the Status Quo in the Western economy. But severe doubts exist whether this treatment is enough to manage radical changes in global economy.

The real challenges are

- energy
- air and water pollution
- waste
- transportation
- education

- social competence and
- the development of a circle economy with
  - decentralized production units closer to the customer
  - different ways to distribute finished products
  - reduction of the use of new fossil material
  - incorporation of the regenerative energy sources

All these challenges have in common that there are opportunities to find completely new technologies, because they require function-orientated, genuine solutions, not necessarily new products.

The first one to enter into the battle of re-distribution starts his learning curve early enough. He will have the expertise, when all others have to start too.

It is smart to do the inevitable before everybody else does it, but it needs a free-will-decision right now.

Can people be changed?
It is not very popular to advocate the opinion that people, or at least their behaviour as economic entities, can be altered to the good of society, since the communist attempt which was meant to achieve that has failed. It is a big challenge for entrepreneurs who have understood the opportunities of the future to lead their people into the right direction.

It is always individuals who make the difference. Why this time, when collectivism has failed, can the individual not lead the way to the next step of human evolution?

Self-restraint in an economic sense must not mean saying farewell to our lifestyle at all. But whoever has reflected on his own behaviour regarding the use of his environment knows that a little more care for our natural riches, in much the same way that we care for good friends, would make a lot difference, without restrictions in comfort and convenience.

It is not realistic to expect that people give up the need for status symbols, but different status symbols can be created. This is a wide open field for creative marketing.

But who is the individual who will save the world? Where does he/she/it live? Everywhere, because it's you and me!

'The environment crisis forces us to reconsider the premises of economic rationality.'

William Knapp, economist, 1973

13 ECO-CONTROLLING: AN INTEGRATED ECONOMIC-ECOLOGICAL MANAGEMENT TOOL

by Stefan Schaltegger and Andreas Sturm

Managers comparing the ecological and financial effects of two alternative products or production processes are often confronted with two choices: an environmental choice – e.g. better quality of water versus a lesser air quality – and an economic one – e.g. reduction in the contribution margin versus increase in pollution. This chapter is not concerned with the concept of environmental auditing but with the idea of life cycle analysis. Eco-controlling as an instrument of precise and continuous formulation of targets, progress review, analysis of differences and reformulation of new targets, was developed as an internal management tool for ecologically orientated decision-making problems without loosing contact with the financial reality.

ENVIRONMENTAL OPPORTUNITY – BUSINESS CHALLENGE BUSINESS OPPORTUNITY – ENVIRONMENTAL CHALLENGE

The natural environment serves a company in particular as a supplier of resources and as an absorber of emissions. Because the public is becoming more and more aware of the over-exploitation of our environment, companies are confronted with a demand for better environmental performance. Management is required to analyze the environmental impacts of their products and production processes, and to improve on them. Companies that are more future orientated than their competitors can gain a competitive edge by convincing their customers that their products cause relatively less environmental damage. Methods of eco-controlling serve to supply and analyze environmental information, to direct and control ecological impacts, as well as to aid the decision-making and communication process. In the following paragraphs the basic characteristics of **ecological accounting** and the **eco-rational path method (EPM)** as the basis of eco-controlling will be explained.

Apart from the values recorded and their units of measurement, the process of eco-controlling does not differ much from customary financial controlling. It equally consists of the definition of target values, recording of actual values, analysis of divergencies, determining the relevance of these divergencies, and recommendations for corrections.

The definition of environmental targets requires a quantitative registration of the ecological impact caused by a company or its products. Financial accounting in its present form is neither useful, nor meant for this purpose. Ecological accounting is therefore a necessity. Since environmental targets are not the primary concern of a company, this form of accounting will in the future have to be integrated into financial accounting.

VALUE ADDED – POLLUTION ADDED

The **target** of ecological accounting is to record and assess the ecological impact of economic activities in order to:
- reduce the negative ecological effects of existing products,
- set benchmarks for product development, and
- enable the creation of an ecologically orientated product range on a rational basis.

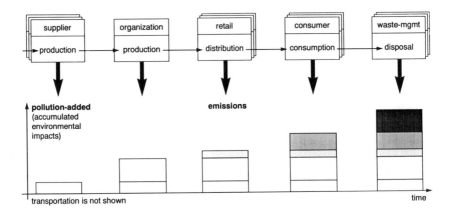

Figure 13.1: Pollution-added life cycle

The assessment of a product's **pollution-added life cycle** is similar to that of a product's value-added life cycle. **Pollution added** is the sum of all the emissions caused during a product life cycle, and derived from their respective ecological effects (see Fig. 13.1). The registration and the ecological weighting of effluents and energy flows takes place by means of **pollution-added accounting**. The imprecise and usually incorrectly used terms 'eco-balance' or 'environmental audit' are best avoided because, in the case of pollution-added accounting, we are actually dealing with a profit and loss account – as is in fact the case with all 'eco-balance' analyses known today. **Eco-balance sheets** give an evaluation of changes in the ecological capital of nature (such as the clearing of woods, soil erosion, existing contamination, etc.). In the following section we will concentrate on pollution-added accounting as a profit and loss account.

Determination of effluent and energy flows

Before we can start a data collection for pollution-added accounting, we have to define our aim and the production processes under consideration. For example paint is made of oil, oil is extracted with the help of machines, machines are produced using other machines, and so on. Since the production of a particular product clearly has an impact on virtually everything around it, it is very important to define the boundary of our analysis. We have to choose a concrete product (for instance Product A) and settle on the analysis and the definition of all processes in connection with this product (the pollution-added centres).

Figure 13.2 gives an example of how a practical representation of all effluent and energy flows caused by all economic activities in connection with a product can be achieved using the effluent flow of a production process in the chemical industry (Ciba-Geigy AG Switzerland). In seeking data it is useful to stick to the saying: 'approximately right is better than exactly wrong'. This wisdom should, however, not be confused with inaccuracy and the principle that all known effluent and energy flows have to be listed is therefore valid in any case. An estimation of flows is better than a failure to list them at all because of their unknown exact value. Whereas emissions into our natural environment have to be determined accurately, it is sufficient to merely indicate the order of magnitude for auxiliary agents such as the cooling water used in chemical processes.

It is advisable to make a clear distinction between effluent- and energy-flow accounting. An energy flow consists of the electricity used in the production process as well as the energy contained in the materials used in kilowatt/hours or joules. In effluent-flow accounting, the unit of measurement is kilograms. Based on the physical law regarding the preservation of mass and energy, the input and output streams of both material and energy should correspond. The calculation of a check balance (input − output) gives an indication of the completeness and, in most cases, also the accuracy of the data recorded. The data sheets need to show whether the data were obtained by measurement, calculation, or estimation (Figure 13.2). Listing all steps 'from cradle to grave' of all the materials in question gives an overview of the relationships within the pollution-added life cycle. A step-by-step record of all pre- and post-production phases provides a clear picture of a product's entire life cycle.

Since matter contains a certain amount of energy, the material and the energy data represent analyses of different aspects of the same flows. Looking, for instance, at an apple, we could either focus on its composition or its nutritive value. In the case of a material analysis the evaluation of fuels (e.g. mineral oil) in joules is therefore considered undifferentiated and wrong. Fuels are material inputs with a certain content of energy and are therefore expressed in kilograms in a analysis of material flows, and only in kilowatt/hours in an energy analysis. Mixing the two aspects leads to misinterpretations. Since energy analyses and considerations of entropy are very time consuming, and the necessary data are usually lacking, it is advisable to carry out material analyses instead. In a pure material analysis, the consumption of energy can be found by listing all the emissions connected with the transformation of energy or its provision. This, however, does not only cover the operation of power stations, but also the whole product life cycle of the fuel (oil, coal, uranium) and related infrastructure. The product is debited with these cumulated emissions, and not the amount of energy employed in kilowatt hours. Only in this way can we show the difference in pollution of the various energy systems. It would not make sense to regard a 'brown coal kwh' and 'hydro power kwh' as equivalent in their degree of pollution. Only when the product is not debited with kwh, but with the amount of pollution caused by the generation of those kwh, does the difference in pollution-added become clear. A reduction of pollution added can be achieved either by changing to a lower emission technology, or by a reduction of the energy employed.

product:	pigment A	*standard quantity:*	100kg	
pollution added:	plant Z, building X	*production quantity:*	897.5 kg	
name of process:	synthesis	*factor of standardization:*	0.11142	
output of the process:	pigment A (wet)		(= 100 kg: 897.5 kg)	

note: atmospheric emissions are cleaned in a multi-purpose scrubber, quantity calculated according to the contribution to total air pollution

input/output	Quality of data	pre/post	kg per production unit	kg per 100 kg pigment A
input				
Product W consisting of:				
main product TT	measured	production A	388.88	43.33
by-product VV	calculated	production A	120.00	13.37
by-product SS	calculated	production A	8.70	0.97
raw material XY	measured	supplier B	250.00	27.86
raw material LL	measured	supplier N	0.70	0.08
polyethylene	measured	supplier V	2.50	0.28
cooling water	estimated	pump station	250 000.00	27 855.15
water	measured	pump station	12 000.00	1 337.05
total input			**262 770.78**	**29 279.09**
output				
pigment A (wet)	measured	drying	**897.50**	**100.00**
by-products (liquid)				
sewage consisting of:				
water	estimated	sewage plant	11 220.00	1 250.1
TOC	calculated	sewage plant	376.80	41.98
AOX	calculated	sewage plant	0.07	0.01
Cd	calculated	sewage plant	0.01	0.001
			11 597.38	**1 292.14**
re- and down-cycled byproducts				
cooling water	calculated	recycling	**250 000.00**	**27 855.1**
emissions				
air pollution from scrubber:				
CO2	calculated	environment	250.60	27.92
NOx	calculated	environment	12.70	1.42
CO	calculated	environment	9.80	1.09
Dust	calculated	environment	0.78	0.09
Cd	calculated	environment	0.01	0.001
			274.89	*31.53*
sewage	–		**0.00**	**0.00**
disposal	–		**0.00**	**0.00**
total output			**262 768.00**	**29 278.00**

Figure 13.2: A practical record of effluent flows

Not all emissions are equal

We mentioned earlier that, since the ecological impact of the various effluents differs enormously, they must be weighted according to their ecological relevance, i.e. their relative harmfulness to the environment. Here it is important that either only the inputs or only the outputs of a pollution-added life cycle are taken into account. Considering that every input becomes an output, failing to observe this rule leads to double counting and weighting. Considering the difference in in- and outputs (i.e. the reduction in value of all the resources used) is another method of measuring ecological relevance.

Since from a socio-ecological point of view the environmental problems caused by emissions are considered to be the most important, we will concentrate on them. This does not mean that we are neglecting the resource aspect. As we have seen earlier, on account of the physical law regarding the preservation of mass input equals output. The consumption of non-renewable resources, (e.g. ores) is not in itself an ecological but an economic problem. The ecological problem lies in the environmental impact of the emissions caused by the extraction, consumption and disposal of these resources. The destruction of resources (renewable or non-renewable) on the other hand causes a change in the ecological capital of nature, and should therefore not be included in pollution-added accounting but in an eco-balance sheet.

Since there are no objective, uncontested and scientifically proven statements on the ecological harmfulness of substances, the ecological relevance of emissions can only be measured in relation to socio-politically acceptable and eco-toxologically based environmental quality targets. An example of such quality targets are the maximum emission levels fixed in the Swiss law on air quality standards (*Luftreinhalteverordnung*). While the maximum emission levels (i.e., what comes out of the smoke stacks) vary from country to country and come under attack from certain quarters, the ambient quality standards (which relate to substance found in the air, water or ground) tend to be of similar levels internationally. In the last few years there has furthermore been a trend towards harmonization of maximum emission levels, in particular within the EC. This trend is likely to continue.

The eco-toxological harmfulness of a substance is represented by the ratio: milligram of harmful material per mol of environmental medium. One mol is defined as 6×10^{23} particles (atoms, molecules, etc.). By expressing the various substances specific maximum emission levels in mg/mol and comparing them to, for instance the level of CO_2 in the air[1], we can get a clear idea of the scale of emission levels, as is shown in Figure 13.3. It also enables us to make comparisons between emission levels in different environmental media. A survey held about a year ago among eco-toxicologists and emission experts showed that this method, despite its simplicity, was seen as correct and acceptable from both a scientific and socio-economic point of view.

Figure 13.3 gives some examples of environmental quality targets.

weighting factor (choice)

	emission standard	expressed as [mg/mol]	weighting factor [PP/mg]
air			
CO_2	579 mg/m^3	13.701272	1
CO	8 mg/m^3	0.189152	72
NOx	0.03 mg/m^3	0.000709	19 316
. . .			
water			
Al	0.1 mg/l	0.001803	7 599
Fe	1 mg/l	0.018031	760
Hg	0.001 mg/l	0.000018	759 852
. . .			

Figure 13.3   Concept of quality target relations

Multiplying the recorded emission quantities (mg) by their material specific weighting factor (PP/mg) gives the number of units of pollution-added points (or pollution points – PP) emitted during a product life cycle. The resulting pollution addition allows us to rank different products according to their environmental impact.

FROM POLLUTION-ADDED ACCOUNTING TO ECO-CONTROLLING

In order to realize sustainable development of a company a decision-making instrument which shows the developmental path that makes sense from both an economical and ecological viewpoint (the eco-rational path) is required. The integration of ecological accounting into financial

[1] Because no air quality standard has yet been set for Co_2, the world CO_2 concentration of 1960 is taken as quality target.

accounting is made possible by the **eco-rational path method** (EPM, see Figure 13.4). This method can serve as the basis for eco-controlling and is explained below.

Looking at Figure 13.4 on the ecological side (left-hand column, EMP module I) the pollution added is measured by means of pollution-added accounting as was demonstrated in the two previous sections. In the EPM module II (left-hand column, second from the top) the ecological advantages are represented as PP per product unit. This relationship between input and output is called the ecological efficiency. Calculation of this ecological efficiency provides criteria for ecological product development and improvement as well as for ecologically motivated adjustments of the product range.

On the right-hand side of Figure 13.4, which is the economic side, cost and revenue are taken over from traditional management accounting (EPM module III). Here, we need to ensure that ecologically determined costs, especially the ones arising from overhead cost centres such as sewage plants, scrubbers, etc., are debited to the products causing the emissions. The precise allocation codes can be determined if the results of the corresponding pollution-added accounting are known. The cost of a scrubber used to filter emissions occasioned by several products can thus be split according to the number of pollution points (PP) each product causes. This means that harmless products do not carry the cost of and therefore subsidize harmful ones.

Economic efficiency criteria such as the contribution margin (CM) for financial efficiency are well known from traditional financial controlling (EPM module IV). When combining ecological with economic efficiency, the economic-ecological efficiency of a product can be expressed in pollution-added points per pound contribution margin (PP/£CM). This factor allows us to fill in the EPM portfolio and to categorize the products into green cash cows, green dogs, black cash cows, and black dogs (see bottom part of Fig. 13.4. The vertical axis plots the environmental impact or the pollution added, and the horizontal axis plots the contribution margin). The EPM portfolio enables integrated economic ecological controlling as well as strategy analysis and development. EPM can serve as a decision-making tool in the development and improvement of products and the cleaning up of a product range.

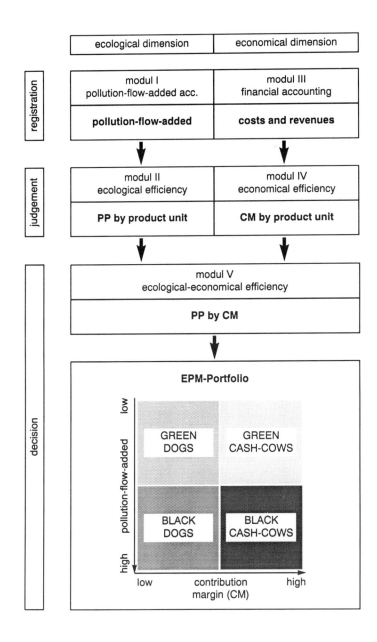

Figure 13.4: The Eco-rational Path Method (EPM)

SIMULTANEOUS GROWTH AND ENVIRONMENTAL IMPROVEMENT

By maximizing the positive contribution margin per pollution-added point and by eliminating products with a negative contribution margin per PP, a company can achieve sustainable growth, i.e. increasing contribution margins without increasing, or even while decreasing, the pollution added. The EPM portfolio shown as an example can refer to either the performance of strategic business units (SBU), or branches. In the EPM portfolio, four basic categories can be distinguished.

- **Green cash cows** are products with a low pollution added and a high contribution margin. Low costs are achieved through integrated 'clean' technologies (prevention, as opposed to 'end-of-pipe' solutions). Their environmental impact needs to be already optimized at their development stage. Apart from relatively lower cost, there are some markets where consumers are willing to pay a price premium for environmentally friendly products, which also results in a higher contribution margins. The development of green cash cows means implementing a sustainable growth strategy within a company.
- **Black cash cows** are the result of a quantitative growth strategy. They are characterized by relatively high financial revenue at a high pollution added.
- **Green dogs** are environmentally friendly, but achieve a relatively low contribution margin. In this category we often find products that have been ecologically improved by using end-of-pipe technologies. Since, in this case, pollution is not avoided but merely reduced at high cost, green dogs generally achieve a comparatively lower contribution margin than products that were conceived to be more ecological through using integrated technologies.
- **Black dogs** are products producing a high pollution added and a negative contribution margin. They are generally economically uninteresting and cause enormous environmental damage. These products should be eliminated or improved economically and ecologically.

To develop green cash cows by maximizing the contribution margin and minimizing the (now known) pollution added of a product is the way forward for companies which take sustainable development seriously.

Competitive advantages through eco-controlling

Apart from supporting management decision making, the introduction of pollution-added accounting and the use of EPM signifies that:

- those with a financial stake in the company (banks, shareholders, etc.) can be shown that investment in environmental protection is applied in an economically efficient way;
- environmental efforts can be communicated better and with more credibility to ecological pressure groups – a statement of the reduction of pollution added is more informative than a presentation of the amount of money invested in pollution reducing measures;
- environmental qualities of a particular product can be communicated to the public using the knowledge gained from pollution-added accounting;
- knowledge regarding the effluent and energy flows of a company can highlight potential savings and facilitates the allocation of the cost of ecological overhead centres (such as sewage plants). This in turn forms a better basis for the product cost calculation which are important for the pricing of a product.
- information on effluent and energy flows can be used to analyze the corresponding cost reduction potential, should marketable instruments of government environmental policies (e.g. emissions trading, emissions taxes) establish themselves.

All these advantages show that ecological accounting does not just pay lip service to environmental issues, but is becoming more and more an economic necessity for gaining and preserving a competitive edge.

MANAGEMENT'S CREDIBILITY

If management does not want to lose credibility, empty words such as 'bio' and 'green' have to be backed up by actions and convincingly presented acts. This is the only way to preserve the increasingly important condition for business survival: social acceptance and the recognition that the environment has only limited capacity as resource base and emission absorber. EPM shows that the apparent conflict between economy and ecology can generally be overcome. Nowadays the realization of a company's sustainable growth is not simply a question of will any more but of survival. Companies who manage to seize their ecological opportunities quickly and make use of them in an innovative, open and sincere manner, will have an enormous competitive advantage over their competitors.

The previously demonstrated instrumentary of information and decision making can be of considerable help in this matter. The sooner environmental aspects are introduced into the decision-making processes of managers, the better. Our natural environment is screaming for action. We either protect it now or – and this is the more difficult and more expensive option – we repair later the damage that can still be (partly) repaired.

INDEX

Note: Most references are to environmental management, unless otherwise indicated.